The Sounds of

AURORA AUSTRALIS

The Sounds of

AURORA AUSTRALIS

A History of Australia's Musical Identity

BEATRICE DALOV

SUSSEX
ACADEMIC
PRESS
Brighton • Chicago • Toronto

2 4 6 8 10 9 7 5 3 1

Published in Great Britain in 2022 by
SUSSEX ACADEMIC PRESS
PO Box 139, Eastbourne BN24 9BP

Distributed in North America by
SUSSEX ACADEMIC PRESS
Independent Publishers Group
814 N. Franklin Street
Chicago, IL 60610

British Library Cataloguing in Publication Data
A CIP catalogue record for this book is available from the British Library.

Library of Congress Cataloging-in-Publication Data
To be applied For.

Hardcover ISBN 978-1-78976-108-5

FSC
www.fsc.org
MIX
Paper from responsible sources
FSC® C013056

Typeset & designed by Sussex Academic Press, Brighton & Eastbourne.
Printed by TJ Books Ltd, Padstow, Cornwall.

Contents

Foreword by Natalie Williams

Australian cultural life has long struggled with a sense of identity. While Australia's First Peoples possess a more-than 60,000-year-old cultural history, European settlers have, in the 233 years since their arrival, grappled with their own sense of social and cultural identity in ways that continue in the present day. This wrestle has not been easy, and contemporary cultural debates are only now finding clearer paths through an uncomfortable history. Beatrice Dalov's book traces this complicated backstory and highlights the challenges and triumphs of a transplanted musical culture and its intersection with the cultures of the traditional custodians of this land.

While Australia's European settlers brought their own musical heritage to the wide brown land—hymnody, salon music and concert hall repertoire—their artists were also influenced by both Australia's unique topography and the music of its First Peoples. John Antill's 1946 ballet *Corroboree* is based upon a traditional corroboree witnessed by the composer in the early twentieth century. Other composers reflected on the mysteriousness of the Australian landscape within their works, including Miriam Hyde's 1975 piano solo piece, *Valley of Rocks*, and Ross Edwards' haunting Shakuhachi Concerto (2004), *The Heart of Night,* which seems to suspend a starlit swamp-land directly within the concert hall itself. Until very recently, Australian "classical" composers (trained in the Western tradition), often seemed unsure of their own sense of nationalistic identity, being acutely aware of the odd dichotomy between European musical heritage and Australian contemporary life. Sculthorpe's output was pivotal in shifting Australia's musical voice toward a clearer sense of national identity—one that recognized and celebrated First Nations heritage—and the cultural musical conversation has continued strongly from there.

Patriotism as an ideology seems to elude non-Indigenous Australians, perhaps resulting from our disconnection with a far-away *motherland* (England) that few of us may have seen. We are then left with a choice to make, as to what our identity "really" is—this presents a precious opportunity to define our cultural future, while deciding to embrace or jettison the weight of history. Within

Australian society itself, the past thirty years have seen an acceleration in cultural change. Indigenous heritage is being rightly brought to the fore, and this trend continues apace. Australia's wider population now actively promotes a greater cultural awareness, the adoption of equality protocols, and a socially-aware approach toward minority voices and their treatment within a diverse cultural milieu. Significant geographical landmarks have been renamed to their traditional names; *Ayers* Rock now known as Uluru (1993), and *Fraser Island* returned to K'gari (2017). The *Welcome to Country* (acknowledging the traditional owners of the land at any gathering of persons) is now almost ubiquitously practiced from major public events, to office boardroom meetings. Inevitably, these political and social changes are reflected in the arts, where a stronger sense of shared cultural identity has also grown.

Musically, these burgeoning societal changes have brought many things. The appointment of an Executive Director of First Nations leadership at the Australia Council (the nation's arts funding and advisory body), gives strong representation to the voices of First Nations composers. The *Ngarra-Burria: First Peoples Composers* program run by the Australian National University in conjunction with the Australian Music Centre, enables Indigenous composers to work with Western classical musicians, presenting newly commissioned works across the country. The recent appointment of Deborah Cheetham AO, a Yorta Yorta woman, as the First Nations Creative Chair at the Melbourne Symphony Orchestra has greatly amplified the voice of a beloved Indigenous creative artist. The commissioning of large-scale works adopting Indigenous musics, such as Paul Stanhope and Steve Hawke's 2014 cantata, *Jandamarra – Sing for the Country (Ngalanybarra Muwayi.u),* has brought First Nations musical heritage into the concert hall arena. These changes are positive, they are intensifying, and they are overdue.

Australia's contemporary musical languages carry many themes, the most exciting being those that reflect upon our shared heritage (examples mentioned above) and those that promise to drive that heritage toward an intertwined cultural future. The fact that we have not, yet, determined any one national identity, suggests that such a pursuit may be futile. To attempt this act surely misses the obvious circumstance of our deeply diverse population—how can the plethora of cultures that share Australia's landscape possibly commit to a sense of any one, singular, identity?

Dalov's book confronts this grit and incongruity between Indigenous and Western musical identities, and the strength of her approach lies in her treatment of their respective sovereignty. She does not attempt to codify or determine any singular sense of identity—which, ironically enough, many Australian writers themselves have attempted—instead, she presents and confronts multiple artistic perspectives and voices, assembling a collection of the leading compositional voices of the modern era. This work amplifies the voices of composers who are deeply attuned to Australia's landscape, its First Peoples, and the delicate progression toward new identities. May this valuable contribution to the literature serve as a pivotal step in the road toward cultural harmony and render the "Nerves of Nationality" a thing of the past.

DR. NATALIE WILLIAMS
September 2021
www.natworksmusic.com

Preface

Great nations write their autobiographies in three manuscripts: the book of their deeds, the book of their words, and the book of their art. Not one of these books can be understood unless we read the two others; but of the three, the only quite trustworthy one is the last. The acts of a nation may be triumphant by its good fortune; and its word mighty by the genius of a few of its children: but its art, only by the general gifts and common sympathies of the race.

JOHN RUSKIN

The mention of Australia immediately conjures dynamic images of kangaroos, koalas, boomerangs, the Great Barrier Reef, the Outback, and energetic urban centers, all unwavering fixtures of the conventional perception of the "Land Down Under." Among the most fascinating nations in the world, its imaginings suggest an enthralling stretch where the boundary between "G'day mate!" refinement and inhospitable wilderness is largely ambiguous.

For a musician, the immediate—and perhaps the only—associations with Australia's culture are the didgeridoo and the Sydney Opera House.[1] When I asked Andrew Haveron, the current concertmaster for the Sydney Symphony Orchestra (SSO), what exactly is performed *inside* their instantly recognizable building, he responded: "we play pretty much the same symphonies as everybody else, but, as you would hope, the homegrown composers are featured too. If they can't be featured in their own country, then there is something wrong in the world."[2] A perfunctory glance at the SSO's calendar establishes the veracity (and, perhaps, the irony) of this statement with an inexhaustible list of reputable "classics," greatly favoring the heritage of "Western" civilization and offering but cursory diversions into their own.

The greatest paradox in this situation is the vast wealth of native culture from which an Australian composer could draw inspiration: the nation boasts a monumental volume of unique characteristics, yet their musicians have long relied on the traditions and practices of Euro-American classical music. Indeed, Australia is unencumbered by the conservative outlooks and expansive histories that hinder Western societies, an advantage that many throughout history have noted, but few have chosen to exploit.

The story of Australia's musical identity cannot, of course, be summarized merely as a stale perpetuation of European traditions. While many of the nation's composers did indeed uphold and imitate the practices of their counterparts in the Western world (most of whom had passed away several centuries prior), there were also those who perceived the necessity of constructing an *Australian* civilization, by means of completing Ruskin's third tome: namely, Australia's "book of art." Thus, the current writing does not claim to be a comprehensive history of *all* Australia's music; it simply strives to trace the lineage of Australia's national consciousness in its music and clarify the evolution of its focused efforts toward a distinctly national art. Other historical accounts often acknowledge the major composers of the late twentieth and early twenty-first centuries as the cornerstones of the country's "conscious" nationalism, in that their music reflected the growing awareness of, and desire for, a distinctive national voice in the wake of numerous social, cultural, and political changes. (Indeed, a significant challenge in authoring this book is the open-ended and ever-evolving nature of Australian music, vigorously developing and refining itself long after my "final" chapter has concluded.) Yet the whisperings of a cultural identity were not limited to the musical developments of the last century—from the onset of colonization, many visionary composers, artists, and public figures recognized the inimitable nature of the Australian continent and sought to encapsulate its character in an equally distinctive music. These earlier individuals largely remain unnoticed in discussions of Australian music (which are, in themselves, few and far between outside—and occasionally within—the nation's borders), and therefore they are presented here in an effort to contextualize recent musical developments within a greater historical context.

Beyond these aims, however, this book is simply an attempt to introduce Australian music to the broader international community. General surveys of music history are consistently remiss in mentioning the activities of this continent, and were it not for such curious (yet endearing) oddities like the platypus, an inhabitant of the Western world may well exist without once hearing anything of substance about this region. It is difficult to conjure a satisfactory answer as to *why* Australia has been so unfairly neglected by the musicological community, notwithstanding its immense geographical isolation. Certainly, it is a dynamic, experimental, and progressive society, developing and flourishing when many other nations have long passed their prime. This book, consequently, seeks to shed light on a vibrant and underappreciated culture long enshrouded in mystery and sustained in the public consciousness by virtue of its sheer exoticism. To borrow a phrase from Australian magician Adrian Kebbe, Australia itself is perhaps "the world's best-kept secret."

Acknowledgements

This project is the cumulative result of countless individuals who have guided, assisted, advised, or otherwise offered me time, expertise, kindness, and patience. I have repeatedly found myself overwhelmed with gratitude for the enthusiasm with which those I contacted throughout the research process responded, and I doubt this book would have come into fruition without these innumerable selfless contributions.

I would like to express my deepest appreciation for my mother and sister, from whom I received unconditional support and inspiration; their patience as I spoke incessantly of Australia was utterly invaluable to me. I would also like to extend a special thanks to my sister for investing a significant amount of time and dedication into the concurrent completion of a recital of Australian music, as well as to my mother for crafting our performance costumes.

To my incomparable undergraduate mentor, Dr. David Dolata, for his unwavering support and encouragement throughout my studies. I have been immensely privileged to work under such a kind and knowledgeable professor, and I endlessly appreciate his unreserved honesty, levity, and well-measured positivity throughout the construction and editing of this research. I simply cannot overstate the fortune I have had to be his student.

To the Florida International University Honors College and my "Advanced Research and Creativity in Honors" (ARCH) mentor, Dr. Jose Rodriguez, for their network of support and instruction in the completion of this work, as well as their generous funding through the FIU ARCH Grant. The infrastructure that has allowed me to execute this research has been transformative in my educational and professional ambitions. I would also like to extend a special thanks to the Dean of the Honors College, Dr. Juan Carlos Espinosa, for listening to my ideas when they were still in a juvenile stage and encouraging me to "get something down on paper and come back to [his] office in a week." The many hours of discussion that ensued from this first conversation offered me the impetus to develop my project to its current state. Thank you, as well, to Mr. Allen Varela for his informative guidance throughout my time in the ARCH program.

To Ross Edwards and his wife, Helen Edwards, for their kindness and generosity with their time. Our interviews and email exchanges were invaluable resources for my book, and it was both a privilege and a pleasure to become acquainted with them. I look forward to studying and performing Professor Edwards's music for many years to come.

To Paul Stanhope, for his time and encouragement. I am immeasurably blessed to have had the opportunity to interview him on his work, and his providing of various resources was an immense help to me in my research. Much appreciation is also due for Stanhope's, Steve Hawke's, and June Oscar's time in reading my work and offering thoughtful suggestions and corrections.

To Natalie Williams, for her warmth, enthusiasm, and persistent support for my work. It was an honor to interview her, and I am always thankful for her kindness in our communications. I cannot exaggerate my gratitude for her time and help throughout my writing and research.

To Deborah Cheetham and Christopher Sainsbury, for their time and advice.

To Andrew Haveron, for directing my path in the earliest stages of my research, and to Emil Chudnovsky, for hosting the podcast in which I came across Mr. Haveron.

To Rebecca Litman (New York Public Library) for her assistance in navigating the remarkable network of library resources, and to Sue Chan (National Library of Australia) for her providing of undigitized archival material from the Peter Sculthorpe Collection.

To my professors Kemal Gekic, Jose Lopez, and Joanne Schulte, for their encouragement and guidance in my preparation of the above-mentioned recital of Australian music. Thank you, also, to my colleague and friend Nicolas Aizpurua, for his participation in this concert. I would like to extend a special thanks to technical director Paul Steinsland, for his patience, support, and audiovisual editing.

To professors David Ake (University of Miami) and Kay Shelemay (Harvard University), for generously allowing me a space in their musicology forums. The numerous lectures I have attended as a result of their kindness granted me exposure to myriad perspectives, opinions, and writings, all of which informed and contextualized my own work.

To all my professors, mentors, and advisors not mentioned here by name. I am immensely privileged to have received your support and guidance, and this project would not have been realized without your input over my educational career.

Finally, to the curious reader, for your interest in my work and truly for whom this book is written.

The Sounds of AURORA AUSTRALIS

CHAPTER ONE

Terra Australis Nondum Cognita

Colonization

The Hypothetical Continent

1768. Captain James Cook, aboard the HMS *Endeavour*, sought evidence of the *Terra Australis Incognita*, its existence first postulated by Ptolemy in the second century A.D. and, in the eighteenth, yet undiscovered. Although its precise circumstances were enshrouded in mystery, "Australia" itself had never been called, conceptually, into question; topographers merely speculated as to its absolute boundaries and its habitability. In 1533, mathematician and cartographer Johannes Schöner had confidently (if not fantastically) proclaimed that what he called the *Brasiliae Australis* ("the southern Brazil")

> is an immense region toward Antarcticum, newly discovered but not yet fully surveyed, which extends as far as Melacha and somewhat beyond. The inhabitants of this region lead good, honest lives and are not Anthropophagi [cannibals] like other barbarian nations; they have no letters, nor do they have kings, but they venerate their elders and offer them obedience; they give the name Thomas to their children [after St. Thomas the Apostle]; close to this region lies the great island of Zanzibar at 102.00 degrees and 27.30 degrees South.[1]

(To expound upon the ludicrous nature of this statement would be to belabor the obvious. Suffice it to say, Schöner's characterization is perhaps too familiar and idealistic for a yet unsighted land and people. It was, at least, the most pleasant description that would be attributed to Australia's Indigenous population for much of notated history.)

Throughout the mid-sixteenth to eighteenth centuries, various "Australias"—alike solely by name—appeared on countless maps, often elaborately charted and always accompanied by a wealth of fictitious details. As might be expected for a concept based on such minimal data and abundant conjecture, its representation varied enormously from image to image. The sole point of consensus was that such a landmass *must* exist, for "otherwise the constitution of the world could not hold together at its centre."[2] Indeed, scientists such as Gerardus Mercator (1569) and Alexander Dalrymple (as late as 1767, only one year prior to James Cook's departure) advocated for its existence, claiming that an unknown landmass in the south was a necessary—and, therefore, inevitable—counterweight to the known landmasses in the Northern Hemisphere.

Thus, the purpose of James Cook's voyage, encumbered by the historical weight of unanimous cartographical opinion, was to find *something*, and thereby to settle a centuries' old conundrum. In April of 1770, the search was concluded: Cook and his crew became the first known Europeans to reach the coast of Australia and thereby confirm its existence.

Though he would recount at length various interactions with Aboriginal peoples and otherwise recognized the substantial number of existing Indigenous inhabitants, Cook declared that the land was *terra nullius* ("no one's land") and henceforth was to be the property of Britain's King George III. While this is certainly not the beginning of Australia's settlement, it is its formal point of intersection within European history and cultural "identity."

For several years after Cook's discovery, general uncertainty presided over what should be done with the long-fabled continent. It was so distant, and had proven so unpromising, that it remained largely untouched for almost a decade. After the American War of Independence in 1783, however, the British Empire was faced with a significant concern that would alter Australia's perceived usability: the newly formed United States refused to accept further convicts from the United Kingdom. Prisons soon lacked space, owing to the British practice of jailing citizens for even minor infringements, which resulted in the overcrowding of convicts held aboard docked ships throughout the Isles and thus raised an increasingly urgent debate about a place of captivity that could sustain long-term growth. (Secondarily, the British felt pressure to establish a colony in the Pacific, so as to counter the French's rivaling imperial expansion.) Thus, in December of 1785, Orders in Council in London were issued for the establishment of a penal colony in New South Wales, Australia; the eleven ships that comprised the First Fleet to Australia, commanded by Captain Arthur Phillip, arrived in 1788. On January 26 of that year, Phillip raised the British flag on the shore of Sydney Cove, and this date has since been accepted as the official founding of Australia.

Because of the origin of Australia's population, the earliest Western musical influences in Australia can therefore be traced to two distinct sources: the large body of convicts, soldiers and sailors in the first settlements, who brought with them the traditional folk musics of England, Wales, Scotland, and Ireland; and, later, the first free settlers, some of whom had been exposed to the European classical music tradition in their upbringing. From both demographics of this period, little has survived; nonetheless, these European musics were pervasive throughout the first years of Australia's settlement, and indeed were the few sources of entertainment amidst an otherwise unfamiliar and unwelcoming habitat.

Among the first examples of European art music brought into the colony is attributed to guitarist Newton Fowell, who had written to his parents that "there is Music for Rosina set for the Guitar. Thank you to send it if the ship comes to Plymouth."[3] Such "refined" (or "high") musics inevitably existed alongside the "crude" (or "low") songs for drinking, dancing, sailing, or feasting, and it is not difficult to imagine their lively iterations that both reminded these immigrants of their distant home and colored their inchoate identities on a new continent. Indeed, a commentator in *The Hobart Town Courier* reflected on these musical activities with the characteristic nostalgia of recent emigrants:

> It is an amiable prejudice that people generally entertain in favour of their national music. This lowest degree of patriotism is not without its merit; and that man must have a hard heart, or dull imagination, in whom, though endued with musical sensibility, no sweet emotions would arise on hearing in his riper years, or in a foreign land, those strains that were the delight of his childhood. What though they be inferior to the Italian? What though they be even irregular and rude? If is not their merit which, in the case supposed, would interest a native, but the charming ideas they would recall to his mind; ideas of innocence, simplicity, and leisure, of romantic enterprise and enthusiastic attachment; and of scenes which, on recollection, we are inclined to think, that a brighter sun illuminated, a fresher verdure crowned, and purer skies and happier climes conspired to beautify, than are now to be seen in the dreary paths of care and disappointment, into which men, yielding to the passions peculiar to more advanced years, are tempted to wander.[4]

These European musics did not exist unaltered once transplanted in Australia, however. Perhaps their most obvious distortion was the misalignment in performing music concerned with well-progressed societies (and luxuries thereof) in an isolated and uncultivated settlement—it is somewhat comical to amuse oneself with themes of frivolous love and wealth when neither could yet afford to exist in Australia. In turn, this cognitive dissonance initiated what would become the "muddy issue of Australianness" itself, defined by the inhabitants' ongoing creation of musical and national identity through the cultural acts of naming, claiming, and, resultantly, owning whatever they encountered.[5] The primary purpose of perpetuating these musics was to evoke pleasantly familiar, but far-removed, locales and ideologies; they no longer expressed the commonplace sentiments of the settlers. Any "Australian" experience was, surely, not embodied within tempered lute transcriptions or lilting parlor songs. These merely represented ephemeral fantasies, memories, and escapes, musics suspended in time and soon no longer relevant even to those Europeans from whence they originated.

The second, more subtle, alteration of imported European "high" and "low" musiscs occurred through their intermingling with various Aboriginal musical traditions, to which the settlers were often exposed. Though many later interactions were quite gruesome and violent, friendly relations between these two groups were imperative for the initial survival of both, and thus myriad instances of shared musical performances are evident from this early period. Captain James Cook detailed several experiences from his first voyage that were undoubtedly familiar to the newly settled Europeans, albeit without parallel mention in Captain Arthur Phillip's *Journals from the First Fleet* (Phillip was known to be not a particularly musical individual):

> A little time after this Tootaha[6] came to the Hutt where I and those that were with me lay, and entertain'd us with a Consort of Musick consisting of 3 Drums, 4 Flutes, and Singing. This lasted about an Hour, and then they retir'd. The Music and Singing was so much of a piece that I was very glad when it was over.[7]

In a subsequent encounter, Cook catalogued the various motions within an Aboriginal dance, evidently impressed by the intricacies of the natives' performance, but nonetheless averse to its musical accompaniment:

> The Musick consisted of 3 Drums, and the Dancing was mostly perform'd by 2 Young Women and one Man, and this seem'd to be their profession. The dress of the women was such as we had not seen before; it was neat, decent, and well chose, and in many respects not much unlike a European dress; only their Arms, Necks, and Shoulders were bare, and their headdress was the Tomow stuck with Flowers. They made very little use of their feet and Legs in Dancing, but one part or another of their bodies were in continual motion and in various postures, as standing, setting, and upon their Hands and

> knees, making strange Contorsions. Their Arms, hands, and Fingers they moved with great Agility and in a very Extraordinary manner, and altho' they were very exact in observing the same motion in all their movements, yet neither their Musick or Dancing were at all Calculated to please a European.[8]

In perhaps his most unreserved description of native performance, Cook noted its comparative lack of variety in instrumentation (generally consisting of percussion and various aerophones) and the apparent savageness of Aboriginal dances; he suggested that their songs are sorrowful in quality, but nonetheless tuneful; and he admired their propensity for rhythm:

> Diversions and Musical instruments they have but few; the latter Consists of 2 or 3 sorts of Trumpets and a small Pipe or Whistle, and the former in singing and Dancing. Their songs are Harmonious enough, but very doleful to a European ear. In most of their dances they appear like mad men, Jumping and Stamping with their feet, making strange Contorsions with every part of the body, and a hideous noise at the same time; and if they happen to be in their Canoes they flourish with great Agility their Paddles, Pattoo Pattoos, various ways, in the doing of which, if there are ever so many boats and People, they all keep time and Motion together to a surprizing degree.[9]

Further to this observation, Cook noted that "the natives imitate any thing said by the English very correctly; indeed so much so, that they have even sung songs after our people, though on the contrary we do not find it an easy task to imitate them." This mechanism of colonial transmission (i.e., rote imitation) subsequently proved to be an exceptionally pervasive method of "civilizing" the Indigenous peoples throughout Australia's settlement, particularly for missionary communities that increasingly encroached upon traditional land and native practices.[10] Interestingly, the general difficulty experienced by non-Indigenous peoples in their attempts to imitate or otherwise accurately notate Aboriginal musics likewise persists throughout Australia's history, though subsequent cultural guidelines established throughout the twentieth century largely prohibit such appropriations of native heritage.[11]

Cook's observation of melancholy and solemnity gradually digressing into an incomprehensibly frenzied state was, almost a decade later, reiterated by Lieutenant Daniel Southwell:

> [Bennelong] sings, when asked, but in general his songs are in a mournful strain, and he keeps time by swinging his arms: whenever asked to dance, he does it with great readiness; his motions at first are very slow, and are regulated by a dismal tune, which grows quicker as the dance advances, till at length he throws himself into the most violent posture, shaking his arms, and striking the ground with great force, which gives him the appearance of madness. It is very probable that this part of the dance is used as a sort of defiance, as all the natives which were seen when we first arrived at Port Jackson, always joined this sort of dance to their vociferations of "woroo, woroo," go away.[12]

It should be noted that this "sort of defiance" gestured and sounded through similar native dances is often found in the various journals of settlers, demonstrating the tense colonial relationship between Indigenous and non-Indigenous peoples that persists through contemporary times. While there were peaceable interactions between the two groups, increasing European encroachment contrarily yielded many instances of hostility and violence; the state of cultural associations at any given time was, therefore, ultimately dictated by the inherent power of the colonizers. Native artistic expression was at times a welcome addition to the traditions of the settlers, and at others a nuisance to be subjugated and eradicated. "Defiant" Aboriginal performance is a virtually constant element post-1770, however, and continues into modern Australian music-making as a symbolic resistance against colonization.

Given that many notated encounters between Indigenous and non-Indigenous peoples occurred during the first years of settlement, it is not unlikely that the highly ritualistic and ceremonial nature of traditional society lent itself to various performances with diplomatic purposes, as well. As Cook indicated, Aboriginal music was quite astonishing (albeit generally displeasing) for those more accustomed to the works of Bach, Handel, Haydn, and their contemporaries; yet it certainly exerted a significant influence on the colonizers' musical curiosities throughout their earliest years in Australia.

One instance of such ceremonial interaction was described by Mr. Bradley William, a lieutenant aboard the flagship of the First Fleet:

> Mr. King seeing some Natives on a point of land, he backed the Boat to them to endeavor to have some intercourse with them, One of the Natives threw a Spear at which all the rest seem'd much displeas'd, after which they came close to the Boat & were quite friendly . . .
>
> The Natives that appear'd on the N.o side the Bay express'd the same wish of knowing whether our People were Men or Women, after

> being satisfied on that head, one of them ran in amongst the Bushes, made himself a Belt of Grass & came dancing out with it round his waist with leaves hung over it . . .[13]

Though music is not explicitly mentioned in this encounter, it is difficult to imagine that such a dance was unaccompanied; drums, flutes, or chant-like songs were likely present.

These instances, which represent merely a sliver of all recorded (and unrecorded) interactions between native peoples and European settlers, occurred synchronously with the flourishing of band, military, and art music. During this early period, however, the musics of these Aboriginal peoples and European settlers scarcely altered one another in any tangible or measurable manner; rather, they maintained a mutual curiosity guarded by a conscious distance. Because of the novelty of native performance and musical aesthetics, a far larger proportion of all surviving documentation from the first fifty years of Australian settlement is concerned with Indigenous music than from any later period; even so, musicologists concerned with Australian music have tended to overlook it in favor of attempting to chronicle settler music, while general historians have, under the pretext of "anthropology," done the reverse. Admittedly, unmediated Indigenous evidence is scarce and early colonists' accounts are often prejudiced, misleading, or altogether incorrect; they are, however, honest attempts to observe and respond to the inquisitiveness naturally aroused by Indigenous contact.

Yet, this initial predisposition toward Indigenous musics persisted only until the 1820s and was definitively concluded by the "Black War" in Tasmania (c.1824–1832), a period of violent conflict between British settlers and Tasmanian Aboriginals upon the former's excessive incursion into native territory. Motivated by the inherently hostile sentiments of these proceedings, *The Hobart Town Courier* patronizingly reported in 1830 that some settled musical amateurs had made progress in transcribing the native melodies of these Tasmanian peoples; unenthusiastic and apparently disapproving of the central subject, the *Courier* suggested that the time and efforts of these amateurs would instead be better directed toward transcribing native bird-songs:

> Many of those who are taking an active part in the present campaign, and who have some taste for the beauties of nature, must [...] derive no small pleasure from the new and striking objects peculiar to the island brought under their notice [...] this enjoyment must be more than usually delightful, for not only every plant but every animal is

> different from those in the old world. The mind of him must be dark indeed, and the heart insensible, that is not touched with new delight when he awakes at early dawn [...] and hears the chorus of feathered race. It has been said that our singing birds have no charms compared to the choristers that enliven our English meads and vales; but [...] we have yet many that approximate in giving delight with these associates of our early days.
>
> The present race of our colonial writers is too much engrossed with political and other ephemeral subjects to have yet devoted much time to chronicle the annals of this new region, a description either prose or poetic of these interesting and permanent characteristics. There is however no doubt now amongst us some rising genius, born amidst our woods and peculiar scenery who will shortly apply his descriptive powers to commemorate them [...].[14]

These earliest contacts between Aboriginal peoples, present in Australia for at least 50,000 years (according to approximations by anthropologists), and European settlers throughout the late eighteenth and early nineteenth centuries were therefore largely haphazard, experimental, and disorganized. All native musics were a curiosity, identified by the same few elements (e.g., percussion, aerophones, and a general unintelligibility approaching madness) yet otherwise indistinguishable by any categorical measure. Immigrants certainly were unaware of Aboriginal clan organization, their creation mythology, or their sociocultural specificities; these Indigenous peoples were little more than "primitives" or, at best, oddities. Each native land-owning group can be defined by their particularities in dances, songs, dialects, tools, and manners of life, yet to the ignorant immigrant, these differences were obscured by the vastness of the unknown and the unrecognizable. Indigenous music, dance, and ritualism were intriguing, but aesthetically displeasing. Settlers maintained almost no association with these peoples and certainly did not consider them as having any legitimate relevance to an emergent "Australian" identity and society. No evidence exists to postulate that settlers attempted to imitate or incorporate Aboriginal music into their own (excluding, of course, Cook's futile attempt to mimic one of their songs), and thus the cataloguing of their music was merely to stimulate their inquisitiveness (or simply pass time) without any intended lasting effect. Indeed, the Tasmanian "Black War," compounded by the continuing retreat of Indigenous peoples' retreat from colonial settlements, effectively eradicated any interest in Aboriginal cultural heritage until the late twentieth century, when the advent of recording equipment galvanized amateurs to conduct "fieldwork" (once again from a passionate, yet fleeting, academic interest in native culture). Simultaneously with the development of phonograph recorders emerged various Christian missionaries who, detaching themselves from the dense European settlements, sought out Aboriginal peoples with generally positive intentions of educating and integrating their youngest members into Australian society, but otherwise negative repercussions on Indigenous culture.

Thus, the first contacts of European settlers with Indigenous Australians were but juvenile, ostensibly diplomatic interactions; they had little transformative impact on the cultures or musical activities of either. Perhaps, subconsciously, the direct contact and cohabitation with such natives invigorated the imaginations of the immigrants, as they previously had merely an abstract, detached conception of such peoples. Throughout Australia's development, the cross-fertilization of cultures certainly became increasingly pronounced, and later generations actively sought to unite the two disparate peoples within music. Yet in the earliest years of settlement, they remained separate and existed on mutually exclusive planes (notwithstanding, of course, the violent confrontations in each instance of European expansion and encroachment upon native territory). It might suffice to assert, then, that settlers largely retained their domestic musical cultures (e.g., art musics, drinking songs, dances, festivals, etc.) while Indigenous peoples upheld their religious, ceremonial, and secular practices, with little alteration or external influence.

CHAPTER TWO

Earliest Compositions and Institutions, 1788–1834

1790. Scarcely two years after the first settlers arrived in Australia, Mr. George Boucher Worgan, a surgeon and amateur musician, imported the first pianoforte into the country. Many immigrants followed suit, and soon, a remarkable number of pianos had been brought to the continent. The immense popularity of this instrument, however, was primarily symbolic and only secondarily musical. In Europe, its presence signified a member of the rising middle-class; in Australia, it designated the elite. Bringing such an unwieldy item incurred a significant financial expense, particularly in the context of an already expensive crossing and the minimal capacity for personal possessions aboard the ships; thus, only the wealthiest—and, therefore, the most "cultured"—of travelers could afford to do so. Yet this accumulation of instruments had little measurable impact on the actual musical activities within the colony, for two reasons: first, the pianos were often transported to only the most remote settlement areas, and second, the long and precarious transport frequently rendered them unplayable. To arrive with a piano was, thus, a superficial exhibition of grandeur, refinement, and a fundamental attachment to the West itself.

Pianos appeared all the gaudier and more obnoxious when considering the economic conditions of colonial Australia. The immediate requirements of colonization and survival superseded the creation of an active musical atmosphere in the country; few could divert both the energy and the capital toward leisurely musical education and performance. Indeed, it was not until the mid-nineteenth century, after the harshest and most demanding years of early settlement had subsided, that the first rousing of public musical activities appeared. Already, then, a stratification of society had emerged, its dividing barrier constructed by those who could champion waste and excess (e.g., immigrants importing pianos) and excluding those who could not afford to do so (the vast majority of colonists). Yet this insistence on (and perseverance in) importing such cumbersome instruments perhaps does not indicate lofty extravagance as much as a resilient commitment to cultural continuity;

indeed, it may have been the foundation upon which the nation's musical idiom was to build:

> There is a long association, in Australia's music history, of women with music as a domestic activity, beginning with those first pioneering women who struggled against such awesome physical odds to bring their pianos with them to the new country. If these women "encompass the universal in the particular", then we may see that the reality of Australia's musical life is rooted in domestic traditions, in amateurism, and strive for a "map of the past" in which that fact is celebrated, not disparaged.[1]

Irrespective, the sacrilegious presence of pianos was limited for a period of time to merely the uppermost echelons of the Australian social "hierarchy," to the extent there was one to speak of. That is not to say that music elsewhere was shunned by culturally bereft settlers, however—quite the contrary. Entertainment was a necessity for many; so much so, in fact, that the colonists were content even to engage temporarily with imagined, rather than real, musical performance. For example, musicologist Graeme Skinner notes a particularly amusing instance at Moreton Bay in 1799, in which this absence of readily available music manifested itself:

> The reporter, George Bass put down native lack of curiosity in the whites' offerings to 'a very bad performance' of a reel by the three sailors, who 'for want of music' danced in silence, unable to coordinate their movements because, one imagines, of the three conflicting inaudible musical performances inside their heads. This curious anecdote is testimony to a reality for many early arrivals, whose musical 'baggage' consisted of dozens of tunes they were perfectly capable of recalling silently (an authentic form of performance nevertheless), but which they had little or no capacity of realizing audibly in vocal or instrumental performance.[2]

The "musical baggage" of the settlers was often not one imbued through any formal training or acute sensitivity for the arts; it was simply their known musics acquired throughout their prior lives in the United Kingdom, which most could perform only poorly, at best. While the singing of and dancing to these songs nonetheless constituted a legitimate musical activity, it was largely spontaneous and undirected, exerting minimal influence on larger national developments. These activities did, however, exemplify the keenness of immigrants to sustain some semblance of a musical atmosphere; eventually, when contextualized within new lyrics and new environments, many of these musics were indeed transformed from European folk songs into colonial "Australian" artifacts.

Subsequently, with the arrival of more musically inclined immigrants, performance developed to encompass audible sound. Military bands emerged as the most immediately available musical resource and were encouraged, although many were merely haphazard arrangements of individuals with tolerable command of one instrument or another. Eventually, these ensembles began to fulfill other, extra-military functions, such as accompanying liturgical services, performing popular opera arrangements, supplementing dance functions, and even serenading during dinner gatherings; indeed, they became the most firmly established aspect of Australian musical life. Nothing particularly "Australian," however, manifested in their music—the works they performed primarily reinforced the ethnic and cultural identities of the colonists' homelands, offering some basis in familiarity that only later was to be adapted and recontextualized into an "Australian" identity.

Yet there were many individuals who were aware of the impending necessity to articulate such "national" identity, if only to arouse a nebulous impression of the "exotic" for musical consumers abroad. Australia was quite unlike Europe, Asia, or the Americas, and offered much from which to create a fundamentally new idiom; it was also sufficiently far from the Old World to stimulate a sense of curiosity and interest. Who was to capitalize on this latent potential, however? Trained musicians were scarce, and the earliest settlers were neither the most adept at, nor the most preoccupied with, original composition. Resources were minimal, and musical institutionalization had not yet commenced on any significant scale. Colonists of lower socioeconomic classes were perhaps content merely to enjoy the songs and dances of their homelands after long days of toil and were not particularly interested in "Australian" renditions thereof. The "elite" society of Australia largely preferred to retain their associations with the West, and they meticulously organized their lifestyles to emulate the Old World as completely as was possible. The necessary precursor to this supposed "Australianization" of music, then, was to attract musicians who were sufficiently capable of experimenting with the wealth of unfiltered musical material on the continent (and who were neither particularly elite nor particularly poor), and to implement an infrastructure that stabilized and furthered musical production.

Fortunately, some such individuals did arrive. Joseph Reichenberg (1789–1851), generally agreed to be the first "legitimate" composer of settler Australia, arrived in New South Wales in October of 1824, and, by 1825, had already advertised his *A First Set of Quadrilles for Australia* in *The Sydney Gazette*:

> Mr. Reichenberg, Music Master of the 40th Regiment, respectfully informs the Ladies and Gentlemen of the Colony, that he has composed *A First Set of Quadrilles for Australia*, with proper figures adapted to it, for the Piano Forte, Flute, or Violin; as also, for a full Band. The same may be had in Manuscript, from Mr. Reichenberg, at the Military Barracks, or at Mr. Campbell's [...], by giving one day's notice. Price 6 s[hillings].[3]

A number of other relatively renowned musicians followed suit and settled in the new colony, such as John Philip Deane (1796–1849), attributed the title of "the father of Australian chamber music," and William Vincent Wallace (1812–1865), nicknamed "the Paganini of Australia."[4] As early as 1835, Wallace was giving concerts on the island of Tasmania, south of Melbourne, and one year later had founded a music school for girls in Sydney. His reign, however, was short—though beloved by the public, he was financially over-indebted and thus fled to Chile in 1838. Isaac Nathan (1791–1864), after establishing a relatively illustrious career in Britain, arrived in Sydney in 1841 and eventually acquired recognition as "the father of Australian music." Indeed, he emerged as a prominent leader of local musical life: he founded the *Singing Academy*, gave numerous concerts, wrote several patriotic vocal works for official or civic occasions, and endeavored to systematically collect Aboriginal chants. Additionally, he functioned as a music adviser both to a synagogue and to a Roman Catholic cathedral in Sydney, and further directed the first (or among the earliest) Australian performances of works of Mozart and Beethoven. His opera *Don John of Austria* (1847), telling of the rivalry in love of Phillip II of Spain and his illegitimate half-brother Don John, is considered the first operatic (or otherwise major work) to be written, composed, and produced in Australia.

Isaac Nathan is, in fact, a somewhat curious figure in Australian culture, in that he was among the few competent musicians who relocated to the continent from an intrinsic desire, rather than by the compulsion of some immediate professional, artistic, or financial strain. Much of modern Australian scholarship on his musical endeavors results from the advocacy of Charles Bertie, a Sydney City Librarian; in a 1921 lecture jointly sponsored by the Sydney chapter of the British Music Society and the Sydney Conservatorium of Music (and preceded, strangely, by a performance of Claude Debussy's *String*

Quartet in G Minor, Op. 10), he rather optimistically emphasized the unusual nature of Nathan's presence in the country:[5]

> I am sure you will ask why a musician with an established reputation should of his own free will embark on such a venture. I think it necessary to emphasize the words 'of his own free will.' Quite a number of professors of the arts arrived in Australia in its early days, but they were unwilling guests—they 'left their country for their country's good.' Not so with Mr. Nathan, he made his own choice, and the events which culminated in his departure have an air of mystery and romance surrounding them.[6]

Nathan, however, was apparently displeased with the atmosphere he discovered in Australia:

> He says that he exercised his profession amongst a 'depressed people,' and it was a fit adjective to use. The Colony in 1841 was still in the throes of convictism, and in the early years of the forties it passed through a financial depression which swamped any interest in such unfinancial things as the arts.[7]

He nonetheless committed himself to combatting the low ebb of the musical tide in Australia (a few years earlier, *The Sydney Gazette* had declared that "concert going, it is said, is out of fashion"), and he began composing music that could be considered, relatively speaking, distinctively national.[8] Among these were the above-mentioned Aboriginal "airs" (i.e., transcribed and harmonized Indigenous songs, the composers of which Nathan apparently held in high esteem), as well as official music intended to celebrate significant celebrations of the new colony. For example, his "Currency Lasses—a song inscribed with the utmost devotion and respect to the Fair Sex of Australia" was composed for the fifty-eighth Anniversary of the Colony (1846), whereas his "Australia—the wide and free—as sung at the great Civic Dinner, December 21st, 1842" commemorated the inauguration of the City Council in that same year. These and other musical ventures have since earned him the title of "Australia's first composer" of the early nineteenth century, which certainly reflects his commitment to the establishment of some form of recognizably "Australian" music (or at least one distinctive enough from the small repertoire of European salon music popular in the colonies at the time); indeed, throughout his twenty-three years in Sydney, he "put a solid foundation to its nebulous musical life, and set a course towards artistic maturity."[9] While Bertie, considering William Vincent Wallace's earlier presence in Australia, could not accurately claim that Nathan was Australia's first *musician*, he could, at least, argue, for his superiority as a composer:

> But I think we can safely claim for our subject the title of 'Australia's First Composer'. Wallace was only a bird of passage, and did nothing of an Australian character, whereas, as we shall see, Isaac Nathan set to music a number of aboriginal airs and was the composer of the first opera written and produced in Australia. He had, moreover, a great influence on the musical life of the young community, and was the first musician of wide reputation to settle in Australia.[10]

Other noteworthy composers who published musical works in this period include Francis Hartwell Henslowe (1811–1878), Frederick Ellard (1824–1874), Charles Edward Horsley, Stephen Hale Marsh (1805–1888), and his son, Henry Marsh (1824–1885). Among these, Ellard emerges as perhaps the most "nationally" minded. Arriving in Australia in 1832, he composed many works that were inspired by the social life and natural environment of the colony—a particularly charming example is his series *National Country Dances* for piano, appearing in five "volumes" in 1853. The fourth of these, *The Australian Ladies*, is comprised of sixteen piano solos dedicated to various women of colonial Sydney's social "elite": they include Lady Gipps (wife of governor George Gipps), Lady Franklin (wife of the former Lieutenant-Governor of Van Diemen's Land, John Franklin), Lady Dowling (wife of Judge James Dowling), Mrs. Forbes (wife of first Chief Justice Francis Forbes), Lady Mitchell (wife of Surveyor-General Thomas Mitchell), Mrs. Edward Deas Thomson (daughter of governor Sir Richard Bourke), and Lady O'Connell (daughter of governor William Bligh).

Beyond these whims of parlor grace and coquettish flattery, Ellard could also maintain a sense of solemnity and austerity, as heard in his *The Sydney Corporation Quadrilles* (1842); even this work, however, is counterbalanced by the levity of dance, suggesting Ellard's own lighthearted nature and atypically comfortable life in the colony. A later piece, entitled *Australian Bird Waltz* (1854), likely remains his most renowned composition, owing to its then-unique incorporation of an Australian bird call. Indeed, it is possibly the first published Australian work to use such material as the foundation of a musical composition; he further includes a preface that explains the piece's genesis and provides a transcription of the original bird call:

> On [a beautiful Australian summer morning] some years ago, when on a visit to the country (the Wollombi district) I was awoke from a beautiful long clear note from a Bird outside the window: and, by the way, I maintain that the birds of Australia have notes as beautiful, as their plumage is brilliant, notwithstanding the contrary assertion by people who in all probability, were never beyond the Botany Swamps, nor ever had an opportunity of judging, and which of course is implicitly believed by the people of the old country.

Though *Australian Bird Waltz* is arguably the first composition to incorporate the distinctive sounds of Australia's birds, it would hardly be the last. Composers frequently returned to this fundamental source of expression throughout the musical history of the nation, subliminally acknowledging Ellard's assertion even if they had not directly encountered his musical works. Amusingly, almost all Australian musicians who have upheld the calls of native birds as an inimitable aspect of the national experience have laid claim to the same epiphany made by Ellard—that the song of a bird, resonating well above the mundane sounds of life perpetually beyond one's window, aroused in them some heightened awareness of the country's soundscape and galvanized them to adopt a quasi-ecological approach to their work.

Concurrently, a growing recognition for the importance of a national "canon" of art was emerging, and publishers had begun to assemble collections of miscellaneous works unified under the title of "Australian Album." Though the first of these was issued in 1854, perhaps the most notable and nationalistically inclined was the *Australian Album* of 1857—elegantly bound and ornamented in gold, it was a luxurious item with the dual intent of symbolizing the nation's recent economic and cultural growth (largely stimulated by their ongoing gold rush) and demonstrating their artistic merits to the larger international community. Indeed, the English journalist and author Frank Fowler wrote of the volume:

> The idea of a purely musical album—that is, a book filled with the original productions of our own artistes—is, I think, peculiarly happy, and one which the Australian public will readily appreciate. The value of such a work must be apparent to every one. They are all new—all colonial. Here, in this city—they were played, printed, and published. True, some of the composers are foreigners; but still this book is as much an Australian production as a cluster of grapes from the German vineyards at Kissing Point. We can send the work home as a specimen of what we can do out here at Botany Bay—as an index of our education, refinement, art-feeling.

And it is fitting we should attest our social progress by some unusual publication of this character. Nothing else will do it so completely and so well. It vindicates our connexion with old-world genius and skill; and proves that we are not destitute of some of the haughty lineaments of European civilization.[11]

Australian newspapers, thus, readily acknowledged the notable increase of "professional" musicians on the continent and offered unbridled optimism for their cultural potential. For example, after one of Wallace's Sydney concerts in 1836, a reviewer commented on the nation's good fortune of attracting dynamic and vibrant young composers:

The encouragement given in a young Country to the Professors of the Fine Arts, is the best and most certain indication . . . of the nascent taste, refinement and liberal spirit of its community—and it has been, therefore, with especial pleasure that we have witnessed first, the arrival on our shores of [these] men . . . and then the enlightened appreciation of their merits . . . and it must, we think, be a source of secret satisfaction to [them] that they may be now laying the foundation-stone of future schools of art that may flourish in this far land, when the Institutions of the older nations of Europe (. . . whose fame has probably already passed its zenith) may be dying and dwindling away into the inertness and inanity of exhausted energy and age-enfeebled efforts. And when we recollect [whether] the genius of the Greek, Roman, and Italian nations, as manifested in their great works in painting, sculpture, and music, did not in a great measure result from the inspiring influence of their fine climates—it is surely not too far-fetched to suppose that the blue cloudless skies, and brilliant atmosphere of our own beautiful climate, will ultimately exercise the same moulding influence on the mental constitution and temperament of our community.[12]

Already, the trope of "blue cloudless skies" and impeccable climate rivaling the fatigued and polluted Old World had become evident; indeed, the notion of a "dying," "exhausted," and "age-enfeebled" Europe was to become a recurrent metaphor in Australia, juxtaposed against the youth, vitality, and liberality of the new continent. The perceived freedom from tradition (likely heightened by the immense physical distance from any martyrs of convention) became the primary impulse for innovation. Nothing inhibited the unbridled experimentation of settlers in Australia, from which something of value was surely to arise.

Ultimately, these and other locally composed musics in the first half of the twentieth century were to exert a since-unparalleled influence on the growth of the Australian musical economy. Given the nation's extreme physical isolation from the remainder of the "civilized" world, replenishing or updating the available musical repertoire was a rare occurrence. Emigrants, both professional and amateur, often brought their personal musical collections with them; upon arrival, however, their hope to acquire additional sheet music rested solely in seldom imports from abroad. The rarity of music, in fact, led to a proliferate market of "copying" (i.e., reproducing) these few available manuscripts and selling them for what were then luxurious sums, often beyond the reach of the working class. Thus, the emergence of "native" composers who could produce—and, later, engrave and print—new music was heavily encouraged, welcomed, and appreciated by the Australian public; even those who had produced but a few works (even if they perhaps did not rival those of the accepted European "masters") were celebrated. Paradoxically, however, many compositions of the era did not sustain any significant popularity and were often forgotten within a few years of their production; resultantly, relatively little survives from this period.

Alongside the increased production of local music came the gradual "democratization" of the piano. Claviers were imported at increasing rates through the nineteenth century, and they had become highly sought after as a symbol of a "cultured household" (often to accommodate the growing popularity of "parlor songs," or Australian *lieder*). This phenomenon occurred, of course, *in tandem* with the growing economic prosperity of the colonies and the establishment of "fixed" international travel routes. Because it was both less costly to produce an instrument domestically and less likely that it would not be substantially damaged after a tumultuous transit, however, local craftsmen soon emerged and began constructing pianos on the continent. Around 1834, the first Australian piano had been built in Sydney.

Likewise, a market for private musical education emerged and was apparent from as early as 1837, and the first music store opened in Adelaide in 1839. Throughout colonial records, shipments of organs, harpsichords, pianos, fiddles, and numerous other instruments are notated in cargo logs and were subsequently advertised for sale to the general public. The expanding access to instruments facilitated the rise of an active network of musicians, who were then solicited to perform at balls, fêtes, levees, marriages, liturgical services, and even annual conferences between administrative officials and Indigenous peoples.[13] Around 1850, concurrently with a fundamental revision of the school system, the first endeavors to institutionalize music education materialized; thus, choral organizations, glee clubs, madrigal societies, and "song tables" (the latter especially favored by emigrants after the European independence revolutions of 1848) proliferated. As described in the *Hobart Town Courier*:

> A Glee Club is about to be established on a footing which will ensure its permanent establishment. Musical Associations have frequently been formed in Sydney, but have never arrived at maturity; owing to their meetings taking place in Public Taverns it has always been found necessary to abandon the idea after a few trials, from the evident impracticability of succeeding. The Association to which we now allude, is of a respectable character, whose Meetings will be held in the house of a private Gentleman, from which all persons, whatever their musical talents may be, who betray an attachment to habits of intemperance, will be carefully excluded.[14]

In the period from 1855 to 1870, choral music established itself as the most important domain of the Australian "professional" music business (paralleled in the amateur realm by the enormous output of domestic "salon" songs), especially for composers who received frequent commissions in this genre.

Instrumental performance, in parallel with vocal activity, likewise began to flourish in the public realm. From the 1830s onwards, numerous orchestras were arranged *ad hoc* for special occasions, mostly for opera or oratorio performances, and the practice of spontaneously organizing such festivals continued into the twentieth century. An "official" institutional lack of these occasional ensembles did not prevent a certain continuity in their regularity: in Melbourne at the end of the nineteenth century, festival orchestras appeared in such regular succession that they were largely equivalent to the establishment of a permanent ensemble. This was, *de facto*, the inception of a professionalization of Australian music. By the 1840s, an active concert life is evident on the continent, pervaded with a European "canon," as it were, of George Frederic Handel, Joseph Haydn, Wolfgang Amadeus Mozart, and Ludwig van Beethoven, as well as Thomas Arne, Christoph Willibald Gluck, and Ignaz Pleyel. (For comparison, fashionable continental composers of the time included Giacomo Meyerbeer, Carl Czerny, Vincenzo Bellini, Sigismond Thalberg, and Étienne Nicolas Méhul, among others.)[15]

This increase in the number of instruments, both for professional use and a household capacity (among which the piano remained the most popular), together with the sustained increase in public performances, necessarily stimulated a demand for sheet music, at least with more regularity, affordability, and accessibility than before. Thus, in the second half of the century, permanent publishing industries emerged, and single-sheet prints of Australian salon music, which were inexpensive and easily distributed, proliferated. There had been previous attempts to engrave music in the colony, however, it was not until the 1830s, together with these general booms in other realms of music making, that continuous music printing became an institutionalized fixture. Frederick Ellard's father, Francis Ellard, emerged as perhaps the foremost engraver and printer of the time. He had established a business in Sydney in which he sold instruments, provided repairs, and imported sheet music, and, since colonists previously only had access to music which they had brought with them, Francis' operations thrived as a novelty. Because he was a skilled engraver himself, Francis soon began publishing new music of local composers, recognizing that, as a counterbalance to the market for European music in Australia, a market for "Australian" music existed in Europe. Thus, among his first published works were of his brother, William Ellard, which featured several nationalistically inclined titles such as *The much admired Australian Quadrilles* (1835). Although William lived in Dublin and never visited Australia himself, he nonetheless attempted to imbue his dances with a slightly outlandish exoticism. Among the various dances were "La Sydney," "La Wooloomooloo," "La Illawarra," and "La Bong Bong"; an illustration of Sydney Harbor (then, as now, a symbol of Australia itself) decorated the cover of the collection. Certainly, these artistic decisions were enough to draw the casual eye—for all the assumed propriety of the Old World, supposed barbarousness consistently fascinates—but musically, there was little to recommend them as particularly "Australian." Above all, they were simply an enterprising appeal to the colonial market at "home."

This approach toward composition is perhaps indicative of the Australia's continued attachment to the British Empire and, conceptually, the Old World. Indeed, the two most popular forms of ensembles—choral societies and symphony orchestras—closely replicated their British counterparts. Most Australian classical composers of this period continued to work entirely within Western models, and those later musicians who sought a professional musical career undertook their training in continental Europe or the United Kingdom. Frederick Ellard was among such individuals—showing great promise as a performing virtuoso at a young age, he became one of the first Australian-educated professional musicians to pursue further studies in Europe. He returned to Australia some years later and advertised himself as a performer and teacher with considerable success; in doing so, however, he established a precedent of seeking education elsewhere, rather than institutionalizing it at an advanced level locally. Frederick in particular cannot be held at fault for his decision, nor, of course, can anyone who chose to temporarily leave their country. Conversely, no single individual can be held responsible for developing the educational infrastructure of an entire nation; the perpetual procrastination of establishing any self-sufficient system of education, however, continues to impact the musical life of the country.

Throughout this chapter, more attention has been directed toward the "art music" of colonial Australia than their convict counterparts. ("Convict" is a somewhat inelegant term that encompasses both those true convicts of the original penal colonies, and those who were simply of a low socioeconomic status.) It is worth discussing, however, the traditions of Australia's "folk songs" that largely date to this period. It is inherently distinct from the folk music of other regions in that much of it did not originate from the musics of "native" peoples, but rather, from the large variety of immigrant cultures dispersed throughout the colonies (e.g., Celtic, English, German, Scandinavian, etc.); Aboriginal musics, which many would rightly suggest are the true product of "native" Australians, were still merely a passing ethnographic interest.

Many of these Australian songs consisted of newly composed poems set to popular preexisting tunes, often sea shanties of the eighteenth and nineteenth centuries. Early Australian "bush ballades" sing of the harsh conditions of the colonial era and of such "stock" figures as bushrangers,[16] swagmen,[17] drovers, stockmen, and shearers; convict and bushranger verses, in turn, often complained of governmental tyranny. (These various characters were, in some regards, an Australian counterpart to those of the Italian *commedia dell'arte*.) A number of poems, additionally, commented on the relationships between white settlers and Indigenous peoples in various regions across colonized Australia.

Part and parcel with these themes were the difficulties imposed by the arid Australian countryside (colloquially known as "the Outback")—immigrants set about the somewhat senseless tasks of clearing native vegetation, growing crops, and shearing sheep, all of which were distinctly British agricultural activities scarcely suitable for the inhospitable nature of the Australian landscape. These activities were, of course, intended to establish an air of familiarity on such jarringly foreign terrains; doing so, however, was almost certainly a futile effort on the part of the colonists, and perhaps contributed to the forlorn and dejected atmosphere so prevalent in their early songs. Poet A.B. Banjo Paterson's "The Silent Shearer" (from his gravely entitled book *The Animals Noah Forgot*) is as good a testament to this as any:

Weary and listless, sad and slow,
Without any conversation,
Was a man that worked on The Overflow,
The butt of the shed and the station.[18]

Not all musics were so single-mindedly despondent, of course. Through the nineteenth century, as Australia became increasingly prosperous and developed beyond its humble origins as a penal colony, the folk songs likewise became imbued with a sense of humor and resilience. Furthermore, a "gold rush" in the 1850s expanded the range of immigrant cultures importing their own folk musics—as a result, North American and Asian prospectors, together with the primarily Northern European convicts, brought their songs, styles, and instruments, diversifying and enriching the nation's burgeoning music. Perhaps the most poignant representative of this era of Australia's folk music is Charles Robert Thatcher (1831–1878), an entertainer who, by "trade," panned for gold in the Victorian fields. His songs describe life among the prospectors in remarkable detail, detailing the harsh conditions, perpetual drunkenness, tensions with authorities, and struggles of daily survival. In spite of these unpleasurable circumstances, however, Thatcher's songs maintain an optimistic and humorous nature that enlivens the otherwise pervasive misery of the time. Indeed, his music is emblematic of the Australian character writ large, portraying an image of strength, resilience, and levity in even the most unforgiving of circumstances. For example, a poem in his *Colonial Minstrel* songbook upholds the virtue of struggle in earning a fortune:

No one out here need toil in vain
If his mind to work he's giving,
In spite of hardships it is quite plain,
Each one may get a living;
So in Australia stay awhile,
And work away with vigour,
For many a one will make his pile
That's now a hard-up digger.[19]

Thus, the ballades of the time exhibit remarkable diversity and individuality. Different poets, understandably, introduced different perspectives and influences to their use of the form: some narrated enthralling escapades that venerated the Australian bushman as a heroic figure; others maintained a reflective, elegiac tone, emphasizing the loneliness and difficulties of the bush life; yet others were profusely comical, almost caricaturing the colonial Australian society. Many, too, are distinctly nostalgic, striving to preserve the coarse beauty of the Outback amidst the gradual modernization and urbanization of nineteenth-century Australia.

Complementing these provincial, yet touching, bush songs were myriad instruments accessible to the poor, traveling classes. Many of these accompanying instruments were derived from European musical traditions and were easily portable to accommodate the transient life of bushrangers and gold diggers—for example, the fiddle, button accordion, tin whistle, harmonica, and banjo were quite common. The last of these was, in fact, so widespread, that it was a central element of A.B. "Banjo" Patterson's musical persona, later canonized by his publishing a collection of colonial ballads entitled *Old Bush Songs* (1890).

In the nineteenth century, the growing popularity of Australian bush poetry augmented the first iteration of a conscious Australian nationalism. Poems appeared with great frequency in periodicals and newspapers of the era, and surviving evidence suggests that these songs were highly mobile, transmitted to and performed in regions where other forms of entertainment were quite scarce. These periodical publications were, in fact, themselves sympathetic to Australian nationalist sentiments; the emphasis on the "bush" as a peculiarly Australian setting, therefore, advanced the perceived creation of a national literature and folklore.[20]

The above-mentioned stock characters were further venerated in literary circles as symbolic of Australian nationalistic and egalitarian ideals, firmly rooted in the sense of equality and anti-totalitarianism fostered during the earliest penal colonies. Indeed, these sentiments were so strongly encouraged that the quintessential Australian expression—"mate"—originated around this time: as historian Russell Ward describes, "a convict-derived ethos of matey anti-authoritarianism embedded itself in the Australian psyche from the beginning"; far from a simple and innocent denotation of friendship, "mateship" evoked the intraclass loyalty, unconditional assistance, and mutual respect pervasive among the early convicts and new settlers.

As with any immensely popular genre of music, however, the bush ballades elicited a substantial share of criticisms. While some felt that they provided an authentic representation of "Australia," others derided their pastoral romanticization of the bush. (It is hard to entirely disagree with this criticism, given the unforgiving climate, omnipresence of lethal fauna, and extreme isolation from established settlements.) Critics noted that the majority of published poets were, in fact, professional writers situated in urban areas such as Sydney and Melbourne, and thus they did not have much direct experience of the bush. Given that the landscape was persistently regarded as among the most distinguishing features of Australia, balladists likely felt it was a universal theme through which to communicate a national "experience"; nonetheless, it is true that writers fantasized and idealized much of the life in the Outback. Furthermore, they often forewent any legitimate representation of Aboriginal society, instead subjugating Indigenous cultures to racial prejudices of the time while glorifying the largely imagined Anglo-Celtic triumph over the environment. This element, however, garnered less criticism then as it does in contemporary scholarship, likely owing to the ubiquity of such biases at the time.

Irrespective of these criticisms, the bush ballade remained a central element of Australian folk culture that was as pervasive, if not more so, than the institutions of "high art" that wealthier settlers were attempting to establish in the colonies. Many of these primarily oral traditions of the early colonial era continue to influence the popular and folk culture of the nation today, and they contributed in no small measure to the formation of a distinctly Australian identity in the arts. In some regards, the undocumented performances of these ballades were perhaps of greater significance than contemporaneous premieres of works by Mozart and other such figures, in that they offered more thematic relevance to the experiences of settlers. Ballades exploited innumerable popular tunes reminiscent of the immigrants' homelands and presented easily comprehensible imagery that accorded with the national atmosphere; contrastingly, Bach, Mozart, Beethoven, and the already extensive canon of European "immortals," though impressive, were largely foreign, unfamiliar, and, quite simply, uninviting, reminding their listeners of the strict social hierarchies and governmental tyrannies of lands now far removed from them. These two bodies of repertoire, juxtaposed against one another, constituted much of Australia's early soundscape.

CHAPTER THREE

Revolutionary Figures and the First Enunciations of a "National Identity"

Late Nineteenth to Early Twentieth Century

I am hitting my head against the walls,
but the walls are giving way.
GUSTAV MAHLER

Perhaps, dear reader, this chapter's title suggests that your effort in sifting through the previous pages will now bear reward; that, after some burdensome prose, we have arrived at a definitive "Australian" music (and that this book may soon be concluded). As the number of remaining pages likely indicates, such is not the case. Almost a century after colonization, any convincingly Australian music had yet to be produced. We are as yet some distance away from a truly "national" music, and somewhat frustratingly so. We must, however, be patient with our Australian composers and remain assured that, eventually, some novel compositions will emerge. We must also be reminded that "nationalism" is rarely an isolated instance of ingenious artistic vision; instead, it is a tedious process, alternatingly galvanized by impulses of national sentiment and suppressed by broader concerns of cosmopolitanism. Compounding this is the general hesitancy toward asserting any overt "Australianness" within the country, as constituents have long preferred to label themselves by other, less forceful adjectives, such as "egalitarian," "naturalistic," or "open-aired."

Thus, we must defer our hopes for but a short while more, and temporarily content ourselves with the various figures introduced in the following pages. Though they may not be considered "revolutionary" by any contemporary standards, their willingness to embrace "Australian" as an adjective unto itself was significant enough to initiate a form of musical "nationalism," however gradual. It is through long-overlooked individuals such as these that a recognizably nationalistic foundation begins to emerge, and the characteristics of an "Australian" music to assume shape. Indeed, it is only after the following composers devoted their artistic lives to "hitting their head against the walls" of European aesthetics that these walls could give way to a regional individualism.

G.W. Marshall-Hall (1862–1915)

Born in London on March 28, 1862, George William Louis Marshall-Hall experienced an adventuresome and unrestrained childhood, imbued with an exuberance for the vitality of life that strongly contrasted the somewhat lethargic nature of British society at the time. Exemplifying this were the parental practices of Marshall-Hall's father, who owned a sixty-five-ton ocean yacht kept "in great measure to give my family fresh air, the opportunity of seeing foreign ports, of leading a healthy life such as cannot be led on shore, and, lastly, not least, to prevent my children from disgracing their Viking extraction."[1] Indeed, much of his youth epitomized a defiance against the standards of traditional society, defining his regard both for music and for public conduct for the remainder of his life.

Marshall-Hall undertook all his training (musical and otherwise) in England and Europe, and thus his musical language assumed the stylistic traditions of the Old Continent; he would later come to be an early, if somewhat peripheral, representative of the "English Musical Renaissance," in that his work would absorb the unmistakable self-confidence and subliminal anti-authoritarianism of his youth. His first educational endeavors, excluding a brief period in Brighton, took place in Blackheath Proprietary School, during which time he enrolled in private music lessons. In 1878, he moved to Switzerland with his family, where he formed a choral society that met regularly to practice in his family's dining room. He began studying organ privately in Berlin under Carl August Haupt; then, in 1883, he enrolled in the Royal Conservatory of Music, studying organ with Walter Parratt, composition with Hubert Parry, and counterpoint with Frederick Bridge. He was subsequently appointed as organist at Oxford Military College; organist and choirmaster at Newton College (1884–1886); assistant to Alan Gray, music master at Wellington College; and, in 1888, director of the orchestra and choral society at the London Organ School and College of Music, where he also taught composition and singing. Simultaneously with these and various other pedagogical activities, Marshall-Hall had begun to author articles on myriad musical subjects, many of which appeared in English newspapers and magazines.[2]

Throughout this early period of his life, Marshall-Hall's paternal grandmother and his great-uncle, both of whom were accomplished and devoted musicians, supported and encouraged his artistic pursuits. His father, however, met these professional undertakings quite unfavorably—he had emphatically declared that he "wouldn't want any damn fiddler in his family" and eventually banished his son without the slightest monetary support. He so strongly admonished him for this apparently base profession that he was not moved even when Marshall-Hall, unable to obtain work on occasions throughout the 1880s, was compelled to sleep in the snow, buttoning his jacket up to the neck amidst "polite society" to conceal his lack of a shirt collar and waistcoat.

Nonetheless, Marshall-Hall's profession was not interminably dependent upon the fragile and unpredictable whims of England's musical economy. In 1890, he was appointed as the premiere Ormond Professor of Music at the University of Melbourne, Australia, tasked with governing the newly created music "department."[3] This employment was, perhaps, a fluke of academia, considering his few formal qualifications for the position: the sum total of his tertiary education was a mere three months at the Royal College of Music, which he left after becoming "impatient with the college's slow ways and slower Professors";[4] his only other relevant musical achievement, apart from freelance musical journalism, had been an 1888 performance by the London Symphony Orchestra of an excerpt from his opera *Harold*. The appointment of Australian university professors at the time was typically based on recommendations from expert committees established for the purpose in London; the deficiency of Marshall-Hall's qualifications for the position is reflected in the fact that, although he was one of forty-eight applicants when the post was first advertised, all members of the London committee declined to make any recommendation. One member argued that although "some eminently respectable men, and good musicians in the ordinary sense of the word" had applied, there were "certainly not five—hardly one—of whom I could honestly speak as first-class. [...] The best men have not become candidates."[5]

Likely hoping for more favorable contenders and still lacking any official appointment, the University of Melbourne re-advertised the position later that year. Marshall-Hall, having attained little professional or artistic success since the first search, nonetheless applied and, again, was not regarded particularly highly. Anxious to fill the appointment, however, the committee succeeded in recommending four names, of which Marshall-Hall was one, to the Council of the University of Melbourne; yet they abstained from ranking these four individuals, perhaps on the premise that none of them were particularly qualified. Although the committee felt an immediacy to produce an individual of merit, given their failed first attempt, their indecision did little to resolve the matter; indeed, the lingering impasse within the Council only delayed it further. It was not until the Council obtained private advice from several musicians largely unrelated to the search, such as concert pianist Sir Charles Hallé and the principal of the Royal Academy of Music, that they determined—somewhat resignedly—the appointment of Marshall-Hall to be the "[nearest] to the mark." Underwhelming and grossly inefficient as this decision may seem, it was to have a significant impact on the musical life of Australia.

Arriving in Melbourne (and thus escaping the-then rule-bound, conservative English musical establishments), Marshall-Hall proved to be a flamboyant extrovert of indefatigable vitality and exuberance, promoting "constant activity" pursuant to a "superabundant life" and "the utmost joy of living." Contemporaries remarked on his loud laughter and his habit of humming operatic airs as he strode around town, of tapping his baton importunately on the podium and glaring at restive concert audiences to inspire silence when conducting, and of writing volatile comments—such as "O superfine Assiduity" and "monstrous ignorance"—in the margins of books he read as a demonstration of his contempt for their writers.[6] He quickly forgot the tribulations of his recent past in London and embraced the energy of his youth, embodying the vicariousness of Australian life in a way perhaps only few could. His coarseness and vulgarity, too, seemed to complement the atmosphere of the time, despite general attempts to implement a sense of "refined society" within the colony. Jocundity and classlessness were the defining characteristics of his personality—controversialist and critic Bernard Shaw vividly described him as "a representative of young genius, denouncing the stalls, trusting to the gallery, waving the democratic flag, and tearing around generally."[7] Marshall-Hall's program note for a 1908 performance of his *Symphony in E Flat* encapsulated these sentiments quite well:

> This symphony was originally conceived of a summer holiday whilst camping out in Sydney Middle Harbour with a couple of congenial comrades. I found that in it I had unconsciously gathered together as a harmonious whole the many heterogenous impressions of Australian life and scenery which my stay in this country had engendered. Hence its buoyant cheerful tone. For what have we Australians, in this fresh unattempted land which absorbs all our energies, to do with the self-questionings, the too often morbid introspectiveness,

> that the gloomy climate and cramped-life conditions of our English ancestral home more and more tend to induce? Here we grow up under a genial Southern sun, amid an environment which makes it a delight merely to be alive. In every direction new paths open before us. Our every faculty, every energy, finds countless fields for healthy exertion. For us the world is only beginning.

A friend of Marshall-Hall's in England, music critic John Runciman, would likewise note the immense influence of the natural environment on his personality and work (undoubtedly with origins in his early travels with his father):

> The strangeness of nature in that strangest of lands [Tasmania] took possession of him; he felt as if existence were an unreal dream; he seemed to be taken back a thousand years to the far-off beginnings of the world. Stillness and sunshine and the eternal sea—these made life.

(Runciman would, a few sentences later, further his underlying implications of exoticism and primordiality by claiming that he thought it "something like a crime that such a man should be wasted on a half-civilised city, in a nearly totally barbarous continent.")[8]

Marshall-Hall's immense enthusiasm for Australia's potential was duly channeled into his musical activities in Melbourne, and, during the next quarter of a century, he exercised an inestimable influence on music education, appreciation, and performance throughout Australia. He was not satisfied with passively presiding over the University's negligible degree and diploma courses; indeed, he bemoaned the lack of sustained general interest in the program, as well as his inability to regulate the practical studies of performance-oriented students (the absence of music faculty apart from himself meant that the students were obliged to take private lessons of their choice in the external community). Thus, to eradicate (or at least minimize) these issues, Marshall-Hall petitioned for the establishment of a university conservatorium. In 1894, legislation was passed to create the first conservatorium in the British Empire within a university, over which Marshall-Hall presided as its ex-officio director. This was to have a significant and enduring impact on the musical activities of Australia, as it institutionalized—and therefore sanctioned—the professionalization of music, elevating it to a status above the colonial-era apprenticeship of performance.

Concurrently with these developments, Marshall-Hall established a largely professional orchestra, named the Marshall-Hall Orchestra, outside the University, which soon began to give an annual series of concerts in the Melbourne Town Hall. Through his access to this ensemble, he introduced a considerable amount of novel orchestral music to the colony and gained a reputation as a fine conductor. From 1897–1902, he acted as the honorary conductor of the Melbourne Liedertafel, a male choir; he additionally continued to compose a vast breadth of instrumental and vocal music, much of which was performed in Melbourne under his direction. Adding likewise to the spiritual life of the colony, he established a body of prayers recognized by visiting musicians as (generally) equal to those in Europe.

Despite acheiving these monumental strides in Australian music, however, Marshall-Hall's unrestrained temper and astonishing public behavior had become overbearing, and his widely circulated articles and lectures became notorious for their "socially outrageous," and otherwise disreputable, nature. Following the publication of his collection of poems, *Hymns Ancient and Modern* (1898), satirically titled and laden with irreligious verses that so strongly contrasted his "serious" body of musical prayers, the press unreservedly accused him of "lewdness, animalism, lasciviousness and anti-clericalism." Soon after, Marshall-Hall delivered an address at a Melbourne Liedertafel concert that, although not strictly indecent, nonetheless upset the Victorian sensibilities of the time in their promotion of sexual liberality and a sensuous enjoyment of life. If that had not borne enough offense, his praise of war among men certainly did: in arguing that such activity is "a good thing. Nay! The best thing. It is a symptom of vitality, energy, super-abundant strength," he appeared to symbolize the imminent disintegration of what was already a delicately balanced colonial society.[9] The fiercely bitter public debate that ensued brought the question of freedom of free speech to the fore; in turn, it stimulated national interest in Marshall-Hall as a personality, but otherwise decimated his professional reputation. Not content with merely upheaving the sensitive moralities of the Australian community, Marshall-Hall proceeded with slandering its ongoing musical activities, asserting that the performances were "execrable," the concert-goers "profoundly ignorant of what music is," and the music teachers "frightfully bad." When private school principals complained about the high failure rate in the matriculation music examination (for which he, in fact, was responsible), he retorted that

> it is fortunate our schools are the last places in the world to which our youth turn for light and understanding, otherwise they would grow up mentally akin to those monstrosities which I remember with dim horror upon the tables of boarding-houses and which go by the name of resurrection pies.

Those who disagreed with his judgements, explosive and unnuanced as they were, found themselves the subject of his impassioned verbiage. Because of such public outrages, his tenure was not renewed in 1900—indeed, opposition to his continued presence was demonstrated by over seventy handwritten notes declaring "I, the undersigned Headmistress of . . . Girls' School in Victoria, beg to enter my strong protest against the re-appointment of Professor Marshall Hall to the Ormond Chair of Music in the University of Melbourne," each with the name of a school inserted and signed by its Headmistress. In defiant response, he set up his own "Conservatorium of Music, Melbourne" (later renamed the "Albert Hill Conservatorium") as a rival to that of the University of Melbourne, thereby dividing the music community's loyalties for an entire generation.

Despite this fervent display of pride and individuality, however, Marshall-Hall was disillusioned by his profound failure and, after the Marshall-Hall Orchestra dissipated in 1912, he returned to Europe to promote his own music, albeit with little success. This trip transpired to be an exceptionally brief one, however—in a strange whim of popular demand, he was reinstated as Ormond Professor in 1915 and returned to Australia in triumph.[10] Six months later, he died of peritonitis.

Strongly influenced by the work of Wagner especially, and Brahms and Puccini to a lesser extent, George Marshall-Hall's compositions display a pronounced individuality and sincerity. Much of his output adopted an ultra-romantic style understood by few in the period following his death, however, and the music fell into near-total neglect. It was not until the 1930s that they were revived by Percy Grainger, who purchased his collection of manuscripts; they thus became the first Australian works to be preserved for his Museum at the University of Melbourne in 1935. It is likewise interesting to note the flourishing of his music as roughly coinciding with the Federation of Australia—as musicologist Peter Tregear notes:

> It is precisely at this time that the country had on the one hand developed the social and economic infrastructure and population base to support a sophisticated level of musical enterprise, and on the other had yet to become inundated with the products of a fast-developing international music industry. Certainly, Marshall-Hall was no crude musical nationalist, but it is also true he saw his creative work as part of a nation-forming project, part of an effort to create [...] a 'heroic New Brittania.'[11]

While it is improbable that "nationalism," particularly as an uplifting of established institutions and supreme civic character, was a primary aim in Marshall-Hall's work, his influence on the musical maturation of Australia was undeniably critical. Indeed, it was both his steadfast commitment to the institutionalization of music and his resilient, vibrant character that would define Australian music for many, even long after his passing. Beyond Marshall-Hall's significant compositional output, it was as a teacher, enthusiastic and free from pedantry, and as an inspiring orchestral conductor that he did his most significant work, and the value of his influence on the musical life of Melbourne can thus hardly be overstated.[12]

A.E. Floyd (1877–1974)

Alfred Ernest Floyd was born on January 5th, 1877, to a pious Methodist family in Birmingham, England. His father, Charles Hulme Floyd, was a minister, and Alfred was therefore regularly exposed to liturgical music and practice; thus, when the family subsequently moved to Cambridge and Alfred Floyd had begun to display an inclination for music, he was accepted as an organ pupil by Dr. A.H. Mann, organist of King's College in the University of Cambridge. Mann's influence on Floyd's musical style was to be inestimable, and it was from him that came Floyd's later stylistic attributes in both extemporization and psalm accompaniment. By 1912, he had completed a Bachelor of Music degree from Oxford University, where he was mentored by J.C. Bridge, C.H. Kitson, and C.H.H. Parry.

Floyd was then employed as a chemist for some time in his brother-of-law's laboratory; he continued musical practice, however, and eventually gained employment as an organist and choirmaster in various parishes throughout England. In 1915, by the recommendation of English organist Sir Walter Parratt, Floyd was selected from over two hundred applicants for the position of organist and choirmaster of St. Paul's Cathedral in Melbourne, Australia.

During his thirty-two years in service at the Cathedral, his influence on and legacy within the nation's musical development were prodigious. He enforced a superlative standard from the choir, and the ensemble was soon lauded as equal to those in England and throughout Europe. Additionally, he introduced annual carol services and offered profound and intricate extemporizations and poetic psalm accompaniments, all of which were met with great enthusiasm from the congregation. His collective advancements to the liturgy and worship within Australia were significant, and it was under his direction that the St. Paul's Cathedral enjoyed an international reputation for excellence; indeed, his contributions were to earn him an honorary Doctor of Music degree in September 1917, conferred on him by the archbishop of Canterbury by the recommendation of a group of leading English church musicians visiting Melbourne.

Floyd did not, however, limit his attention to the immediate activities of the church; rather, he maintained a continuous interest in Melbourne's educational infrastructure and development. He was in constant demand as an adjudicator throughout music festivals in Australia; served as an examiner over several decades for the Melbourne University Conservatory of Music; lectured in music for the Workers' Educational Association and, until 1963, for the Council of Adult Education; and even made a foray into musical journalism and criticism for the *Argus*, enjoying the routine of attending concerts despite its enormous demands on his schedule.

Yet where Floyd arguably acquired his greatest acclaim was neither in the spiritual nor the pedagogical realm of Australian society—rather, it was from his recurring radio sessions with the Australian Broadcasting Commission. From 1944, at first in Victoria only and then nationally, he appeared on air each Sunday afternoon; then, from 1948, his "Music Lovers' Hour" was broadcast weekly for twenty-four years, (almost) without interruption. Through a simple, unpretentious, and straightforward approach to music discussion, he was soon widely beloved by audiences across the nation; as the pianist Lindley Evans would later recount: "He could charm the last sixpence from the canniest Scot, had he chosen to do so. In common with thousands of listeners I am filled with affection and admiration for this gentle man and fine musician." Musicologist Ian Burk commented that "A.E. Floyd had the ability to make music interesting and accessible to the musical public. By the 1940s, he was a household name in Australia particularly as a result of his music broadcasts, which always ended with the words 'and now I'll say goodbye 'til next time.'"[13]

These engagements, alongside his pedagogical pursuits at the Melbourne Church of England Girl's Grammar School and the Methodist Ladies' College, furthered the performance and appreciation of music on a broad level (both institutionally and culturally) throughout Australia, and more generally contributed to the sense of a positive and fulfilling education that he sought to inspire through his work. Unlike G.W. Marshall-Hall, the impression Floyd left was one of a mild, caring individual, sincerely devoted to the cultural advancement of Australia without the pretenses of public scandal. Neither was he limited to the imitation of English musical practice and standard—

indeed, he enthusiastically advocated for the support of Australian composers of "serious music," writing:

> The encouragement of our own composers, and especially perhaps of those who are brave enough to embark upon the writing of works on a fairly large scale (things which can hardly ever be what are called 'paying propositions') is a matter of the very first importance.[14]

It was a primary aim of his to "support home industries," as it were, and offered four specific manners in which the nation could do so: performance, publication, radio transmission, and recording. Approximately simultaneous to Floyd's writings, the Australian Government issued a Broadcasting Act that mandated the devotion of a certain percentage of airtime to "locally composed" music; thus, recording and broadcasting were among the most practical (and welcoming) pursuits in which a young musician could hope to garner attention. Further to this end, Floyd increasingly repurposed his "Music Lovers' Hour" to advance what he deemed to be "worthwhile" Australian composers, particularly after his radio broadcasts had achieved national exposure. His humble justification for doing so, particularly in defense against the general avoidance of any immoderate exposure to "Australian music," was that national "composers are not figuring quite so prominently at the moment. I try to do something about it on Sunday afternoons." On two separate celebrations of Australia Day (January 26th), Floyd's entire program was exclusively devoted to Australian works (which was, in itself, a venture rarely attempted and largely regarded as predestined for failure).

In his programming, Floyd often placed emphasis on the works of young, emerging composers; for example, he championed the music of Margaret Sutherland (1897–1984), Fritz Bennicke Hart (1874–1949), Peter Sculthorpe (1929–2014), Percy Grainger (1882–1961), Clive Douglas (1903–1977), and John Antill (1904–1986), among others. Significantly, the works he chose often adhered to functional tonality and otherwise Western compositional traditions, although this likely had less to do with an obstinance for convention than it did with his subdued, unchallenging demeanor. Throughout the mid- and late twentieth century, experimentation, dissonance unmediated by any tonal conventions, and a growing aversion to the ordered systems of harmonic and melodic motion were becoming increasingly popular throughout Europe; reactively, what was referred to as the "cultural cringe" permeated Australian music education, in which a strict adherence to and replication of European modernism was demanded of students. Although few truly enjoyed this idiom, which composer

Ross Edwards (b. 1943) would later describe as "convulsive" and "nihilistic," it had become the predominant musical force in the nation. Floyd, however, perhaps recognized its lack of promise within Australian music and thus did not promote it. Indeed, he asserted on numerous occasions that the musical training in Australian academic institutions was, in fact, detrimental to the creativity, individualism, and innovation of national composers. For example, he wrote in an article entitled "New Musical Education" that:

> The courses of study prescribed in many a college, or conservatorium, or university, are calculated to break and spoil the musical spirit of all but the most resilient students. One of the greatest living theorists told the present writer that his degree work (he was a graduate in music of an ancient and honourable university) had killed his originality.[15]

Thus, the predominant aesthetic that Floyd preferred to advance was confined within the immediate post-colonial period of Australian composition, largely reflecting an English pastoralism and European neo-classicism. The music's stylistic conservativeness was, likewise, to accommodate his desire to remain accessible to the general listener. He did not include any composers who came into prominence in the 1950s and 1960s, such as Felix Werder (1922–2012), Don Banks (1923–1980), Richard Meale (1932–2009), or Nigel Butterly (b. 1935), as he was staunchly opposed to their modernist, avant-garde, or otherwise "Second Viennese School" approach to their work; instead, he diplomatically circumvented their music by labeling it as "different," but unsuitable for radio broadcast.

Beyond Floyd's individual musical preferences, his programming choice was, at least partially, a result of his campaign to advance music listening and appreciation in Australia. Floyd sought to stimulate listeners without excessively challenging them, and therefore he presented works that were sufficiently "Australian" (and, thus, distinct from established European traditions), but that did not meander too far into the alienating and uninviting. Only once did he offer an example of traditional Aboriginal musics, albeit modified to accommodate the conservative restraints of "civilization." (He did, however, recognize the political ramifications of their music, stating that "we've taken nearly all their land, and now it's our duty to take care of them and learn something about them."). He noted "the intervals not clearly defined" and "an element of repetition, a matter of very great importance" in their music—both of these characteristics would, interestingly, emerge in the works of composers who later sought to achieve "Australianness" through Aboriginality.

Thus, Floyd was a significant catalyst for the advancement of Australian art music. His range of aesthetic tolerance was certainly limited; yet his encouragement of Australian composers, both publicly and in private, was not. Scant appreciation for, or engagement with, local music production was a significant impediment in the post-colonial period, which undoubtedly hampered an unrestrained flourishing of a new, national idiom. In embracing the Broadcasting Act's programming stipulations (particularly at a time when few dared to), however, Floyd subverted Australian hesitation toward their own composers. He sought to contextualize Australian music-making within the larger developments of England and Europe, but consciously strove to do so in a manner that was validating, rather than denigrating. His work received official recognition in 1948 when he was appointed an Order of the British Empire (O.B.E.), and in 1971 when he was awarded an honorary Doctor of Letters from Monash University. He died in a suburb of Perth, Western Australia, on January 13th, 1974, predeceased by his wife and survived by two sons.

Fritz Bennicke Hart (1874–1949)

Born in London and undergoing his musical training under the conservative English influences of Charles Villiers Stanford, Gustav Holst, and Ralph Vaughan Williams, Hart is often regarded as a British expatriate who, although enormously influential in promoting "serious" art music within Australia, did little to advance a nationalistic idiom of any esteem. This perspective is not wholly without credibility—indeed, Hart maintained a firm allegiance to and appreciation for the Victorian landscape of his home country, and he insisted that it was "absolutely impossible for a school of Australian creative music to arise that is not founded directly upon British music" there.[16]

Perhaps as a result of such perceptions, as well as his somewhat abrupt relocation to Honolulu, Hawaii toward the end of his career, Hart's legacy has largely faded into obscurity within Australian music history. What remains well-known is a supposed "rivalry" between him and Marshall-Hall, which had less to do with music than it did the chauvinistically anti-German and pro-British sentiments that had run amok in the aftermath of the two World Wars: Marshall-Hall having left for London, Hart assumed his lecturing duties at the Albert Hill Conservatorium in 1913; when Marshall-Hall announced a year later that the Conservatorium was to be closed, however, his staff refused to resign and appointed Hart as the new director. Then, after Marshall-Hall's reinstatement as the Ormond Professor at the

University of Melbourne in 1915, its predominantly German staff resented the greater popularity that Hart's British-oriented school attracted.

Yet such politically entrenched controversies did not define Hart's contribution to Australian culture. Despite his conservative compositional style, marked by a keen sense for text declamation coupled with the melodic fluency of English folksong, he contributed one central work that was distinctive for both its complexity and its subject matter: namely, his symphonic suite *The Bush* (1923). This work, too, is evidently "founded directly upon British music" in its pastoral nature, remarkable lyricism, general avoidance of dissonance, and the absence of that overwhelming ferocity that would come to define later Australian depictions of the untamed "bush." All sections are richly diatonic, and although Hart achieves climaxes of grandiose proportions that suggest something of the vastness of the Australian continent, the overall impression is of poised regality rather than inhospitable wilderness. (Musicologist Christopher Mark commented that "the work could just as easily have been entitled *Picnic on the Downs*."[17])

Nonetheless, the work represents the overall consciousness of early twentieth-century Australians that their landscape, in its singular diversity, merited attention in their concert music. Hart understood the character of the country in a distinctly British manner: its mysteriousness imbued a sense of majesty in its expanses, as unattainable as a sheltered maiden for a chivalrous knight; without any potential of direct contact, therefore, he transformed it into an object of wonder and idealization. This romanticization of Australia's geography is a recurrent trend in the nation's history, as evident in their music as in their practical use of the land—until today, sheep herds and winsome colonial homes remain "distinguishing" features of many regions, largely deriving from the quaintness associated with ruralism in Britain. Thus, Hart represented the conservative notion of what the "bush" was to the English listener, albeit soon to be replaced by other, more modernistic representations. He would dismiss those later idioms, however; in discussing an interview with Hart, the Australian poet and journalist Louis Esson would emphasize his predisposition for nostalgic pastoralism:

> Complexity for its own sake is no virtue. It takes a big man, he remarks, to say a simple thing simply. At the risk of being considered old-fashioned he is utterly opposed to the spirit of jazz, and the hysterical, sensational, Negroid element that permeates so much modern art. Admitting the difficulty of judging contemporary art, he yet takes

> Stravinsky as an example of a composer who was great up to a certain point and then, as in "The Rite of Spring," was content with primitive rhythms that had the power, akin to the beating of drums by negros, of rousing a civilized audience to frenzy. Such work, like a great deal of modern music, is only physically, not spiritually, stimulating. He believes that music is a leisured art, not expressive of the psychological conditions of a rushing, mechanical age, and in its essence serene and consolatory. He warns us not to be deceived by the easy doctrine that change necessarily means progress.[18]

Notwithstanding his present obscurity from both the Australian and the international musical community, Hart was a renowned entity of his time. In the same article, Esson wrote that:

> In his charming but workmanlike garden-study, with his piano and some favourite books and pictures, Fritz Hart is happily working at his original compositions. Composers are rare in Australia, and we are, indeed, fortunate to have in our midst a musician of such rare natural gits and fine equipment. Though Fritz Hart is English by birth and training, he has become so Australian in spirit that we can justly claim him now as one of our own. It was in Australia, as he gaily admits, that he first really discovered himself. Indeed, in some curious imaginative way, he was always an Australian, seeking like an old mystical Spanish voyager an ideal Terra Australis, a great free Southern Land of the Holy Spirit.[19]

The desire—and perhaps even the necessity—to appropriate British composers as "Australian," irrespective of whether their music truly communicated a distinctly Australian experience, is evident in this brief extract. Hart emigrated to Australia on the premise of a conducting contract with theatrical entrepreneur J.C. Williamson; that this engagement was merely an excuse to pursue a greater spiritual expedition, however, is inconclusive. Indeed, such relocations often arose from practical and professional concerns. England's musical environment at the time was quite saturated with remarkable compositional figures, and for some, the hope for recognition rested in establishing oneself in a different country, where not only "talent," but composers altogether were "rare."

Though Hart could not "be accused of any narrow, nationalistic views" given his conservative, and perhaps even chauvinistic, English predilections, he nonetheless strongly advocated for the future of Australian art music. The challenges to a composer posed by a young and self-conscious nation such as Australia did not go unrecognized;

Hart, however, embraced those characteristics that are seemingly synonymous with "Australia" themselves, so frequently are they applied to eminent composers of this era:

> Though a composer has a hard road to travel in a young country like Australia, Fritz Hart is happy in his surroundings, in his music, in his love for our great sunshiny country, the bush and the sea and with his Pan-like spirit, his gaiety and eternal youthfulness, he is a good illustration of Rodin's saying that, for all his troubles and disappointments, the artist is the only happy man.

Hart's idealistic sojourn in Australia was, unfortunately, rather brief. In 1931, he was invited to Hawaii as a guest conductor of the Honolulu Symphony Orchestra, and, in 1937, he accepted the post of permanent conductor; he was also appointed as the first professor of music at the University of Hawaii. Thereafter, he visited Melbourne only once, for the jubilee of the Albert Street Conservatorium. During the remainder of his life, Hart continued to compose, paint, and author twenty-three unpublished novels. He passed away on July 9, 1949 of cardiac disorder.

Percy Grainger (1882–1961)

The most commonly asked question in response to this book on Australian music (aside from "why *Australian* music, of all things?") was "is the book about Percy Grainger, then?" What often ensued was a feeble explanation that Grainger was not, in fact, as Australian as his singularity in non-Australian histories of music would make it appear. Such assertions, however, are generally received as philistine at best, and sacrilegious at worst.

Quite ironic in this perception is that, until not so long ago, it might have been appropriate to awkwardly extol Percy Grainger's virtues as an underestimated, if not entirely "neglected," composer (which, of course, the author has shamelessly done with several other figures in this chapter). Indeed, it was not until the late twentieth century that Grainger's presence in the periphery of both the popular and the academic musical consciousness became noteworthy, owing in part to such projects as the British recording company Chandos' "Complete Grainger Edition" on CD (advertised in 1997 as "one of the most important recording projects of the decade," and only completed in 2021), as well as a series of books and sketches on his "artistic" legacy.

Certainly, Grainger's eccentric personality has amassed significant attention from biographers, or at least far more than almost any other Australian composer to date. This attention arguably owes much more to his eccentricity, however, than to his musical work—writers cannot help but gossip about his professed despise for his primary instrument, the piano, which he unflatteringly described as nothing more than "a box of hammers"; his affinity for garish, self-designed clothes made from towels, often so bizarre that passerby mistook him for a vagrant; his peculiarly close relationship with his mother, which invited rumors of incest and formed the basis of the movie *Passion* (1999); and his sexual fanaticism for self-flagellation, which eventually became so pronounced that he proclaimed his creativity to be inseparable from his whip. Amplifying these social indecencies is his uncomfortable lack of clandestineness; rather, Grainger appears to have been quite proud of his unusual personality. In 1938, for example, he endowed a museum in his birthplace of Melbourne and entrusted it with a large collection of whips, pornography, and blood-stained shirts. "Music is the art of agony," he noted. "It derives, after all, from screaming." These unsettling characteristics, particularly when juxtaposed against a performance career laden with impressive achievements, have since procured for Grainger a reputation amongst musicians as "an Australian composer" (if not "*the* Australian composer"), further cultivated by his remarkable volume of self-procured publicity.

Nonetheless, the myth of Grainger's inherent "Australianness" is challenging to debunk. Such perceptions may owe, in part, to his taint as an "outsider." Few of Grainger's compositions exceed ten minutes in length (and thus are considered "miniatures), and they often feature unconventional orchestrations with harmoniums, banjos, theremins, or ukuleles, among other atypical instruments. His disdain for classical form extended to a determined rejection of Italianate terms for tempo and dynamic markings—for example, Grainger's scores indicate to the performer to "louden" rather than "crescendo," or instruct the player to interpret a passage "with pioneering keeping onness." Toward the end of his career, Grainger rejected "canonized" compositional practices altogether in an attempt to bypass what he believed to be the "absurd goose-stepping" of standard notation; indeed, he eventually came to the opinion that Western music was arrested at a state of two-dimensional artifice, much like the conventionalized forms of Egyptian bas-relief, which he would then endeavor to counteract by constructing a machine capable of generating a scaleless, pulseless, synthetic sound termed "Free Music." The harmonic innovations that arose from his unwillingness to conform to "traditional" composition resulted in his structural motion "in unresolved discords," characteristic of his mature style, about which musicologist Malcolm Gilles stated: "to the best of my knowledge, such a procedure was unknown at that time and must be considered an Australian contribution to musical progress."[20] Grainger would, in a 1952 lecture, more explicitly clarify the intents underlying this experimentation:

> 1. Melody freed from the tyranny of harmony; 2. Harmony freed from the narrow conceptions of concordance; 3. Intervallic freedom unrestrained by the hampering confines of scale & key; 4. Rhythm freed from the constant in-step-ness-with-Jim (coincidence between the rhythms of the various voices); 5. Musical form freed from unsuitable 'architectural' conceptions. In other words: FREE MUSIC.

Naturally resulting from such concepts was music foreign and unsettling to an audience otherwise accustomed to pleasurably tonal music, thus necessitating a lecture from Grainger, tinged with unsettling overtones of racial supremacy, on "The Goal of Musical Progress":

> 'Free music' [...] will be the full musical expression of the scientific nature-worship begun by the Greeks and carried forward by the Nordic races. It will be the musical counterpart of Nordic pioneering, athleticism, nudism. In all these respects it will be cosmic and impersonal, and thus fundamentally differentiated from the strongly personal and 'dramatic' music of non-Nordic Europe with its emphasis upon sex, possession, ambition, jealousy and strife.

(Alongside America, Britain, and Scandinavia, Grainger regarded Australia as belonging to the Nordic race; he excluded, however, Germany.)

It is therefore the sheer oddity of Grainger's approach to his personal and artistic existence that has almost intuitively granted him popularity as an *Australian* composer. (An "odd Australian composer" would perhaps be redundant.) For a time, Grainger embraced this association and "used to insist that he was an Australian composer" who simply "lived in the U.S."—when, in 1917, he revealed his intentions to become an American citizen to British music critic Robin Legge, he made particular note that:

> In wishing to become an American I do not love Australia less, its incomparable scenery, its glorious ultra-democraticness, its myriad nature appeals to me. It is because I am such an ultra-democratic, ultra

> Colonial [sic] Australian, I think, that I find in America such intense satisfaction, such a realisation of my inborn ideals.[21]

His later founding of the Grainger Museum in Melbourne likewise bears testament to his aim of (if not his intermittent obsession with) becoming Australia's "first renowned composer."[22] Yet, this insistence on a national association was merely sentimental and emerged concurrently with the increasing popularization of an Australian national "identity"; otherwise, it scarcely gained realization in his musical output. He moved to the United States in 1914 and, aside from a few brief tours in Australia, directed his attention primarily toward performance, composition, and pedagogy; furthermore, his attention to his homeland's music was vastly overshadowed by that of England and Norway throughout the entirety of his career.

In fact, he spent only the first thirteen years of his life in Melbourne before relocating to Germany to pursue his musical studies at the Hoch Conservatory, and thus he wholly detached himself from the musical activities of his homeland. His decision was motivated primarily by a lack of professional opportunities in his Australia—a tradition unto itself in the country—and, after the outbreak of World War I, he permanently established himself in the United States. (He later subverted the implications of this decision, claiming that he felt his ambitions made it *necessary* for him to live away from the country that supposedly "inspired his creativity.")

Thereafter Grainger had little direct impact on, or consistent involvement in, Australia's young compositional culture. He is occasionally mentioned as one of the earliest composers to attempt the creation of an Australian "idiom" (most notably, in Henry Tate's *Australian Musical Possibilities*) as a result of his composition *Colonial Song* (1912), in which he sought to evoke the loneliness of "vast virgin countries" and the "struggles against natural and climactic hardships (rather than against the more actively and dramatically exciting counter wills of their fellow men)." The sentimentality, idealism, and pastoralism he portrayed, however, have more often been ascribed a quality of self-aware "kitsch" than as any genuine representation (colonial or otherwise) of Australia. Yet his use of, or allusion to, folk song, and the then-emerging nationalist discourses are united in that the "the verbal art of the peasantry" had become, in the nineteenth and twentieth centuries, the primary means by which such discourses could legitimize their claim to "authenticity." Indeed, the presumed value of folk repertoire (or, in the case of Grainger's *Colonial Song*, an *invented* folk song) was that it could transform "an experience of individual transcendence" by the "folk" composer, such as what Grainger temporarily aspired to become, into a benign symbol of national "unity"; somewhat ironically, then, he was contesting the increasing desensitization and de-popularization of music that the emerging modernist aesthetic was espousing, thereby encouraging an Australian reaction against its dogmas.[23]

Notwithstanding this isolated attempt at contributing to an Australian musical idiom, which itself was largely overlooked by the general public, it is challenging to identify any explicitly "national" traits within his catalogue of music. One could perhaps argue that Grainger's most Antipodean characteristic was the manner in which his musical scores manifested as a "vast, virgin" soundscape open to all outside influences, and thus they reflected his opinions and attitudes of Australia itself. Further exemplifying this was his own system of ranking composers, in which he placed Bach first (and himself ninth, with especial strengths in "experimentation" and "complexity") because, he said, "if he were living today, I feel Bach would include ragtime, Schonbergism, musical comedy, Strauss and all the grades in between." Above all, Grainger maintained that music was a universal art: "As a democratic Australian, I long to see everyone somewhat of a musician, not a world divided between undeveloped amateurs and overdeveloped musical prigs." His egalitarianism would, in turn, become evident in his compositional practices—he argued, for example, that his "musical creed (to which I do not consistently live up) is 'musical democracy,' my definition of 'democracy' being 'a chance for all to shine in a starry whole.' I would like each voice, at all times throughout my music to enjoy equal importance & prominence."[24]

This progressive and liberal attitude, reminiscent of the classlessness of convict Australia, was certainly revolutionary for its time; yet outside of these philosophies, Grainger offered little of tangible value to the composers after him. Indeed, Grainger merely influenced the *concept* of a distinctively Australian music, rather than a specific style or realization thereof, offering a vision analogous to the monotonous landscape and Asian-Pacific location of the country that inspired following generations without providing any clear point of departure. Perhaps this lack of commitment to any particular "national sound" arose from his somewhat detached understanding of the nation itself, given his seldom-interrupted status as an expatriate. Among his most succinct contributions to theoretical discussions on what Australian music *might* be were his ideologies about its necessarily inherent diversity, in which he

> [suggested] at various times that it might exhibit a deliberate monotony (reflecting the long spans of Australian landscape, in contrast to the segmented nature of European topography and much of its music); become a clearing-house of Pacific, Asian and Aboriginal styles; engage by natural inclination in wistful sentimentality on the model of music in other pioneering countries (cf. Stephen Foster in the USA); be democratically equal in its part-writing and happy-go-lucky in its assignment of voices and instruments; or show an affinity, because of its origins in a predominantly warm climate, for broad Italianate dynamic shading and Italianate vocal and instrumental timbres.[25]

Overarching his musical continentalism, however, was his belief that the music must seamlessly develop across great expanses of time, rather than perpetually repeat and manipulate small groups of self-contained material (as, paradoxically, was often the case with his own folk-song miniatures, and which continues to be evident in the works of contemporary composers).

A slightly more decisive demonstration of the influence Grainger would have over the following generation of Australian musicians is in an anecdote of his encounter with the young composer Peter Sculthorpe (1929–2014). Sculthorpe reportedly met Grainger at the age of nine while walking with his mother in the Melbourne Botanic Gardens, and, upon disclosing his desire that he, too, was to be a composer, Grainger exclaimed "my boy, you must look north, to the islands!" (Presumably, Grainger was referencing the Asiatic islands.) This conversation would, ostensibly, motivate Sculthorpe to reconcile and unite Eastern and Western musical cultures in his compositions, and thus it was a source of inspiration for many of his later musical endeavors. Such encounters exemplified Grainger's capacity for inspiring, either directly or inadvertently, composers of the next generation to reify those ethereal "Australian" qualities so uniquely embodied in Grainger's persona, if not his own music.

Conceivably as a result of these philosophies, many Australian musicians and critics considered Grainger an unequivocal product of their nation. A.E. Floyd wrote, for example, that

> Australia and Melbourne have abundant reason for being proud of this unique personality. A very intelligent observer has declared that everything he says, writes, or does is different from what anyone has said, written or done before; also that the 'open-air' influence can be felt in all his work, in other words that no musician has ever less suggested the atmosphere of either the drawing room or the study.[26]

It is perhaps this legacy alone that justifies Grainger's universal "Australianness." He was among the few to sincerely embrace the endearingly odd nature of his country, thus popularizing and legitimizing the concept of "Australia" itself—indeed, considering the perpetual unease with which its constituents regarded their nationality, it was rare to find one who continually advocated for its relevance and viscerally exuded a "nationalism" through both his persona and his "pedagogy."

Clive Douglas (1903–1977)

Born in Rushworth, Victoria, on July 27th, 1903, Douglas's early life was punctuated by the death of his father in 1906, his mother's remarriage, and the family's frequent relocations; thus, his educational and artistic pursuits were quite unsettled. Like many composers of this era, Douglas could not lay claim to a privileged background, and he therefore began a full-time job as a bank clerk from the age of fifteen (in which he was to remain for another eighteen years). In his spare time throughout the 1920s, he played in amateur regional orchestras and dance bands as a violinist and pianist; concurrently, he pursued lessons in theory, orchestration, and conducting with Alberto Zelman. Otherwise, any "serious" musical ambitions were postponed—it was not until 1929 when, on the basis of his first attempt at a fully scored opera, Douglas secured a scholarship that enabled him to pursue a Bachelor of Music in composition at the University of Melbourne Conservatorium.

In 1936, Douglas was appointed as a staff conductor at the Australian Broadcasting Commission, the impact of which was threefold: first, he now commanded a professional orchestra through which he could promote his own work; second, his engagements around Australia fostered his admiration for the nation's diverse landscapes; and third, he acquired an interest in Aboriginal music, melody, and culture as a symbolic representation of the nation itself. It is in the latter regard that his music displays significant novelty, however—he was among the first of the nation's composers to truly embrace and incorporate Aboriginality within Australian music, successfully merging the two cultures through masterful orchestration and imagery. Indeed, it was during his time with the ABC that Douglas sought to capture the fundamental quality of the national landscape and its Indigenous peoples (despite lacking any first-hand encounter with the latter), and thus to find a musical idiom "so Australian that no other influence can be felt." From this perspective, he was perhaps the first composer to demonstrate a sincere interest in articulating an "Australian" quality in his music, and his program notes often depict his work as consciously and deliberately nationalistic.

Furthermore, Douglas is noteworthy for the invention of what may be considered the "Australian" symphony. Throughout the mid-twentieth century, symphonies composed by "native" Australians for local audiences were scant, largely outnumbered by English-born composers who later settled in Australia (such as Marshall-Hall). The primary motivation for the local creation of such was the 1951 Commonwealth Jubilee Composer's Competition, which encouraged musicians from across the British Commonwealth to compose a symphony of no greater than forty minutes duration. (The title, of course, referenced Australia's fiftieth anniversary as a federation in the same year.) In addition to a first prize of £1,000, a separate award of £250 was reserved for the best Australian submission, in the event that an Australian was not the overall winner (an apparently foregone conclusion by the organizers, headed by the conductor of the Sydney Symphony Orchestra, Eugene Goossens). Douglas, enthused at the notion of composing a large-scale work on a national theme, submitted a sizeable symphony entitled "Jubilee" for consideration. In his program notes, under the "Aboriginal" pseudonym "Karawora," he wrote:

> The thought of writing this symphony occupied the composer's mind for two years prior to its completion in March 1951. Always keenly interested in creating a musical style germane to Australia, the operas and symphonic poems of Clive Douglas have exploited aboriginal folklore as a means of national musical expression. He has become convinced, however, that modern Australian life demands a more elastic idiom and that aboriginal art, however important in its own right, obviously expresses nothing of the life and thought of the average Australian.
>
> The symphony is thus not only a conscious attempt to break away from the traditional laws of harmony and melody which were developed in Europe, but is also the composer's first step towards a musical language arising more directly out of the atmosphere of Australian life. One result is a strong tendency to atonality as in the scherzo of this symphony where the composer uses harsh atonal harmonies to suggest some of the harsher aspects of Australian life.[27]

Writ large, the symphony is unified by a single theme that Douglas entitled "Spirit of Adventure," meant to "suggest a national characteristic of ruggedness." He describes the first movement, which dutifully adheres to Western convention through its use of sonata form, thus:

> The spirit of adventure dominates this movement with the strong opening subject for the brass section against soaring passages for strings and woodwind. . . A more jocund second subject conveys a feeling of freedom and subsequent sections reflect varying moods—the mystery of a vast unknown land, the drama of its early exploration, moments of strife followed by periods of tranquility and even romance. However all these moods are fleeting and give way to the dominant force of the opening.

The second movement is contemplative, reflecting the "solitude of the inland plains" and the "vast dead heart" of the desert. His description of the "Scherzo", the third movement referenced in his original program notes, is especially evocative and pictorial, if not a bit hyperbolic:

> Frequently atonal and harshly discordant, the scene of the Scherzo is set first in the din of cities, changing shortly to wide, wind-swept pasture lands and the stark, overwhelming devastation of an inland dust storm (and an allusion to the panic-stricken bleating mobs of suffocating sheep). The rhythm continues, leading to a great outburst of the "Spirit of Adventure" theme by the full orchestra in unison. Then follows the clanging of steel foundries, the pounding of a modern locomotive, the whir of textile mills, the crystal sounds of glass making—a return to the cities of an industrial empire.

Finally, his notes for the last movement affirmatively declares his commemoration of Australia as a nation, so strongly worded that, to the modern reader, Douglas appears a bit bombastic and perhaps unattuned to the nuances of his suggestions:

> The finale reflects the dignity of Australia taking its place in the affairs of nations. Lighter moments appear suggestive of a sport-loving people, but the more serious tones of national achievement predominate. With the measured rhythm of the drums of war as a background, the symphony ends as a song of freedom rises in simplicity and strength pointing towards a yet unformed future.

Throughout these descriptions emerges two central aspects of Douglas's approach to conveying nationalist sentiment: namely, programmatic titles and Aboriginality (although he confusedly denies any presence of the latter in his work). He often found it necessary to defend his preference for "fanciful [stories that] aid the listener's understanding," claiming that "involved [analyses] of theme and development [are] often highly technical and beyond the comprehension of the average concert goer," whereas "a simple number at the top of a score" is simply unhelpful. Nonetheless, more conservative figures of the era, most of whom adhered to modernist or otherwise European techniques, derided the use of Aboriginal legends, modes, and rhythms as catalysts for an Australian nationalistic music. Among the most vocal proponents of this ideology was the tempestuous composer and critic Felix Werder, who asserted that

> There does, however, exist an amusing apology for Australian music when some composers attach to their impressionistic outpourings some such label as 'On the Road to Wagga-Wagga' or 'Murrumbidgeeana'.[28]

Douglas, however, rarely sought to superimpose any singular narrative on his works, all of which could otherwise be enjoyed purely from an abstract appreciation of their orchestral brilliance. He stated:

> None of these works are programme pieces in the material sense—the 'story' to each is meant merely as an aid to the listener. Remove the title and the synopsis and the music becomes purely abstract—it does not pretend to 'lead' any school of Australian composition, but is entirely personal. It is not held as a model for others to follow—this is left for posterity to decide. Sincerity of purpose has always been the aim of serious minded composers, and this is the ideal I try to follow.

The second element of Douglas's idiom—Aboriginality—is slightly more contentious and has been met with harsh rebuke from contemporary commentators. His music lacks any distinctive ethnography or otherwise legitimate representation of Indigenous peoples, primarily owing to his neglect in conducting fieldwork or establishing contact with those diverse peoples whom he sought to signify. Throughout Europe (and, subsequently, Australia), "armchair anthropology" was the primary mechanism of study, in which musical "research" was wholly based on the often-outdated writings of amateur ethnographers who, despite presenting claims to fieldwork, employed methods lacking scholarly or ethical rigor. Douglas, too, adhered to this methodology, and he studied the publications of Frank Gillen and Baldwin Spencer, among the foremost Australian anthropologists of the era who frequently worked jointly on Aboriginal reports. Novel and valuable that their writings were, they were nonetheless oversimplified, and at times rather cloddish, in their juxtaposition of the "civilized white man" against the "primitive aborigine." Furthermore, their emphasis on "primitivism," totemism, magic, mythology, and ritual—all of which was analyzed from a "behaviorist" perspective, rather than from any emic understanding of Aboriginal language or society—served more to excite the popular imagination than it did to offer a model of ethnographic study. Indeed, their mere advertising that Gillen had lived amongst representatives of the "Stone Age" was enough to validate their findings to the general public and instill a national interest in Aboriginality, to which Douglas likewise succumbed.

This primitivism espoused in Gillen and Spencer's books is quite evident in Douglas's musical compositions. His compositional style incorporates colorful and evocative orchestration (with, notably, a level of skill and expertise uncommon in Australia at the time); assertive chromatic melodies, occasionally punctuated by brief periods of diatonicism and even lyricism; and frequent parallel harmonies, often emphasizing tritones, fourths, and fifths that recall early chants and religious musics (albeit tinged with a sense of frenzied "tribalism"). In his description of his 1951 *"Jubilee" Symphony*, Douglas admits to "exploiting aboriginal folklore as a means of national musical expression," though it is unlikely that he would have considered this confession of "cultural appropriation" (or, quite literally, "exploitation") as anything inherently negative. Nonetheless, this attitude (in conjunction with his reliance on Gillen and Spencer's works) lent an atmosphere more akin to European primitivism than to its Aboriginal "origins" in his music, emphasized by his use of modalism, dissonance, driving rhythms, and continual reference to the "exotic." In turn, this quality has encouraged present-day musicologists to declare him "guilty" of cultural imperialism, of shameless colonialism, and of consciously misrepresenting Aboriginal culture—all common charges that, while justified from a contemporary perspective, are perhaps a bit too scathing in the context of mid-twentieth century Australia.

Douglas's musical Aboriginality consistently reappeared as a trope in his works between 1938 (with an orchestral work *Bush Legend,* which was subsequently reworked as *Kaditcha* and submitted for a Doctor of Music degree in 1958) through 1959 (with *Terra Australis*). Indeed, he was the first symphonic composer to holistically integrate Aboriginal musical elements in his work, far predating later (albeit more popular) works by contemporaries such as John Antill or Peter Sculthorpe; he was, likewise, among the first Australian composers to successfully undertake large-scale musical forms such as a symphony, offering the earliest iterations of what their "national" manifestations might be. By 1963, however, all references to Australia or Aboriginal motifs had conclusively dissipated with his *Third Symphony,* and he thereafter embraced a personal adaptation of twelve-tone serialism that was to define the remainder of his work. This compositional shift partly owed to the increasing aesthetic dominance of post-war modernism, which Douglas followed with a commitment rivaling that of his earlier "nationalism." In some respects, he was one to welcome experimentation with the (often European) trends of his time, emerging with remarkably individualistic works that spoke to the sentiments of their period. Somewhat ironically, however, Douglas also encouraged a "defiance of precedent," reminding his audience of the unique sociopolitical condition of Australia as compared to the Old World:

> Since there is no musical idiom which can be regarded as essentially Australian in style, nor any folk song source, an attempt has here been made to write music of national significance by creating a tonal thesis wedded to the land itself . . . The real Australia is that vast and little-known interior; the environs of the aboriginal painter, Namatjira . . . A land of vast distances and a grim, remorseless and forbidding desolation of sandy desert or gibber plain, contains incredible mountain formations and geological wonders unique in the world. It is a dramatic land conforming to no ordered pattern, a law unto itself.
>
> It is beyond the limitations of words to describe might be conveyed in the abstract quality of music—a music which, like the land, must be defiant of precedent.

Though Douglas's music itself was not quite so theoretically or artistically radical as his program notes might suggest, he was nonetheless a foremost contributor to the realization of a distinctly Australian music. He has, in recent times, unfortunately fallen into obscurity, and his works are seldom performed in favor of later, more progressive composers. Yet, he was among the most decisive and steadfastly assertive of Australian nationalism, and in no small measure contributed to the tiresome task of breaking down the wall behind which a new and revolutionary idiom patiently laid waiting.

John Antill (1904–1986)

Born in Sydney at the turn of the twentieth century, Antill remains in that unfortunate category of composers who remains a known entity solely on the basis of a single composition; even more unfortunate is that this same work, though still significant, is now disconcertingly outdated.

Earning the majority of his income for some time as a mechanical draftsman with the New South Wales Government Railways, he remained unfalteringly committed to music and soon overcame his father's reservations about the unreliable nature of a career in such field. He was surprisingly quite industrious during this period and composed a number of ambitious works (mostly operas and ballets), confirming both Antill's untiring energy and his passion for the theater. It is perhaps worth noting that Antill's formative years occurred immediately after a particularly productive period in Australian theater and musical drama: it was during this period of engagement of opera that composers such as Alfred Hill (1869–1960), Marshall-Hall, and Hart had premiered relatively accomplished operas, which undoubtedly influenced and encouraged Antill in his own compositional activities. He formally initiated his career by enrolling in the New South Wales State Conservatorium of Music, where he studied composition, violin, voice, and, tangentially, bass clarinet. During these years, the intensity of his curriculum prevented his producing such major works as during his "amateur" endeavors, but this should not be mistaken for any sudden decline in motivation. Quite to the contrary, his diary entries display an ever-increasing commitment to his musical aspirations, albeit tempered by his regret of not pursuing them earlier. For example, his entry on January 29, 1925 reads: "A bit brighter today full of ambition. I have made up my mind to become famous some day but how to do it I don't know." Remarkably, Antill was among the few Australian musicians who never embarked on what was otherwise considered an obligatory period of study abroad; he later claimed that he was "glad that [he] never went overseas to study as [he thought] it's important we in Australia should work things out on our own."[29]

Then, in 1936, Antill joined the Australian Broadcasting Commission as an assistant to the federal music editor and as a conductor of the Sydney Wireless Chorus, where he remained for another thirty-three years until his retirement. He was appointed as federal music editor himself in 1949, in which capacity he curated the selection of new Australian and overseas compositions submitted for broadcasting.

Antill contributed much to the general appreciation of Australian music during his service at the ABC, however, it was to be his 1946 ballet *Corroboree* that securely placed him within the canon of "national" composers and thereby advanced the public perception of a local idiom. As a young child, Antill had witnessed a "caribberie" (or "corroboree") and was enraptured by the costumes, ritualistic reenactments of sacred mythology, and propulsive energy of the Aboriginal peoples throughout the gathering. He claimed to have notated melodic and rhythmic figures that particularly intrigued him, preserving them for use several decades later in what was to be a watershed moment in Australian culture and nationalism. (Antill dates his visit to La Perouse, the site of the attended corroboree, to 1912 or 1913, when he was not older than nine years of age; other musicologists give the year as 1911, at the age of seven. In either instance, it seems a rather precocious time to be notating Aboriginal music.) Much variation exists in the often-recounted story, inevitably casting doubt as to its authenticity; nonetheless, this touristic endeavor continually remained the official genesis of the work, perhaps in an attempt to render it a "legitimate" depiction of Australia and its Indigenous peoples. By qualifying that the work was "not a literal interpretation of an Australian Aboriginal corroboree," however, Antill granted himself full license to pursue a fantastical entertainment that merely suggested to a non-Indigenous person something of the nature of Aboriginal spiritual practice, following the general contour of the ceremony without strictly adhering to its path. Laden with driving rhythms, pungent dissonances, and a rampant exoticism, *Corroboree* immediately intrigued its audiences and was the foremost cultural success of its time. Eugene Goosseens, the conductor at its premiere in the Sydney Town Hall, enthusiastically claimed that it was, "in my opinion, the most significant work from the pen of a contemporary Australian composer I have been privileged to examine."

Notwithstanding the work's somewhat popularized representations of native religion and costume, Antill sought to offer a solemn commentary on the cultural and political condition of the Aboriginal peoples within the greater framework of Australia's history. *Corroboree* opens with a clapstick ostinato, unnervingly stable and persistent in its syncopated repetitions. The (Western) symphonic orchestra grapples with its presence, challenging the solitary clapstick through ominous, predatory growls performed by low strings and percussion; with sudden, frantic energy, the violin section emerges with dissonant, bird-like shrieks; finally, recognizing its inability to intimidate its rival, the entire orchestra gradually awakens in an attempt to subdue him through brute force. Yet in each moment of dynamic recession, the clapstick emerges resonant and determined, persisting despite the industry and modernity of the Western orchestra.

The haunting metaphor of Antill's "Welcoming Ceremony" cannot be overlooked. This was not, as he portrayed, the (rather unwelcoming) opening of an Aboriginal corroboree; it was the volatile clash between Aboriginal and colonial populations, in all its ferocity and mutual vehemence. The clapstick served as an unsettling reminder to the listener that Aboriginal people had been on the continent long before the arrival of Europeans, steadfast and assertive of their heritage; for the colonizers to sustain their perceived dominance over both the land and its Indigenous peoples, they must remain cognizant of their own fragile presence. The clapstick remains calm and unfaltering despite its displacement from its original context; it is the Western symphony that becomes, all too quickly, agitated and hysterical.

Antill was further commenting on the determination of colonial and post-colonial Australia to eradicate, or at least appropriate, the culture of the native peoples. Colonizers consistently oscillated between their outright denial that Aboriginal society had any relevance to the nation at all, and their fanatical attempts to borrow, incorporate, and—inadvertently—claim it as their own. In either instance, of course, they sought control over this alien, non-European portion of their country, though it remained unclear to them which of the two mechanisms was better suited to their purpose. By denying what was so evidently a legitimate aspect of Australia, they achieved little more than temporary ease of mind, yet one always underlaid by that sense of uncertainty so agonizing to the egotistical desire for power. Alternatively, recognizing Aboriginal presence granted them the perceived ownership that derives from the act of naming and transformed it into something palatable—an object of satire, of caricature, and of exotic entertainment. Colonizers, then, dictated that Indigenous culture could persist only in the realm of stylized entertainment, under the close watch of urban life and removed from any potential of resisting the dominant, European culture. Antill's use of the clapsticks subtly reminded his audience of this legacy, the simplicity of the unassuming instrument belying its cultural and metaphorical power. Thus, Aboriginal music—just as Aboriginality itself—remained an unwavering fixture in the non-Indigenous Australian subconscious, fluctuating in its presence but never entirely disappearing.

To claim that *Corroboree* is merely a fetishized Aboriginal caricature, therefore, would be both unjust and inaccurate. Certainly, it is a period piece reflecting dated views of Indigenous Australia, and it should not be perceived as a strict ethnographical account of Aboriginal culture. Antill did, however, commit himself to a certain standard of anthropological awareness and accuracy that was regrettably uncommon for the time. In a 1946 typescript entitled "Corrobboree: A Ballet Suite for Orchestra," Antill wrote that:

> it took well over twenty years of study and research, visiting libraries, collecting volumes, and seeking information from all sources (which are unfortunately too few) before deciding the form and procedure upon which the work finally emerged.[30]

While contemporary commentators will argue (and not without cause) that no amount of academic study can replace thorough and consensual ethnographic research, Antill's efforts are nonetheless commendable and demonstrate a sincere desire to portray Aboriginality with a degree of veracity. For example, he notated several "totems," such as "Cockatoo" and "Medicine Man," as well as copied transcriptions of Aboriginal songs across the breadth of existing literature at the time, duly incorporating them throughout the work.

This reliance on anthropological literature, however, was a doubtful advantage. Though Antill was likely acting in good faith, the culture of the time neglected the finer nuances surrounding Aboriginal culture—namely, its processes of initiation and social passage, and, therefore, selective secrecy. The concept of cultural appropriation scarcely existed in Australian society of the time, and even less so during the era of the ethnographic accounts on which Antill depended. For example, Spencer and Gillen's books contain photographs of material traditionally revealed only to senior, initiated Indigenous men; women and children (as well as non-Indigenous peoples) were forbidden, often at the penalty of death, from knowing certain elements of native culture. Through their publication in the commercial market without the permission of Indigenous advisors, images of such prohibited material circulated unchecked amongst the Australian and international public; Antill further exacerbated this unacknowledged concern by incorporating them into his own widely performed ballet.

Even in instances when the orchestral suite was performed without the accompanying ballet (which itself always neglected to cast Aboriginal dancers), Antill breached the profound secrecy of Aboriginal society by incorporating a "bullroarer" into the scoring. An exceptionally sacred instrument used in initiation ceremonies and burials to repulse evil spirits, bad tidings, and women and children, bullroarers are considered "secret men's business" across Aboriginal clan groups, and their sound is forbidden to the uninitiated. In some Indigenous systems, it is believed to represent the Rainbow Serpent, the primary creator god in Dreamtime mythology; in others, it is the symbolic voice of Daramulum, a sky hero. Yet in Antill's work, the bullroarer was, above all, a device intended to evoke the perceived primitivism of Aboriginal soundscapes, encumbered by the overarching presence of modernistic dissonance and rhythmic propulsion that denies the listener the spiritual reflection inherent to the sacred instrument. Its most prominent appearance is in the final movement ("Procession of Totems and Closing Fire Ceremony"), supported with a climactic *ffff* tutti sections and dissonant choral ostinatos that unambiguously communicate chaos, frenzy, and destruction. Antill then quotes the following passage from Spencer's book as the culmination of the work: "sparks falling in all directions and a mass of howling, dancing men, with their bodies grotesquely bedaubed, formed a scene that was a little short of fiendish." "Fiendish" is perhaps generous of Spencer; his depiction inspires nothing less than the most fearsome imaginings of hell itself. If Antill intended *Corroboree* as a celebration of Aboriginal culture, his positive objectives were not realized; instead, the work reinforced the settler's experience of Aboriginality as a distant, untamed, and foreboding, yet unchangeable element of Australia itself.

Long overdue in this discussion is a mention of Stravinsky's *Rite of Spring* (1913), an inevitably necessary comparison to Antill's *Corroboree.* Stravinsky's work enjoyed its Australian premiere in August of 1946, the same year Antill composed his singularly famous work; Antill, however, denied any knowledge of the suite. Certainly, the parallels between the two works are evident: they both demonstrate an emphasis on exotic primitivism, modernist dissonance, propulsive rhythms, irregular and frequently changing meters, and an overarching sense of savagery and frenzy that unfailingly reminds one of the earliest accounts of Aboriginal contact written by the first settlers. Little had changed, it seems, in the perception of the non-Indigenous Australian over a century and a half after colonization. Though little evidence exists to demonstrate any direct correlation between Stravinsky's work and that of Antill, their temporal proximity is nonetheless indicative of the primitivist-modernist aesthetic pervading musical culture of the time, as well as the interest of the general public in attending such aggressive, theatrical performances.

Interestingly, it is possible that Antill initially conceived this work as something "suitable for performance at the orchestral concerts for school children," only later incorporating dance and theater "because aboriginal culture is so bound up with dancing." In an early version of *Corroboree*'s inscription, he wrote:

> Therefore I dedicate this work to the Children of Australia. Trusting that they will appreciate the true place
> These true Australians

> [Yet?] they may be encouraged to study further and appreciated the lives and [adventures?] of these true Australians.[31]

Indeed, Antill "had long considered it a pity that [...] at the children's concerts all the music was European in influence. He wanted to make all young Australians realise that music was part of their lives and of themselves."

Corroboree, ultimately, was to realize for Antill his early goal of becoming "famous some day," albeit at the expense of overshadowing the remainder of his compositional output. It also unambiguously categorized him as a distinctly nationalistic composer, despite the fact that his later works are generally European (and specifically modernistic) in character. Musicologist Rhoderick McNeill stated that it was "the most important and successful Australian composition of its time"; others have claimed that the very inception of modern Australian composition can be traced to this pivotal work. *The Bulletin*, somewhat colloquially, called it "racy of the soil."[32] On his eightieth birthday, Antill said that he wished people would listen to some of the many other ballets he had written, rather than simply reiterating *Corroboree*.

Nonetheless, he displayed an evident preoccupation with developing a nationalistic school of music for several years following the first performances of *Corroboree*, and he advocated for and defended the creation of such in the wake of the positive (and nationally inclined) reception of the work. While explaining the genesis of the ballet suite, Antill wrote:

> As I became more mature I became more sceptical [sic] about the people who said there was no Australian school of thought, musical or otherwise, and that our country had nothing of its own to use as a cultural idiom. I personally believe that there is a mine of rich material available.[33]

For much of Australia's history, this "mine of rich material" largely consisted of Aboriginal cultural heritage, whether it was imagined and idealized, appropriated outright, or utilized in direct collaboration with Indigenous peoples (which did not become common practice—relatively speaking—until the late twentieth century). This inclination largely owes to the fact that, in the perception of the national composer,

> there was little in Australian musical culture, whether in the church, folk music, popular urban music or the concert hall, which marked a

> distinct national flavour. In contrast, Aboriginal culture presented a unique Australian voice; it was also undeniably connected to the topography and spirit of the bush.[34]

Antill shared this perspective and thus employed Aboriginality, both in a literal and metaphorical manner, throughout his *Corroboree*. A few other works of his likewise engage with Indigenous cultures to a certain extent (e.g., *The Kurrajong Song*, *An Outback Overture*, or *An Australian Rhapsody*), however, none have ever paralleled this particular ballet suite in either commercial popularity or nationalistic fervor. Within the ramifications of this book's proposed intent, therefore, the discussion on what is but a negligible percentage of Antill's composition must suffice.[35]

While this is scarcely a comprehensive list of the composers active in the early twentieth century—indeed, these do not even represent all significant figures of the time—it is perhaps the most expedient overview of their gradually emerging consciousness of an "Australian" identity in music. Certainly, each individual displayed varying approaches to what constituted a "nationalistic" aesthetic, manifested either in their own compositions or the works they sought to promote: some evidenced a sustained interest in producing a regional idiom, others composed but one or two pieces that could be attributed a vaguely "Antipodean" character, and yet others espoused the ideology in abstract only. Irrespective of their discrepancies, however, they unequivocally advanced the public perception of a legitimate national school of music, thus preparing the foundation for those pivotal figures soon to succeed them.

CHAPTER FOUR

"The Nerves of Nationality"

Australian Musical Possibilities (1924) and its Impact on Australian Music

> *Sound civilisations are based on sound ideas. A good tree bears not evil fruit. If the fruit is evil the tree is doubtful. Is it any wonder that men who live in the age of the Great War should not only raise the question whether the politics or religions which made that war possible are not imposter politics and religions, but should also suspect that the Art, the ethics and the poetry which allowed that war slowly to ripen are bogus Art, ethics and poetry?*[1]

Thus begins Melbourne poet and musician Henry Tate's (1873–1926) pivotal, though largely overlooked, 1924 treatise on the then-hypothetical concept of an "Australian" musical idiom. Ashamed of the lack of a recognizably Australian music, particularly in the context of the already well-established nationalistic parallels in both visual art and literature, Tate openly voiced the deficiencies of the country's composers that had been too long ignored (or, at best, uncomfortably explained away). Many were adept at imitating the prevalent Euro-American musical aesthetics of the time, and some had indeed achieved a considerable amount of fame abroad. None, however, had emerged as a representative of the "Australian nation," in the same manner that Richard Wagner was considered synonymous with German "music drama," Giuseppe Verdi with Italian *risorgimento*, or Béla Bartók with Hungarian ethnomusicology. Tate emphasized that there was no dearth of raw environmental, anthropological, or cultural heritage inhibiting the emergence of such a composer in Australia; rather, the primary impediment was that few were willing to sacrifice their careers in the honorable act of experimentation, which in its earliest stages inevitably promised little more than failure:

> Early Australian composers, in their turn, must be prepared for misunderstanding, neglect, and disappointment. The act of creating a

> national music such as the Russians have lately achieved is no simple task. No single composer could accomplish it, but he may light a torch which will show where the path begins to others, who will press further into the jungle of the unknown. Those who would follow and help our national music must be prepared to see our first composers advance with faltering steps. Much effort must be consumed in experiment, and every experiment will excite the jibes of the inconsiderate and the indifferent. The towering names of the great masters will be used to shut out the sunlight of appreciation from our pioneers.[2]

Certainly, such statements appeared less than enticing for young, ambitious composers. Many were deterred simply by the enormity of the proposed undertaking, in which great professional risk was not counterbalanced by greater artistic success and recognition (quite the contrary, in fact). Even if one were to attempt formulating a nationalistic musical idiom, what was a convincing point of departure? Australia is a uniquely individual continent, and its deviations from Western culture and society are only exacerbated by its immense physical isolation. If we are to reference the Balkan nations (which are not such a far cry from Russia) as examples of successful cultural experiments, it is prudent to remember that each country need only glance over to its neighbors when wanting in ideas.[3] Australia, however, lacks the formatively beneficial conditions of ongoing transnational contact (e.g., historically active trade routes, immediately bordering countries, etc.) and regions that are substantially similar to itself.[4] The individuality inherent to traversing such a virgin path as articulating an Australian identity prevented a composer from utilizing convention as a standard against which to determine the "quality" or "correctness" of their music; indeed, many Australian musicians were not entirely certain where this "path" began altogether. Tate's final prediction would likewise prove true, as evidenced by the near-total lack of contemporary discussion on Australia's earliest cultural "revolutionaries" in favor of those later, more matured figures of the twentieth and twenty-first centuries.

Furthermore, devoting oneself to articulating a convincing national idiom necessitated not only an intimate understanding of Australia, but also an unfaltering commitment to its advancement, a sincere belief in its yet unrealized potential. From where, however, was this confidence to be derived? Institutionalized musical education was still sparse, and those seeking professional opportunity felt that "Australian composition" was a contradiction of terms; indeed, they maintained that little could be more absurd than such a concept (making reasonable exception for the platypus, of course).

It was not merely the prospect of blatant failure that dissuaded emerging musicians from dedicating themselves to Australian cultural advancement. Composing overtly nationalistic music—and being among the first to do so within a country—requires more of an individual than knowledge or innocuous patriotism: it demands audacity. As jazz pianist and historian Ted Gioia notes,

> a new psychological model of the artist emerged with Wagner and Verdi. They no longer saw themselves as *serving* the nation; instead, they believed they *represented* the nation. They saw themselves as embodying the most powerful movement of their time, and this notion gratified their egos and inflamed their pride to a degree previously unknown in the annals of secular music.[5]

Although his language is perhaps a bit strong for the purposes of the present discussion, Gioia nonetheless presents a crucial consideration of "national" (or "nationalistic") music—namely, that its composer inadvertently emerges as a sounded symbol of the nation itself. Proclaiming that one's work is not merely music, but *Australian* (or German, or Italian, or Hungarian) music, immediately relativizes the composer within a social and political context of national representation. "This," the musician says, "is emblematic of our national experience." "This is who we are, how we think, and how we perceive the world around us." Because it is not possible for the composer to survey all constituents of the nation he is striving to represent in his music, he must necessarily extrapolate his own experiences, thoughts, and perceptions as relevant to those of his neighbor, and thus he assumes a significant degree of responsibility for the nation's image to the global community. The composer therefore becomes a spokesperson for "his" country, establishing a divide between those who understand and empathize with the significance of the music's national symbolism, and those who can do little more than appreciate it as an outsider. Nationalistic music is at once an affirmation of oneself and a declaration to others. It establishes a community and its criteria for inclusion, and, in doing so, sets boundaries for those who do not "belong" within it.

Australians, however, are not so unabashedly assertive. Their sociopolitical history demonstrates their relatively unconfrontational nature, and the Australian Values statement presented by their Department of Home Affairs repeatedly emphasizes the nation's belief "in peaceful disagreement and above all the right to be safe and free from violence and intimidation." Musical nationalism, of course, is not inherently violent, but it undoubtedly connotes a degree of pride otherwise uncommon in the Australian character. Thus, attempting to create a national idiom firstly demands *amour propre* from a composer to overcome the psychological inhibition of initiating this process; it secondly requires humility and patience from the same composer upon encountering failure in its earliest manifestations.

There is perhaps no less promising perspective from which to approach Australian musical nationalism. Optimistically enough, these seemingly unfavorable, or at least uninviting, circumstances did not daunt *all* composers; if such was the case, then this book would not exist. Some bravely offered themselves as martyrs for the cause, however, the resultant work was dismissed as unsuitable for public consumption in an insultingly prompt manner. Far from heeding Tate's advice to support and encourage these young composers, critics ungraciously looked upon their work as akin to "musical pollution," if such a term may be used. Nonetheless, amidst the contemptuous clamor of these largely conservative opinions, quite a few individuals entertained noble ideals of "discovering" the works of young musicians and selflessly "advancing" their careers, shouldering the indignity of "sifting through the rubble," as it were, to elevate the cultural standing of the nation as a whole.

Eventually, however, the creation of a national musical idiom became less of an idle pastime than a sociocultural necessity. In the early post-war era, described in the opening quote of this chapter, young Australian artists found themselves disheartened by the severity of the carnage they had witnessed in Europe. The excessive destruction of life and property, coupled with the extreme politicization of various art musics (and their respective composers), instilled doubts in Australian artists as to the credibility of Western systems. The Continent was no longer an irreproachable beacon of civilization, an imposing paradigm of human creativity and tradition; instead, its soils were tainted with blood, and its institutions were representatives of archaic, dysfunctional ideologies. Indeed, much of the subsequent demand for a distinct national idiom may have arisen from Australia's increasing embitterment with Europe's sociopolitical and economic upheavals. In a lecture regarding their development of art music, the prominent Australian composer Ross Edwards (b.1943) stated:

> It's often claimed that the great social upheavals of the first half of the 20th century, having shattered values and traditions already drained by the European Scientific Revolution and the Enlightenment, had initiated a period of disenchantment followed by a virile new secular aesthetic which set about clearing away what Pierre Boulez called the

> 'dust and crap'. It's not surprising that many young European composers of the post-war generation, having witnessed the destruction at first hand, felt a need to turn away from traditions that seemed stale—that had seemingly let them down—and strike out bravely into the unknown in search of sanity.[6]

Thus began Australia's reevaluation and adaptation of previously sacralized European aesthetics, discarded in favor of national sentiments that sought rejuvenation, individuality, and separation from now-stagnant traditions. It was a gradual process, rife with uncertainties and disquietudes, but one galvanized by the impending suffocation of "native" composition. "Sanity," it seemed, was an equivocal aim, but it was the singular unifying motivation for Australian musicians amid the social cataclysms throughout the remainder of the world.

These circumstances, in turn, were the background against which Henry Tate authored his collection of essays entitled *Australian Musical Possibilities*. Indeed, he was among the first to attempt a codification of such an elusive concept as an "Australian" nationalist idiom, and, in doing so, offered both encouragement and guidance for emerging national composers with a remarkable degree of prophetic clairvoyance. A considerable number of his intimations, predictions, and aesthetic ideologies are evident in the work of those composers now regarded as "pioneering" in the realm of Australian art music, and it may well be that Tate's modest pamphlet exerted an influence far greater than that suggested by contemporary scholarly interest in his writings.[7]

He initiates his discussion by dismissing the pervasive belief that Australia lacks traditions and heritages of its own, asserting that the nation's composer may both derive inspiration from the cultural heritage of the world writ large, and simultaneously revel in its freedom from the oppressive weight of tradition:

> It is customary to regard our country as lacking in folk-lore, folk-song, mythology, and historic tradition, and it is quite easy to regard this lack as a misfortune and a hindrance to the development of a national type of Australian music. A more resolute scrutiny of the situation discovers that such a conclusion is not by any means as sounds as it appears to be; that there are possibilities which are easily overlooked; resources that are only masked; and even advantages that may prove to be unique. [...] We may lack Australian folk-lore and folk-song, but we have that of all the world. [...]

> Our history is short, but it does not lack characteristic features, and our story is interwoven with that of the old world in a way that only requires a deep-sighted interpreter to display its novelty and richness of interest. Our animals, our birds, our flowers and trees exhibit traits which are peculiarly their own. Our blue-grey distances, suffused with clearest sunlight, have a voice if we could hear it. The green light of our gullies does not vibrate with memories of the past, but it is eloquent with the deeper music of the future. Our social and political ideals have commanded the admiration of the whole world, and surely they will provide many a glorious theme in the days when genius will have set the "billows of sweet sound" in motion.
>
> But if we have no more, we have a virgin page. On the palimpsest of old-world literature, legend, and song can be traced the faint lines which show the vanishing imprints of aeon upon aeon. The very absence of the factors which have seemed to mould the great movements of the past makes our position unique. An ordained and unavoidable development along definite and comparatively confined paths is not forced upon us, and we are in a position to wrench our music from silence by sheer intellectual power. The range and freedom of our choice of resources is unparalleled in all the world's history, and we have good reason to hope and believe that some day the music of Australian composers will be recognized as national and take a worthy place in the world's treasure house of tonal art.[8]

He further recognized the primal, visceral nature of nationalistic sentiments, proclaiming that

> art must have material, and the nerves of nationality, which have carried such deep and vivid impressions to the throbbing centres of musical inspiration, are not likely to lose their value till mountains and seas, climate, race, creed, and history have themselves vanished. Music that achieves nationality is on the way to rise above nationality.

Indeed, he maintained that the fundamentally pathetic nature of nationalism is what would contribute to its effectiveness within Australian music, as it relies on the instinctual predisposition of its listeners toward what they perceive as their homeland and its constituents. A number of generations had already passed in which Australia was regarded by its residents as the "motherland," yet a chasm of impersonality existed in that there was no music that was distinctly "national" and representative of an *Australian* experience, as separate from that of the geographically remote Great Britain.

Precisely this gap was what Tate sought to remediate, further suggesting that the finer specimens of such music would (eventually) transcend the attention of local audiences and assume a place in the canon of humanity's collective cultural heritage:

> If Australia is to come into line as one of the countries whose national characteristics have inspired great music, Australia must have composers who will study their own country, and aim to achieve in their music an inherent distinction that will arouse interest in it as Australian music.[9]

Thus far, Tate espouses an optimistic attitude that is undoubtedly supported by similar trajectories in nationalistic idioms across music's history: repeat futile attempts, followed by local and, eventually, international success and recognition. One cannot fail to note, however, his lack of specific advices or suggestions. Where should a young composer seek inspiration? What are the most remarkable elements of the Australian nation that could effectively be translated into musical language?

His primary recommendation for "natural" material that may be used in the formation of a distinctly "Australian" music rested in the rhythmic, melodic, harmonic, and modal characteristics of native bird calls. Indeed, he devotes much energy to cataloguing the various species of Australian birds and their idiosyncratic songs, even suggesting that the scalar patterns on which they sing are in themselves sufficiently unique for a composer to utilize. (Here, he draws comparison to Bartók's use of "deflected" scale patterns found in Magyar folk-songs and suggests that the use of atypical or altered modes, when coupled with an acute understanding of "the mental outlook of [one's] race," yields work of "worthy artistry.")[10] He further encouraged composers to evoke Australia's inimitable environmental features, such as the topography, native flora and fauna, and intersecting soundscapes of the "bush"; daily life "reflecting the Australian experience"; and theoretical developments from the "Old World" (i.e., Europe).

This last suggestion, however, must be followed with great caution. While Tate indicated that there were many beneficial aesthetic elements from the canonic Western tradition, he simultaneously warned that "the sunlight of European inspiration, however lustrous it may be in its own environment, fades to a dusk in climes that know far different skies." Australian composers must be apprehensive of any "lazy adherence to the stereotyped formulae of old-world musical methods," striving instead to imbue them with renewed vitality and relevance for national audiences. Such juxtaposition of ancient against contemporary narratives eventually proves to be a recurring theme within Australian music, and, indeed, manifests the somewhat conflicted history of the nation as founded upon the ideals of the Old World, yet uniquely situated within a land untouched for longer than most by Western civilization.

Although valuable in its own right, Tate's list of national characteristics is somewhat superficial. He has, thus far, represented Australia as entirely devoid of human presence, and he implies that the "bush" is a landscape untouched by any peoples prior to the first British settlers. This apparent oversight is both misleading, however, and contradictory to nationalistic musical movements throughout history. Quite often (if not almost always), nationalistic musics incorporate elements of folk or "native" cultures, whether these be embodied in transient peoples (e.g., Franz Liszt's allusions to the Hungarian gypsies, most of whom were nomads but were nonetheless renowned for their execution of local musics), early settlers, or indigenous communities. Indeed, this tendency seems rather intuitive. Tate, however, maintains a dismissive opinion of Aboriginal culture and its relevance to the creation of an Australian nationalist idiom. Although he admits that the musics, dances, and rituals of native peoples could exercise some minimal claims of artistic value, these submissions are reluctant and often disregarded in the same breath they were uttered. Furthermore, his descriptions of Indigenous musics imply a base, primitive quality: he suggests that they are interesting not because they are derived from any virtuous activity, such as intellectual study or experimentation, but rather because of their purportedly unrefined, uncivilized, and animalistic nature. The intensity of labor that would be required of a composer to elevate Aboriginal musics from their unfiltered state to something serviceable and relevant would hardly advance Australia's music, he argues, and therefore the endeavor should be avoided altogether:

> The Australian composer, searching for native peculiarities to build a national music upon, must soon give attention to the very essential matter of striking and characteristic rhythms. There may be original and suitable rhythmic patterns in the dance music of our aborigines, but, if so, they are difficult to get at. In any case, they are scarcely characteristic of the real life of Australia to-day, and their interest will soon be too remote to be readily identifiable.[11]

In a later essay, Tate asserted that,

> interesting as the possibilities may be, it cannot be denied that the aborigine is more or less estranged from the psychology of the modern Australian.
>
> It is entirely different with our bird calls. They are with us always, and they supply us with an unfailing reservoir of varied and charming rhythms.

The reader will perhaps recall a previously mentioned report in the October 1830 issue of *The Hobart Town Courier*, in which its author advanced a notion uncannily similar to that expressed by Tate—namely, that the time and efforts of amateur "anthropologists" conducting fieldwork on Aboriginal peoples would be better directed toward transcribing native bird-songs. Indeed, the only possible value, nationalistic or otherwise, that Tate perceived in Indigenous musics was for "composers who may wish to incorporate and develop traits of native minstrelsy in their own work"; after almost a century, published musical opinion had changed naught.

Later in his treatise, however, Tate appears to contradict this opinion, stating:

> The music is surprisingly interesting. Wild and barbaric as much of it sounds, it is rich in rhythms and themes, that, once annotated and fixed, will supply a copious reservoir of melodic germs and rhythmical fragments of the type that composers all over the world are continually seeking.[12]

So much for their psychological estrangement. It is in moments such as these that Tate appears self-contradictory, in that he proclaims both the universality and inaccessibility of Aboriginal musics, thus simultaneously recommending and discouraging their use. While Tate's opinion is neither singular nor conclusive, it represents the uncertainty that continues to pervade approaches to composition of Australian art music: should one, or should one not utilize Aboriginal musical cultures?

At best, Tate suggests utilizing already existing transcriptions of Aboriginal dances and chants, of which he offers several for the curious reader—in essence, he deems it most efficient for an amateur "ethnomusicologist" to confine, with much intellectual labor, native musics into something approaching Western musical notation, which a composer may then interpret (or deform) at leisure.[13]

Other musicians of the time, such as Clive Douglas (1903–1977), likewise engaged in that strange model of advocacy that communicates at once fascination and repugnance:

> The absence of a national music in the white man's idiom adds to the difficulties which confront an Australian composer who attempts to infuse his music with a recognizable Australian identity. Unless some link can be forged which will serve to connect the composer's thoughts to the land itself, the music written will be strongly derivative of what has been recorded in some other country earlier. A musical idiom must be found which is so entirely Australian that no other influence can be felt [...] only there, in the mystical 'dream-time' of antiquity can be found the all-important link—the tribal ceremonial chants of the brown man.[14]

It is uncomfortably ironic, however, that the custodians of this supposedly "recognizable Australian identity" were both denied the fundamental rights granted to those who were *articulating* this identity, and that their relative merits were dismissed as quickly as they were lauded. In the same 1956 essay from which the previous quote is taken, for example, Douglas describes Aboriginal song as "undeveloped," "unmusical," "crude," and "monotonous." Furthermore, he suggests that the value of Indigenous musics extends only insofar as they can be removed from their original context and manipulated as repetitive, persistent cells, reduced into a distant underlay of sound that is always present and recognizable, yet scarcely understood by its listeners. Much like Henry Tate, therefore, Douglas suggests that Aboriginality is imbued with an exotic pagan mysticism that vitalizes the spirit and evokes an inimitable quality of "Australianness," but otherwise must be entirely removed from its traditional context, and all issues of appropriation (or misappropriation) quietly ignored. When all else fails, Aboriginality is an expedient mechanism for escaping "Europeanness" and imposing "Australianness." Indeed, the aims of this movement were most succinctly expressed by musicologist Roger Covell:

> [...] basically it is a kind of longed-for 'short cut' to cultural maturity and national identity; an impatience with the slow process by which a literature truly nationalizes itself in a newly settled country and a desire to, as it were, take advantage of the experience of the Aboriginal inhabitants of Australia and their uniquely close relationship with the county.[15]

Tate's philosophies surrounding the use of Indigenous musics, thus, were contextualized within the growing public interest in Aboriginal culture throughout the early twentieth century. Composers that sought to incorporate these native influences often did not conduct ethnographic research of their own (as did Béla Bartók and Zoltán Kodály in Hungary, for example); instead, they relied on antediluvian anthropological reports and recordings. Ultimately, Tate's aesthetic preferences remain ambiguous: he concedes that Aboriginal musical cultures are quite dynamic and unique, catalogues several transcriptions of native songs that he perceives to be valuable, and encourages composers to synthesize "old-world" traditions with the soundscape of the Australian bush (which, necessarily, includes the musics of Indigenous peoples), yet he denies their relevance to the urban Australian. He opposes—or corrects—himself several times over the course of his book, and the most well-intentioned and open-minded reader is nonetheless encumbered with doubts on this aspect of his ideologies.

All of Tate's recommendations are, of course, easier said than followed. To avoid any potential accusations, therefore, of his offering abstract ideas without implementing them himself, Tate provides two musical examples of his own composition. The first is a pianoforte solo entitled *Morning in the Gully*; the second is a work for voice and piano named *The Australian Thrush*. In keeping with his emphasis on the endemic fauna of Australia, both works exhibit much influence from birdsong—the bass lines in *Morning in the Gully*, for example, feature many variations of his own transcriptions of pied butcherbird calls.[16] He often defies—or is simply puzzled by—the notion of bar lines throughout the piece, and thus he creates asymmetry and a sense of naturalism by composing phrases without regard for strict metrical divisions. Many of these bird calls are utilized as motifs or cells that, in turn, serve as the structure of the works through repetition and elaboration. Furthermore, in *The Australian Thrush*, Tate frequently incorporates the "deflected" scale so strongly emphasized in his booklet and therefore departs from the stereotypical Western character of European art songs; this is further amplified by the austerity of the accompaniment and unusual melodic contour. Admittedly, both pieces are somewhat idyllic and pastoral in nature, but they nonetheless encapsulate Tate's suggestions throughout his treatise with remarkable effectiveness. Many of the characteristics present in these two pieces, such as their repeated melodic and rhythmic cells, unusual modes and harmonic inflections, deviations from typical Western theory, and apparent simplicity or barrenness, can likewise be readily observed in the works of numerous later composers, such as Peter Sculthorpe or Ross Edwards.

Aside from these two brief works, Tate illustrated his aesthetic ideologies in numerous compositions for pianos, songs, and orchestral tone poems, many of which remain unpublished and unperformed.

Among his more ambitious works are a sixteen-part piano cycle, *The Australian,* first performed in 1915; *The Dreams of Diaz,* a musical play about a fictional Portuguese discovery of Australia; and *Dawn,* a rhapsody based on Australian bird calls. His advocacy for an Australian mythology and musical identity was largely overlooked in musical circles of his day, however, but welcomed by leading nationalist writers and dramatists who, in turn, encouraged him to lecture and present his music. (Perhaps this reception of his work is unsurprising, given the lack of an acute national consciousness in Australian composers that was present in contemporaneous visual artists and authors. Interestingly, his musical theories are often considered more valuable and influential than his music itself.) Thus, Tate's writings have gained historical, rather than an explicitly practical, value.

Nonetheless, it was among his central aims to create an "Australian school of music," a daunting and ambitious goal that was to be echoed *verbatim* by Peter Sculthorpe merely a few decades later. To a certain degree, it is unfair to dismiss his work as having little tangible effect on composers in his or following generations—although his musical compositions never achieved any prominence or posterity, his ideas were eloquently preserved in writing and at least tolerably cast in music. It is likewise improbable that figures such as Peter Sculthorpe, Ross Edwards, Paul Stanhope, and others did not have any direct contact with Tate's treatise, given the often-overlapping themes and aesthetics in their works. Thus, it is worth considering Tate's contributions to Australia's musical heritage as not merely incidental and abstract, but critical and tangible (albeit dated); certainly, his ideologies formalized the evolving recognition of a national consciousness in the arts and confronted the marked absence of such identity in the country's music. Indeed, his writings addressed the "nerves of nationality" and galvanized a new generation of ambitious, dynamic, and experimental composers, all of whom were to reify Tate's notions that were holistically formed in abstract, yet still unrealized in music.

CHAPTER FIVE

Interlude

Patriotism, Nationalism, and Somewhere in Between—The Turmoil of the Twentieth Century

Civilization means something more than energy and will and creative power. It needs a sense of permanence. Civilized man must feel that he belongs somewhere in space and time; that he consciously looks forward and back.

KENNETH CLARK[1]

In his immensely popular documentary *Civilisation*, historian Kenneth Clark extolled much effort in defining a "civilization," as separate from its precursor, a "society." When regarded cursorily, his primary examples—namely, settled and well-established European cultures, such as Ancient Greece, juxtaposed against intransient and "barbarous" peoples, such as the Vikings—exist in stark relief as two extremes of social structure, separated by vast chasms that permit no nuance in classification. Within this rigid binary, it is unlikely that Australia, especially in its present condition, would share the same categorization of a violent, superstitious, and piratically heathenistic nation that Clark attributed to those early nomadic peoples. Yet, for some time, it was perhaps equally unlikely that Australia could confidently be identified as a "civilization."

To examine the nation's history through the framework posed by Clark, the delineation of Australia's musical history must somewhat awkwardly be paused, and a looming concern addressed: namely, "the muddy issues of Australianness" itself.[2] Until the mid-twentieth century, the country was meandering the ambiguous boundary between a "society" and a "civilization." "Energy and will and creative power" it certainly displayed; permanence, a sense of belonging, and perspective enough to look "forward and back," however, was lacking. Creating anything that was distinctly Australian, or even organizing such a thing as a national history, was approached with a marked discomfort and a strained self-consciousness. Settlers were palpably unwilling to accept the constancy inherent to calling themselves "Australians" (better stateless than "Australian," it seemed), and those who attempted to compose something "national" did so without entirely casting off their concomitant shame and uneasiness. It is as though people living on the continent maintained that their presence was merely temporary; that, eventually, they would return to "civilization," and Australia would regress into its primeval condition of isolation and inconsequence. "Nationalistic" musical works of the period, then, unsurprisingly assumed a cliché, mawkishly sentimental, and forced character. (Bush ballades were perhaps the most overt example of this.) Of course, it is not quite fair to deride these early attempts; considering the general hesitation of the populace toward developing a modest local canon of art, it was courageous enough that such a thing was attempted at all.

This artificially romantic nature of "Australian" music was augmented by its reliance on European aesthetics. To some degree, the inspiration to create Australian art may have derived in itself from the ongoing independence movements throughout the Old World and its colonies; thus, composers would borrow the lush and sentimental musics of these regions as their model and loosely adapt them to the character of their own nation. What resulted, however, was something neither European nor Australian. Opulence and romanticism were intuitive derivations of European society, legitimized by the breadth of their histories and maturity of their cultures. Australia, contrastingly, was a barren, unornamented land, in which frivolousness translated into little more than vain wastefulness.

Yet, for a time, this superficially lavish, bourgeois attitude had dictated Australian music. Musicologist Roger Covell, in his 1967 book *Australia's Music: Themes of a New Society*, signaled that:

> Music in Colonial Australia wore a frilly bonnet and a crinolined dress and sometimes a military uniform—at least as far as it was recognised in the journals and newspapers of the Australian colonies and, by extension, in all accounts of Australian music gathered from those newspapers and journals.[3]

Nonetheless, Covell acknowledged the critical role that such music assumed during the colonial era:

> In a sense, the more frivolous and empty-headed the music was the more it seemed to provide assurance of a life removed from the grim realities of Botany Bay. Quadrilles and waltzes, sentimentally homesick airs and martial songs of a conventionally patriotic kin were charms against the night and the unknown.[4]

Gradually, however, such aesthetic inclinations lost both their illusory quality and their relevance to the maturing Australian society, although composers had yet to relent on their production. This resulted in a disheartening "betwixt and between" for Australian composition, in which previous European models had grown unsatisfactory, but novel idioms were lacking. Though the process of articulating a cultural identity is neither as superficial nor as problematically "nationalistic" as it is often contrived to be, Australian composers were then (and, to a lesser extent, continue to be) restrained by a lingering uncertainty as to what constitutes their "national" sound. The colony remained an extension of the United Kingdom, however, its inhabitants' experiences had become increasingly remote from those of Europeans. Their vast physical distances from the "center of civilization" negated any potential for Australians to remain abreast of social, cultural, or political developments, and thus their existence was largely self-contained. Yet despite this *de facto* autonomy, their musics left much to be desired in terms of a nationalistic idiom.

A lingering uncertainty heretofore unaddressed is how "nationalism" is to be defined for the purposes of the present discussion. Until this chapter, the term has been used somewhat loosely, in a general and purely evocative sense. As Australians began to refine and clarify its perception of itself, however, it becomes necessary to specify what nationalism is (and is not).

Conceptually, "nationalism" is often discussed in proximity with violence, revolution, and extensive battles for political power, and is thus contextualized within greater international movements for regional autonomy. It is rarely considered a process confined to a single nation, but rather one that, by nature, must involve at least one other self-defined "nation." These involvements are not passive, but instead active, disruptive, and competitive, inherently upsetting some prior condition or cultural paradigm. "Nationalism" is not merely perceived as how one nation defines itself; it is also how it separates itself from others.

Australian "nationalism," however, was not a reaction to oppression or an assertion of independence; it was not an anthem of organized rebellion or a preparation for a concerted upheaval of an overarching power; it was not even overtly political in nature. While nationalism and aggression approached disconcertingly close to one another on several occasions in the country's history, Australia's nationalism more generally indicates a gradual development of an idiom capable of expressing their constituents' shared historical and cultural experiences, which were wholly detached from those of

Europe or the Americas. Because Australia was colonized throughout the late eighteenth and early nineteenth century predominantly by British settlers who transplanted an infrastructure based on familiar European models, its citizens sustained for some time the illusion that they were little more than a remote outgrowth of the United Kingdom. A repeated disinterest from the Commonwealth's governing institutions to act in the interest of Australia, however, led to a growing disenchantment within the country that their social, cultural, and psychological associations with Britain were primarily ceremonial, and scarcely beneficial. Simultaneously, the social models that functioned remarkably well in Europe had begun to prove unsustainable in Australia.[5] Most formal associations with Great Britain had largely disintegrated; yet, Australia's constituents could not espouse a holistic national identity without first constructing such an ideology for themselves.

Cumulatively, these developments widened the inevitably increasing separation between the United Kingdom and its distant colony, Australia. It was not merely carelessness from the British, however, that embittered Australians; the apparent dissolution of order, stability, and control throughout the Old World likewise shattered their perceptions of its functionality. It had become evident that to unquestioningly follow their models was to espouse chaos and social disintegration. Thus, Australians embarked on the complex and intimate processes of consciously constructing a national identity that was relevant to their aims, needs, and experiences.

Europe in the twentieth century: The dissolution of tonality and tradition

Europe's emergence from the nineteenth century was largely triumphant and optimistic—international tensions, a seemingly constant element of life on the Continent, had been relatively minimal since the conclusion of the Franco-Prussian War in 1871; significant and frequent advances in science and technology contributed to an ever-improving quality of life; and the arc of Europe's colonial dominion was only widening, stimulating an unparalleled economic growth. Indeed, Europe appeared a bastion of civilization and a sanctuary for benevolence among men, impressing upon the world an image of a peaceful utopia in which material—and perhaps even social—problems would soon find resolution. The years preceding World War I were thus hopeful, driven by a collective belief in the upward motion of the human race. Viennese novelist Stefan Zweig, in his recollections of this period, commented about the prevailing attitude:

> This faith in an uninterrupted and irresistible "progress" truly had the force of a religion for that generation. One began to believe more in this "progress" than in the Bible, and its gospel appeared ultimate because of the daily new wonders of science and technology. In fact, at the end of the peaceful century, a general advance became more marked, more rapid, more varied. [...] Comfort made its way from the houses of the fashionable to those of the middle class. It was no longer necessary to fetch water from the pump or the hallway, or to take the trouble to build a fire in the fireplace. Hygiene spread and filth disappeared. People became handsomer, stronger, healthier, more robust. [...] Small wonder then that this century summed itself up in its own accomplishments and looked upon each completed decade as a prelude to a better one. There was as little belief in the possibility of such barbaric declines as wars between the nations of Europe as there was in witches and ghosts. Our fathers were comfortably saturated with confidence in the unfailing and binding power of tolerance and conciliation. They honestly believed that the divergencies and the boundaries between nations and sects would gradually melt away into a common humanity and that peace and security, the highest of treasures, would be shared by all mankind.[6]

The subsequent outbreak of World War I, and the sheer magnitude of physical destruction and human misery that accompanied it, would demolish these illusions. It was a crisis few at the time believed still possible amongst civilized societies, yet one that, in retrospect, appeared to be inevitable. Indeed, the utopian prosperity evident over several decades was merely an artificial construct, a lustrous veneer obscuring the undercurrents of social unrest, international disagreements, and stifled originalism. Such control was perhaps necessary to maintain the absolute sociopolitical stability of the prior era, yet the repression of creative thought in the early twentieth century had fostered resentment and restlessness among Europe's more progressive artists and philosophers; their disillusionment and dissatisfaction was likewise evident in their work, evincing their determination to separate themselves from the outworn conventions of an enfeebled manner of life. In the visual arts, there developed a gradual rejection of realism and objective experience, as exemplified by painters such as Pablo Picasso (1881–1973), Max Ernst (1891–1976), and Salvador Dali (1904–1989); some writers adopted a "stream of consciousness" technique that ignored logical continuity and instead favored inner reflection, popularized by Marcel Proust (1871–1922) and Virginia Woolf (1882–1941); and music dismissed the traditional conventions of tonality and structure that had essentially dictated its structure since the eighteenth century, embodied by notions such as Arnold Schoenberg's (1874–1951) "Emancipation of Dissonance" or Edgar Varèse's (1883–1965) "organized sound" (the latter famously claimed that "to stubbornly conditioned ears, anything new in music has always been called noise," a statement which compellingly summarized the general sentiments among radical thinkers of the time). Across these disciplines likewise arose an interest in "primitivism," regarded not necessarily as derogatorily "exotic," but rather as a legitimate counterpart to the excessively structured castes that had defined European society, as though it could liberate art that was on the verge of suffocating itself with the entangled strands of "civilization."

Amidst this turmoil and sudden disintegration of stability across the Continent, Australians could no longer predicate its identity on that of Europe or the West writ large (indeed, scarcely any cohesive "identity" remained across those regions). The essential threads of society had all but unraveled, and, throughout the crisis of two world wars in rapid succession and the traumatic cynicism in mankind thereof, Europe no longer appeared a desirable nor sustainable model of civilization. About this transitional period, musicologist Deborah Crisp noted that:

> The habit of imitation was by now deeply ingrained, yet it was becoming increasingly difficult from such a distance, to assess the value and importance of the many different directions [European] music appeared to be taking. Australian composers had three options: to follow European trends as best they could, to find another leader to follow, or to set themselves up as authorities in their own right. Many preferred to ignore the problem altogether, and continued to write as if Debussy, Schoenberg, and Stravinsky did not exist. Others clung to the Europe of this century, hoping that improved communications would eventually solve the problem of isolation. A courageous few regarded the confusion in Europe as an opportunity for escape from traditions which had held them captive for far too long, and began the slow process of forming a style of music which could contain the vast distances of Australia and express the unique quality of its society.[7]

Prior to these immense upheavals, Australia's "feeling of cultural inferiority inescapable in a neo-colonial or provincial society" (and resultant desire to mimic the Western world) was, perhaps, understandable; afterwards, however, it would be senseless.[8] A distinct national identity, it seemed, had become crucial to the nation's survival in the new post-war era.

How does a national identity emerge, why is it important, and what are the relevant concerns?

A "national identity" is defined as "a sense of a nation as a cohesive whole, as represented by distinctive traditions, culture, and language," necessitating a psychological "awareness of difference" between "we" and "they." Individuals recognize commonalities, such as having a common descent and common "destiny," and they therefore form an "in-group" among themselves. This process, however, is not an inborn trait; rather, it is almost entirely socially constructed. A nation's identity, and the degree to which it permeates its inhabitants' personal beliefs and values, directly results from a concentrated and sustained presence of what a community determines to be their shared national "symbols," such as a common language, history, collection of cultural artifacts, significant landmarks, or other "folk" elements.

To develop an acute sense of an "in-group" (i.e., an identification with a nation) and an "out-group" (i.e., the exclusion of other nations), those elements that distinguish a given nation from the others must first be identified; these may include unique geographical or topographical features, a dynamic anthropological history, exceptional biodiversity, a substantial innovative capacity from its citizens, or a variety of other features and combinations thereof. When examining Australia's "native" identity, a plethora of inimitable attributes are uncovered, many of which were noted at least in passing by composers wishing to espouse a form of national music: but a few are the country's extraordinary natural sites, astonishing flora and fauna, and the fascinating reservoirs of the oldest continuous culture in human history, collectively offering a convincing foundation for a resounding national heritage. Yet, many of these resources were overlooked by composers of "serious" art music and dismissed (or satirized) by entertainers.

Establishing "in-groups" and "out-groups," as well as concepts of "inclusion" and "exclusion," is a necessary point of departure when creating a national identity. It does not have to be done in such a hostile or aggressive manner as the written word makes it sound; merely a psychological awareness of the nation's individuality will suffice. Yet, in even suggesting these boundaries between "self" and "others," Australia's national identity uncovered a fissure. With the gradual increase of locally born inhabitants in the generations following the first settlers, the nation's residents nurtured both a Euro-centric identity (i.e., one which did not encompass Indigenous peoples) and a "native identity" (which did incorporate Aboriginality, albeit reservedly). Problematically, neither appeared to complement the other well. Perhaps believing that the two were mutually exclusive, the settlers clung to the familiarity of their Euro-centric identity. They embraced Western art and its derivatives as emblematic of contemporary culture, established policies and frameworks that were reminiscent of their countries of origin, and associated "being truly Australian" with transplanted markers of belonging, such as the ability to speak English. Under the criteria of identity as a concrete *differentiation* from others, however, the Euro-centric approach emerges as little more than a generic amalgamation of staple Western elements; furthermore, it staunchly resists influence from Aboriginal cultures.

Rather than reconciling the Euro-centric identity with its "native" counterpart, however, settlers chose to aggravate their differences. Thus, the "in-group" and "out-group" perception that typically arises among discrete nations was instead fostered between the non-Indigenous and the Indigenous peoples within Australia. The tensions nurtured through this ethnocentric approach to an Australian identity resulted in an "ethno-national conflict," so passionately espoused that it continues to engender hostility and separation between the two groups through the present day.[9] Owing to the widespread eradication of Aboriginal culture throughout Australia's colonial period and the post-colonial legacy of suppressing Indigenous heritages and languages, Aboriginal populations now "identify less or do not identify with the national identity of being an Australian," instead choosing to preserve their "ethnic identities" as distinct.[10] Though numerous composers discussed later in this book have since attempted to unite the two cultures within their art music, much has yet to be remediated.

Despite these glaring sociocultural considerations of the relationship between non-Indigenous and Indigenous Australian peoples, historian Neville Meaney argues that a homogenous British identity has generally been quite functional for the Australian nation. Throughout its gradual estrangement from the Commonwealth, he asserts, Australia's primary population base of transplanted migrants embraced European traditions with little desire to forge a separate Australian identity. Any attempt for nationalism in Australia was "short-lived," duly superseded by a "positive support to multiracialism and multiculturalism" (i.e., the antithesis of a singular unique people).[11] Though this is a rather optimistic perspective that perhaps accounts for the current demographic diversity of the Australian nation, it is nonetheless a historically simplified and romanticized representation of the historical exclusion of non-European peoples that only recently has begun to dissipate.[12]

This consideration of Australian identity and self-realization, although ostensibly detached from the overarching discussion of its musical manifestations, is important in evaluating the nation's sociopolitical circumstances and the sentiments of its constituents. What becomes evident, then, is a strong contrast between the development of nationalistic trends in Australia and those of other countries throughout history. For example, post-1848 nationalism in Europe (musical and otherwise) was largely motivated and sustained by the ongoing separatist movements across the continent, in which the notion of independence demanded of each nation a discrete identity. Additionally, many European nations were motivated by a collective opposition to the traditions of an artificially imposed uniformity—for example, the Balkan nations have long maintained unique identities that did not submit well to the demands of the Ottoman Empire, the Austro-Hungarian Empire, or the Soviet Bloc. Australia, however, was not forcefully subjected to such strict uniformity and otherwise has not experienced direct conflict with its Mother Country; therefore, it has ostensibly lacked the motivation to redefine its existing identity.

Yet Australia did not have as positive a relationship with the Commonwealth that the prior statement perhaps suggests. In fact, one of the most universally beloved aspects of Australian culture—the phrase "g'day mate!"—is irreversibly associated with Australian blood lost, however inadvertently, by the hand of the British Empire.

In the present day, the above greeting is an amicable symbol of Australian camaraderie and sociability. Its origins, however, can be traced to the nation's engagement in World War I and II and is embodied in the term "mateship," intended to connote the supreme moral virtues of Australian soldiers; this association was solidified during their catastrophic 1915 Gallipoli landing, which Australians now commemorate as "Anzac Day."[13] The legacy of these gruesome events persists in the national consciousness—for example, the Australian Army Recruit Training Centre lists the "soldierly qualities" they seek as "a will to win, dedication to duty, honour, compassion and honesty, mateship and teamwork, loyalty, and physical and moral courage."[14] "Mateship," as a concept, became so symbolic of the Australian experience and its relationship with the Western world that, in 1999, it was almost included in the preamble of the Australian Constitution: in consultation with the Prime Minister of the time,

John Howard (b. 1939), the Australian poet Les Murray (1938–2019) wrote that "Australians are free to be proud of their country and heritage, free to realise themselves as individuals, and free to pursue their hopes and ideals. We value excellence as well as fairness, independence as dearly as mateship." Ultimately, opposition from the Australian Democrats (who maintained the majority in the Senate) resulted in the removal of "mateship" from the preamble, on the basis that it was "blokeish" and "not a real word." Howard met this decision with great reluctance, as he felt that the term had "a hallowed place in the Australian lexicon" as a result of its complex and extensive implications surrounding Australia's history with Great Britain and their growing recognition for the need of a self-sustaining identity.

Though these military escapades are seemingly tangential to the development of a national consciousness in Australia's music, one cannot overlook the evident correlation between the country's developing sense of individuality and the substantial struggles the citizens endured to achieve this independence of spirit. These challenges were not merely physical, such as in surviving the harsh demands of colonization or valiantly fighting on behalf of the increasingly unprotective Commonwealth, but also psychological. To articulate a decisive cultural separation, settlers had to recognize themselves not as immigrants (or descendants thereof), detached from the Australian land and perpetually associated with another, but as members and citizens of a *new* nation, one in which they are responsible for constructing novel traditions and thus establishing a sense of permanence in a virgin territory.

Musical Nationalism

The previous section offered discussion on the political and social ramifications of an Australian identity; it did not, however, encompass the musical manifestations of these developments. Thus, it is necessary to delineate the implications of "musical nationalism" as they have evolved throughout Western history and their relationship with Australia's culture.

As a musical movement, nationalism emerged in the nineteenth century in connection with the above-mentioned European political independence movements, and it is characterized by an emphasis on national musical elements, such as the use of folk songs, folk dances or rhythms; the adoption of nationalist subjects for operas, symphonic poems, or other forms of programmatic music; or the use of religious music associated with a particular nationality (e.g., the German chorale of the Lutheran tradition). Additionally, "nationalism" refers to the various national "schools" that consciously sought to separate themselves from the "cosmopolitan" standards set in the Classical period by the French, Italian, and particularly the German traditionalists;[15] conceived to differentiate itself from the pan-European tradition, nationalism was itself a pan-European tradition in its ideological pervasiveness.

Such definition, albeit relatively discretionary, is perhaps the most functional when considering the "nationalistic" output of a nation's composers. Within the evolving Australian "school" of composition, all aforementioned elements are present: their "folk" music derives primarily from convict heritage and secondarily from Aboriginal musical traditions, either directly quoted or merely imitated; a considerable volume of music is composed in commemoration of national landmarks, historical events, and significant individuals; and religiosity, both of the Aboriginal peoples and of neighboring East Asian cultures, features prominently in Australia's music. (Certainly, an overreliance solely on one's folk music to construct a recognizable nation idiom is not entirely effective, as a nation's history encompasses the entirety of its existence, and not merely the presence of its earliest inhabitants; it is, however, a frequently recurring point of departure for regional composers.)

Musicologist Richard Taruskin defines musical nationalism as an inherent evolution of the social and communal sentiments established by a common language, thereby manifesting the language community's "specific contribution to the treasury of world culture." Furthermore, music is regarded as expressive of the "specific truth of the imagined community" and necessary in determining "its self-definition." Particularly interesting, however, is his statement that "modern political nationalism is most often defined as the belief that political division between states should accord with the ways in which populations define themselves as communities."[16] Thus, if musical nationalism is deemed representative of pre-determined language groups and self-designated allegiances, then it must be considered whether the incorporation of Aboriginal culture in the classical music of Australia can be categorized as nationalistic, given that the Aboriginal peoples do not identify themselves with the post-colonization trajectory of the Australian nation? In consideration of the ongoing ethno-national conflict between the Indigenous and non-Indigenous peoples of Australia, is the insistence on Aboriginality as a "truly Australian" characteristic a form of cultural appropriation? Does this limit the extent of the music's authenticity within a national idiom?

These cultural dualisms of European "tradition" and Australian "identity" maintain a significant role when considering the complex sociopolitical environment of Australia's musical output. There are two distinct circumstances, historically, in which "nationalistic" music arises, both of which necessitate the presence of formally established countries: the first is when a nation or national style is trying to assert itself on the international stage, typically contextualized by similar countries unified by language, temperament, and culture; the second is when one nation is subjugated by another. Both conditions suggest a political process accompanied by transnational hostility, in that they are causally related to the deliberate assertion of national pride and the articulation of a newfound independence. Certainly, then, these relationships are substantially imbued with overarching political aims and a focused "psychological awareness of difference between 'we' and 'they.'" Parallel conditions exist within Australia, albeit in the absence of overt transcontinental aggression: the nation's composers are attempting to establish a recognizable musical tradition amidst the longstanding presence of the distinct traditions of other countries, and, in doing so, are formulating discourses surrounding the ethno-national and ethical concerns of incorporating Indigenous cultures.

There is, however, a *third* style of musical composition in Australia derived from the processes of *colonialism*, the historical implications of which remain pervasive in considerations of inclusion versus exclusion. While Australia's formal connection to Britain is maintained through psychological preconceptions of attachment rather than a forced imposition of culture, it is not a wholly independent nation.[17] Furthermore, the concept of colonialism exists within multiple scales in Australia. On a grand scheme, the modern Australian nation is a product of British colonialism and is comprised of individuals who brought their cultures, traditions, and values with them. Any subsequent development of either the nation or their music had little in common with the preexisting Aboriginal peoples, who were largely ignored in favor of customs familiar to the colonizers. On a smaller scheme, those colonizing Australia were then appropriating and subjugating Aboriginal culture. The practical distinction between this circumstance and the second condition for nationalism, however, is that Aboriginal peoples constitute neither a European nation nor culture.[18] The cumulative result of these conditions is that the transplanted immigrants likely felt little obligation to consider themselves a separate nation from Britain and as such did not consciously initiate a "nationalistic" style, nor did they seek to incorporate Indigenous culture as an integral element of their own identity.

Colonialism predates both patriotism and nationalism. Certainly, the first musics in Australia were created under this aesthetic, as the first settlers were merely relocated British citizens and thus had little impulse to deviate from their established traditions. Furthermore, a large percentage of the first settlers from 1788 onwards were there involuntarily as convicts and therefore did not necessarily display the requisite love for their country that defines "patriotism"; this trend did not begin to dissipate until the mid-nineteenth century (c.1850s), when the discovery of gold in eastern Australia prompted a significant influx of suddenly enthusiastic immigrants from both Europe and Asia. "Nationalist" sentiments, discussions of which originated around the 1920s and persist to the present day, are the evolution of imposed colonialism and passive patriotism to encompass the conscious assertion of a distinct sense of identity. These evolutions of cultural identity and their associated sociopolitical regard for Indigenous peoples have significantly influenced the development of a "sounded" national consciousness, and therefore remain a critical element of consideration when discussing "nationalism" in Australia's musical history.

The Development of an Australian National Identity in the Other Arts

A recurring consideration when discussing Australian composition is the acknowledgement that musical "nationalism" often failed to keep pace with similar movements in the visual, literary, and theatrical arts; it was, perhaps, the last of the creative fields to convincingly manifest an "Australian" identity, and it clung to conservative Euro-American ideologies for much longer than evident in other artistic realms, both within Australia and the Western world. Nonetheless, these analogous trends served to influence and contextualize later developments within Australian music, and thus merit discussion as to their origin and defining characteristics.

Political Australian nationalism largely dates to the late nineteenth century, as Australia gradually developed a culture and identity distinct from that of Britain and began to view itself as a unique and separate entity, rather than an extension or a derivation of British culture and identity. Until that point, Australia was administered as a series of six largely self-governing colonies that were spread across the continent. Attempts to coordinate governance had failed in the 1860s, primarily owing to a lack of popular support and backing from the British government, but by the 1880s, alongside the rise of nationalist movements in Europe, the efforts to establish an Australian federation began to materialize. British imperialism had become a significant catalyst for this sentiment, as such consolidation of otherwise disparate settlements in Australia would centralize and propagate British jurisdiction in the South Pacific, promote economic growth and investment, and expand the perceived breadth of the British Empire. Indeed, this "federation may thus be seen as a meeting point of nationalism and imperialism; both futures seemed to be implicit in it and that ambiguity helps explain the divided and unsure response in both countries."[19] The impact of organizing these independent colonies was both practical and psychological: federation minimized the logistical concerns surrounding Australia's settlement through territorial consolidation, and it granted its settlers a single title under which they could recognize and identify themselves.

As a response to these events, there emerged an upsurge of authors, artists, and performers who actively sought to express a distinctly "Australian" identity in their art throughout the first half of the twentieth century. Literary developments in the mid-1930s, for example, centered around the "Jindyworobak" movement, which recognized that the basis of a recognizably Australian literary culture lay in the overt expression of a relationship with not only the landscape, but also the history and traditions of both the Indigenous and non-Indigenous populations.[20] It was heavily spurred by three distinct ongoing trends: first, an economic depression, which focused the popular attention on comparable hardships of an earlier era (i.e., the early 1890s); second, the vast influx of "alien" culture that threatened to overwhelm the developing Australian literature; and third, a general increase in the number of reverential accounts from travelers describing the then-enigmatic Outback.[21] The Jindyworobaks found inspiration in the Australian "bush ballad" tradition, D.H. Lawrence's novel *Kangaroo* (1928), and P.R. Stephensen's *The Foundations of Culture in Australia* (1936), as well as the aesthetic ideals of their contemporaries in the arts, such as writer Xavier Herbert (1901–1984), painter and printmaker Margaret Preston (1875–1963), and modernist-primitivist composer John Antill (1904–1986).[22] Given that this movement occurred before Aboriginal peoples were granted citizenship in 1976 and in the midst of various racially charged policies, such as the "White Australia" legislation and the "Stolen Generations," Indigenous peoples were not contributing members to the body of literature produced at the time. Thus, the Jindyworobak writers garnered criticism for their largely idealized, and even fabricated, representations of Indigenous life, and the movement was deemed culturally insular and overtly nationalist.

In the visual arts, Margaret Preston sought to foster an Australian "national art" through the use of Aboriginal motifs in her work; indeed, she was among the first non-Indigenous artists to do so. Preston, like many Australians who desired a thorough education, studied in Europe and was trained in the German modernist tradition; she grew disenchanted with its philosophies and denounced the aesthetic, however, proclaiming that "half of German art is mad and vicious, and a good deal is dull." She eventually returned to Sydney and began to advocate for the need to develop a distinctly national identity in art, espousing a "conscious crudity" and a "daring engagement with deliberate primitivism" that, albeit founded in European post-impressionism, assumed a markedly Australian character that pointedly rejected imitation of tradition.[23] From 1932–1939, while she resided in the bush suburbs of Berowra, she pursued this concern most intensively, incorporating Indigenous symbolism, natural-pigment color schemes, an attention to asymmetry, and forms developed through repeated patterns in her works.[24] In 1937, Preston was awarded a silver medal at the *Exposition Internationale* in Paris, thereby raising the international recognition and perceived value of the native cultures of Australia, if only through the secondary mechanism of a non-Indigenous artist.

In the early 1970s, as a result of Aboriginal people working with the non-Indigenous art schoolteacher, Geoffrey Bardon, the widely recognized "dot painting" on canvas evolved in central Australia. In 1972, the artists established their own company, Papunya Tula Artists Pty Ltd., now housing approximately 150 Aboriginal artists and perpetuating the renowned Western Desert Art idiom. Though it is now a highly successful commercial endeavor, the artists' manager, Paul Sweeney, explains that the first paintings were not intended for monetary gain or widespread distribution:

> [They] were produced by people who were displaced and living a long way from their country. The works were visual representations of their own being. They painted sites that they belonged to and the stories that are associated with those sites. Essentially, they were painting their identity onto their boards, as a visual assertion of who they were and where they were from.[25]

More recently, another medium of Aboriginal visual art is gaining recognition as "the greatest contemporary art in the world"—namely, memorial poles.[26] Now an archaic funerary tradition, in which the bones of a deceased individual were placed inside a decorated eucalyptus tree trunk, documentarist and art collector Dennis Scholl is stimulating its awareness internationally as an astounding art form that "embodies the universal themes of life, death, love, and memory." (Another significant installation was curated by the National Gallery of Australia in 1987–1988, entitled "The Aboriginal Memorial.") Though it is still in a somewhat formative stage as non-functional art, such poles are a "powerful metaphor" in "our increasingly interconnected world" about "our cultural differences and shared humanity."[27] The creation of a memorial pole is remarkably similar to that of a didgeridoo, further reflected by their analogous cultural functions; it is indeed only in the final cosmetics that any differentiation between the two items may be found, thus raising considerations as to their cultural symbolism surrounding music, ritualism, and rejuvenation.[28] Interestingly, many creators of memorial poles seek to imbue a "singing quality" to their imagery through regionally specific cross-hatching and line work, thereby unifying the various elements of a traditional mortuary ceremony that are typically accompanied by song and dance.

Dance, similarly, had a nationalistic movement in the early twentieth century. In 1931, after several decades of "imported" ballet productions, Louise Lightfoot and Mischa Burlakov founded the First Australian Ballet; it was subsequently disbanded in 1956 and replaced by the Australian Ballet in 1962, now the largest classical ballet company in Australia. The roots of the Australian Ballet itself are in the Borovansky Ballet, a company founded in 1940 by the Czech dancer Edouard Borovansky. While visiting Australia on tour with the renowned Russian ballerina Anna Pavlova and the Covent Garden Russian Ballet, he decided to remain in the country and establish a resident ballet school in Melbourne. Following Borovansky's death in 1959, the British dancer and administrator Peggy van Praagh DBE was invited to become the artistic director of the company. Despite the nationalistic intentions that prompted its founding, however, the company continues to showcase predominantly European classical and "heritage" works (e.g., *Swan Lake, Coppelia, The Nutcracker*, etc.), rather than demonstrating or projecting an identifiable national image.[29]

Concurrently with the Borovansky Ballet, the British dance company Ballet Rambert toured Australasia in 1947–1949, and over the course of six months, grew into a two-nation troupe, attracting Australian dancers at a consistently increasing rate. They attempted in 1948 to premiere a ballet based on Australia's history, entitled *Dhoogor*,[30] but a lack of public interest ultimately prevented the project from materializing, and it therefore was forgotten.

Among these various artistic developments, perhaps the most internationally successful venture in encapsulating the Australian nation was Colleen McCullough's 1977 novel *The Thorn Birds* (despite critical derision that it was a "commercial," rather than "serious," work of fiction). Set primarily on Drogheda, an imaginary sheep station in the remote Outback, it is the best-selling book in Australian history with a record of over thirty-three million copies distributed worldwide.[31]

In comparison with these dynamic and widely recognized evolutions of nationalistic sentiment in other realms of the arts, the history of Australia's musical nationalism appears relatively lethargic. Indeed, it was not until the early twentieth century that composers openly acknowledged their absence of nationalistic composition, and, burdened with recurring reminders that they had fallen behind, sought to forge a parallel Australian identity.

Re-adaptation of European tradition

Perhaps the greatest impediment to the creation of an Australian musical idiom was the stubborn perception among composers that the nation was little more than a cultural vacuum, lacking any inherent element of interest or diversity as compared to the Old World. Though this sentiment was punctuated at times with a curiosity in the nation's Indigenous peoples or, more passively, its landscape, the presiding sentiment of bareness remained. In 1963, for example, composer Dudley Glass wrote:

> Australia's contribution to the art of music is all the more remarkable when one considers the lack of musical background. In the case of Europe people developed that fertile source, folk melody, in times of peace or national struggle; master composers emerged; vocal and instrumental activity grew over the centuries. The Orient has its age-old themes, and the New World adds to the symphony of the red man more mature notes from European nations who brought their own cultures.
>
> But Australia, the timeless land with claims to be the oldest of all the continents, is very young in matters musical. Even the 'native woodnotes wild' are so different that Adam Lindsay Gordon, rough-rider poet of the outdoors, writes about the land of 'songless bright birds.'[32]

This perspective is, of course, both rather cynical and quite contradictory to the developments heretofore presented in Australia's history. (After all, bush ballads earned recognition as some form of "folk" music in the late nineteenth century; "master composers," however few, were evident; and vocal and instrumental activity, albeit less developed than their Euro-American counterparts, had nonetheless thrived. Even if one wishes to contest these three arguments, the birds of the Australian bush scarcely merit criticism as "songless," particularly considering the many instances of admiration expressed by composers enchanted by their singularity.) Yet Glass's pessimism was not an isolated incidence—it merely exemplifies one extreme of Australia's existential pendulum, perpetually oscillating between pride in the nation's heritage, and dismay in its supposed absence of tradition.

His attitude may further be explained by the educational infrastructure for Australian musicians of the time, which predominantly transmitted the ideologies of the "refined civilizations" of Britain and the West (accompanied by a resentment for anything outside these ideologies). Inadvertently arose the national self-deprecation so evident in Glass' statement, reflecting the perpetual embarrassment of their country's heritage—try as they may, Australia could never be contrived into the image of England. Yet composers did not feel they had the freedom to construct and articulate their own identity; as though in purgatory, they meandered between the unattainability of profound Western art and a novel Australian idiom. As Ross Edwards describes:

> I studied in Europe for several years in the early 1970s. At that time, it was more or less obligatory for young composers to spend time in either Europe or North America, and it was expected that would imbibe their culture, bring it home, and use it as models for our own work. This attitude, which was cynically referred to as the 'cultural cringe,' was based on the assumption that we didn't need a voice of our own, a voice that reflected our own experience, because it was widely considered that they did things better over there in the hub of civilization. Better than anything we in our remote outpost could expect to achieve. For this reason, Australian composers of an earlier generation and my own often chose to remain abroad. Since then, we've made a lot of progress in recognizing that it's essential for us to develop a musical culture relevant to our own society, although it has to be said that vestiges of the 'cringe' are still alive and well in some quarters.[33]

Though many Australian composers refer to this process as a "rejection" of Western traditions, it is not an accurate representation in the literal sense of the word. Rather, their philosophies serve as an *adaptation*, because they choose to retain the same structures, systems of notation, and general theoretical principles. While this may not be sufficient to create an idiom so unique as to be considered "Australian," Western classical music is also a genre heavily bound to tradition and gradual in its evolution. In addition, Australia still relentlessly attaches its identity to that of Britain and the Western world and has only begun recently to shift its perspective to other regions, thus further inhibiting any substantial modifications in compositional practice. Nonetheless, the experiences of Australia's citizens are vastly different from those of their British counterparts and thus necessitate different mechanisms of expression. Such adaptations are both organic and gradual, as they are a response to the accumulation of minute cultural deviations over substantial periods of time.

From this framework, then, the delineation of "patriotism" and "nationalism," as well as the ambiguous intermediary, may be addressed.

The first preserved patriotic song, written for a band by Mr. Thomas Kavanagh (the Irish-born Master of the Band of the Third Regiment), is titled *The Trumpet Sounds Australia's Fame* (1826). Though certainly not a conscious attempt at nationalism, this demarcates an origination point in which the residents of the continent recognized that, firstly, they constitute an independent community, and, secondly, that this community merits distinctive, "patriotic" musical representation. Premiered by the then-recently formed Sydney Amateur Concerts, the work was heralded by the *Sydney Gazette* as an embryonic example of an "Australian School of Music":

> A new song, The Trumpet sounds Australia's Fame, the music by Mr. Kavannah, Master of the Buffs' Band, was given with considerable effect by the composer, and drew down great and deserved applause. The martial style of this air, its highly effective accompaniments, and the animating patriotic character of the poetry, imparted considerable satisfaction and delight, and demonstrated the effect which music wedded to immortal verse, produces on the soul of feeling and sensibility. The following may serve as a specimen of the poetry.
>
> *Live, live, Australia! Land of future kings;*
> *Land where new wonders each new sun disclose!*
> *Land where the young renown luxuriant springs;*
> *Land where the silent patriot worth reposes!*
>
> [...] Taking every circumstance into consideration, it must be allowed, that the Sydney Amateur Concerts, present a considerable degree of

> excellence both vocal and instrumental, and their continued success cannot fail to be a desideratum with the inhabitants of Sydney, who, notwithstanding so small a beginning, may yet consider them as the germ of an Australian School of Music. 'E parvis magna'.[34]

"E parvis magna," translated as "Thus great things from small things (come)," is "a not inapt motto" when considering the emergence and development of an "Australian" musical idiom. Though a relatively minor work with no surviving musical manuscript, it indicates something of the gradually maturing consciousness of Australian country, peoples, and experiences, its bravura and grandeur even intimating national pride. Similarly, in 1859, "The Gawler Institute" awarded twenty guineas for a brief patriotic work of Carl Linger (ironically, a German immigrant) entitled *Song of Australia*; its lyrics, written by "Mrs. C. J. Carleton," inspire the same patriotism and sense of immortality attributed to Kavanagh's work:

> There is a land where floating free,
> From mountain-top to girdling sea,
> A proud flag waves exultingly,
> And freedom's sons the banner bear,
> No shackled slave can breath [sic] the air,
> Fairest of Britain's daughters, fair,
> Australia!

Many such compositions, however, inextricably overlapped with instances of "nationalism." In 1823, for example, the New South Wales poet Barron Field sent to London for journal publication a music-and-words transcription of what he identified as an "Australian National Melody," subtitled "Harry's Song"; notably, this is the first recorded instance of such a "national" epithet being applied to any musics produced within the continent. Furthermore, Field asserted that:

> From the neighbourhood of our settlements we have scared the kangaroo and the emu, and left these poor lords of the creation no created food but a few opossums, and a tenancy in common with us of fish. Together with their numbers, their customs and manners are in a state of decay [...] But the *corrobory*, or night-dance, still obtains. This festivity is performed in very good time and not unpleasing tune. The song is sung by a few males and females, who take no part in the dance. One of the band beats time by knocking one stick against another. The music begins with a high note, and gradually sinks to the

> octave, whence it rises again immediately to the top. I took down the following Australian national melody from Harry, who married Carangarang, the sister of the celebrated Bennilong; and I believe it to be *the first that was ever reduced to writing*.[35]

In 1824, Parisians Charles-Alexandre Lesueur and Pierre-François Bernier published three additional examples of Indigenous melodies, endearingly entitled *Musique des sauvages de la Nouvelle-Galles du Sud* (undoubtedly influenced by Jean-Phlippe Rameau's opera and keyboard work by a similar title). The first is a chant lacking any text; the second is sophisticatedly titled "Air de Danse"; the third is an exceptionally brief "Cri de Ralliement." It is perhaps an exaggeration to categorize the third as a self-standing piece of music, given its brevity and rather formulaic construction (it consists simply of three iterations of a rising fourth interval), but it was nonetheless included as a representative work of Australian "natives."

In 1826, the above-mentioned Kavanagh compiled a set of colonial musical works entitled *Original Australian Music*. His widely disseminated advertisement described this collection of marches, songs, and airs as a "specimen of national music" and, indeed, are the "earliest non-Indigenous music to claim that description"; yet any specific relationship to Australia, apart from their repeat performance for local governor generals, is undiscernible.[36] Though this compilation, together with similar contemporaneous volumes (such as Reichenberg's 1825 *A First Set of Quadrilles for Australia*), constitutes a significant addition to the otherwise scarce body of documented colonial music from this region, there is nonetheless little that musically distinguishes it from its European counterparts. Indeed, much like the numerous maps of "Australia," construed for several centuries prior to the continent's colonization, these compositions are united solely by their arbitrarily applied "national" title.

In some respects, the treatment of such music was subject to the whims of fashion, as the "novelty" of these and similar works had a growing market with English (and, more generally, European) publishers; secondarily, a steadily increasing percentage of inhabitants born in Australia—and thus with no inherent psychological attachment to the United Kingdom—were undoubtedly seeking to represent themselves through what they perceived to be "original" composition. Given that the minimal number of musical institutions in Australia were developed from British models, however, the resulting musics were not particularly "Australian," or at least not any more than they were English, French, German, or Italian. In amalgamating these various styles within a "national" music, yet lacking any distinctive or individual approach to their application, many of these compositions advertised as "Australian" (interchangeable elsewhere with "exotic") scarcely satisfied in that regard.

Even disseminated musics of the "natives" or "savages" were not legitimately "Australian." Many who transcribed Indigenous songs unnaturally compressed them within Western diatonic systems, and then often entirely eradicated whatever "authenticity" remained by harmonizing them. Though there was likely no intent to distort the impression of native musics, Field's statement that *Harry's Song* was "*reduced* to writing" is an unintentionally accurate interpretation. Aboriginal tradition is, by nature, oral. Its pitch systems, performances, and contextualization are inherently dynamic and ephemeral; to petrify them within (foreign) immutable transcriptions is indeed a "reduction" of its various social and cultural meanings. Furthermore, many musics within their myriad ceremonial performances are taboo, or otherwise severely restricted for those who have not passed certain initiation procedures, and therefore were not intended to be notated, "discovered," circulated, and performed by any with a passive curiosity.

Additionally regarded as a "nationalistic" work is *A Song of the Women of the Menero Tribe Near the Australian Alps* for voice and piano (1834) by Dr. John Lhotsky, which he regarded as "the first specimen of AUSTRALIAN MUSIC" (this remains the earliest-known piece of music to be printed in Australia) and advertised in *The Sydney Gazette* as following:

> SHORTLY WILL BE PUBLISHED, A SONG OF THE WOMEN OF THE MENERO TRIBE, NEAR THE AUSTRALIAN ALPS ARRANGED With the assistance of several Musical Gentlemen, for the VOICE AND PIANO-FORTE, Most humbly inscribed as the first specimen of AUSTRALIAN MUSIC, TO Her Most Gracious Majesty, ADELAIDE, QUEEN OF GREAT BRITAIN AND HANOVER BY Dr J. LHOTSKY, Colonist, New South Wales [...] THIS SONG has been declared by the most competent judges as 'very pretty'; by others, even as a 'sublime' production [...].[37]

Reputedly, this piece was composed after Lhotsky attended a "Corrobery" in the Australian Alps, which he described as imbued with a "majestic and deep melancholy [that would not dishonour a Beethoven or a Handel."[38] This performance, however, was witnessed in the course of a broader scientific survey of the Monaro district, for which Lhotsky had attained government funding, and its documentation was largely based in a scientific, rather than artistic, interest in

Aboriginal peoples and culture. Nonetheless, it remains among his most lasting contributions to Australia's musical environment; yet his excessively energetic personality and "blatant self-promoting," together with his status as a "foreigner" (i.e., a non-British Bohemian arriving in 1832 from Brazil), expeditiously negated any camaraderie with his fellow colonists, and he was all but deposed from Australia by 1838.

A few decades later, Moritz Heuzenroeder (1849–1897), a German immigrant, composed *Immomeena* (1893), deemed the "first genuinely Australian opera in terms of composer, librettist, plot, and scenery."[39] Though Heuzenroeder initially operated a jeweler's shop in Gawler (South Australia), he sustained a passion for music and returned to Stuttgart to study piano and voice; upon his return to Adelaide, he advertised himself as a teacher of singing. As described in an article that affectionately chronicled his life, the writer, a Ms. Elizabeth Wood, rather pithily stated:

> Why he came [to Australia] is impossible to discover. It seems unlikely that he was one of the disillusionned [sic] German intellectuals and bourgeoisie who were assisted by the Schomberg Migration Society to escape from a revolution-torn Germany after 1848, and who numbered many talented musicians including the composer famous for his 'Song of Australia', Carl Linger of Berlin. Perhaps he sought independence and adventure. Whatever the cause, he soon found that the precocious musical talents he had shown since early childhood, when he was so 'devoted to his art' that he often spent all day at the piano, oblivious even of hunger, could scarcely be advanced in a new colony without further training, so he enrolled at the Royal Academy in Stuttgart to study composition with Dr. Sebert for several years before again taking up a career in Adelaide in 1872.[40]

His legacy in Australia, albeit rather geographically limited, was nonetheless valuable in expanding the breadth of amateur musical production beyond more densely populated urban centers—for example, he founded an orchestra in Tanunda, a choral society in Angaston, and the Adelaide Harmonie Society. In the last of these organizations, Heuzenroeder often premiered his operettas and comic operas, many of which followed in the Germans *Singspiel* tradition and were received quite favorably by the public. *Immomeena*, however, likely achieved recognition as a particularly "Australian" work because of its libretto, which was written by the journalist Harry Congreve Evans and based on articles in *Quiz and the Lantern*, a weekly humorous and satirical publication. In the above-mentioned article, Wood described the work as an "outstanding operatic venture," vividly describing:

> Set in a homestead on the banks of the River Murray, the loose-knit plot was described by a contemporary critic as 'a lyric of the Australian bush . . . of merry-making and holiday-keeping amongst cultured people as well as the stockmen, the rousabout and the ordinary stationhand'. It thus presented a more realistic picture of colonial society and the democratic spirit than most 'exoctic' [sic] indigenous dramas. Characters include Harry Crosby the squatter, his cousin Kitty and her friend Violet who are both intent on amorous intrigue with the handsome Police Trooper Alex Fergus and his friend James Main, a bush adventurer. Visitors to the fancy-dress party in the homestead's ballroom include a pompous Alderman who is looking for his long-lost son, an eccentric scientist and 'new chum' Professor Bingham who is looking for the mythical Bunyip and succeeds in an unconvincing scene with the help of Billy-the-Hatter, a crazed shepherd-stockman 'gone daft in the sun'. An ingratiating fellow caller Harold Montague is described by his creators as a 'masher' and an 'exquisite', whilst an Irish servant girl, Maggie, sings sentimental ballads about the 'little green isle of the sea'. Choruses of stockmen, stationhands and girls crowd the stage for dances and spirited choruses.[41]

While convoluted, the plot did, indeed, appear quite Australian in character, and it was met with resounding optimism by the quaint Barossa Valley township. Reviewers remarked on Heuzenroeder's "great melodic facility, his bright, swinging style, and the boldness of the experiment which was essentially new and Australian and deserved to succeed not only in the colonies but as a novelty at home (viz, England)," and, were it not for the unfortunate loss of the musical manuscript, *Immomeena* would certainly have persisted as an opera laden with themes of a vibrant colonial culture. It even contained a resounding note of nationalism in its finale: "At its conclusion the cast grouped before an allegorical tableau depicting bush scenes and sang a patriotic 'Song of Australia' glowing with local pride and fervour." Although aggrandized, and perhaps intentionally satirical in nature, its "romantic and hyperbolic drawing-room" nature was undoubtedly capable of inspiring a sense of Australian place and belonging in his audience; revealingly, the greatest criticism leveraged against the work was the unfortunate omission of "some *real* natives of the soil."

In many of the presented works, the categorization of "nationalistic" is, of course, used somewhat loosely; these works are defined as such primarily because they demonstrate both inclusion in their conscious use of Aboriginal culture and exclusion of those cultures that do not claim explicit Aboriginal heritage (i.e., Britain). Nonetheless, they far predate what is considered to be the start of a "consciously" nationalistic style in the 1960s and 1970s, and thus provide crucial historical context for the evolution of this idiom. Furthermore, there is a secondary discourse on the connection to place and the relationship to one's "homeland," particularly when contrasting the majority of imported music at the time against the local experimentation with native elements.

The reader may note that the term "Aboriginal" has been used somewhat interchangeably with "national" throughout the preceding section. Though this perhaps appears a narrow interpretation of "nationalistic" art within Australia, the works of this period—both musical and otherwise—largely rest on the assumption of their synonymity. Throughout Australia's artistic history, periods of uncertainty as to what constituted a "national" idiom consistently reverted to a single-minded attention on Indigenous culture, despite the simultaneous denigration of its merits by composers until quite late in the twentieth century. For example, in the same 1963 work discussed above, Dudley Glass wrote:

> The first people of Australia—the aborigines—gave little to music. Strange to talk of them in this heart of London, with so many musical associations crowding round: across the Thames the Royal Festival Hall, in Covent Garden the Royal Opera House, along the Strand the Savoy Theatre, home of Gilbert and Sullivan. Stranger still to hear these aborigines by means of recordings; to listen to tribal chants in unison (no attempt is made at harmony) that have a monotony as they start on a high note and drop down in the scale. The crude 'orchestras' are no more than sticks, boomerangs or shields struck together . . . didjeridoos (hollow tree-limbs about five feet long with a resonant drone) . . . drums of wallaby skin . . . and bull-roarers (thin slats of wood whirled on a string, to produce a terrifying sound).[42]

Yet Glass praises the use of Aboriginality in national music, claiming that "to hear such a work as [Antill's] *Corroboree* [...] is to realize the spread of instrumental music in Australia." These "crude," "monotonous," and "terrifying" sounds so unfavorably described above became, in turn, the "deliberate," "minimal," and "revolutionary" attributes that would define the nation's music. For example, a Sydney journalist wrote that "a distinctly Australian note has been introduced into modern music," enhanced "by the weirdness and beauty of aboriginal rhythms hitherto unknown in their wonderful possibilities."[43] Likewise, composer August Siede somewhat artfully stated:

> [T]he bush vibrates with magical rhythms; the very air palpitates with hidden melodies [...] The growing Australian multitude, virile and strenuous, surges to and fro in economic conflict, presenting materials for an epic of original mould, which transformed to tone, well might beget an immortal tune.

In this transitional era of patriotism, nationalism, and the ambiguously vast chasm in between, Aboriginality emerged as the most explicit manner in which to connote nationalism and locality; composers even sought to acquire the innate "spirituality" and "belonging to" the land they felt Indigenous peoples represented by utilizing their cultural material, thus usurping the perceived power of Aboriginal society over Australia itself.

CHAPTER SIX

"The great composer who came to define Australia's sound for the rest of the world"

Peter Sculthorpe, 1929–2014

It is perhaps impossible to attempt a thorough summary of Peter Sculthorpe's biography in the limited pages of this book. Indeed, the meticulousness with which Sculthorpe documented and preserved the minutiae of his life, the cumulative result of which is now held in the Sculthorpe Collection of the National Library of Australia, lends an intricate record of his existence, one which has yet to be fully surveyed and organized. It is as though he was aware of the inevitable national magnitude of his work, or at least conscious of its possibility, and prepared for its biographical repercussions accordingly. It was an explicit aim of his to articulate a distinctly Australian voice in music, an act that he was acutely cognizant had been attempted and failed not a few times before him; in the case that he was to succeed, a sanctioned record of its process surely must exist. While his personal record is rampant with self-contradictions, it has been partially edited, organized, and recounted by several notable scholars such as Deborah Hayes, Michael Hannan, Graeme Skinner, and (ironically) even Sculthorpe himself. Nonetheless, there is much room still left for scholarship; Skinner himself states that "the full Sculthorpe story is, as yet, far from complete."[1] Such endeavor, however, is beyond the scope of this work and truly merits a separate project altogether. Of primary concern in this book is the formation of a distinctly Australian idiom; it must suffice to assert, then, that Sculthorpe was unequivocally considered, both by his contemporaries and by present-day artists, as the "key player" during a "watershed era in Australia's musical development."[2] He had seemingly delivered on the purpose of creating an Australian musical idiom by 1974, scarcely forty-five years into his illustrious musical career. A trove of matured material far more indicative of the incipient *Australiana* style, however, is to be found in his later compositions and therefore will be given their due discussion as well.

In order to justify such monumental claims of his formulating a national identity, the setting in which Sculthorpe acquired such a status must first be established.

In 1933, when Sculthorpe was merely a few years old, the newly established Australian Broadcasting Corporation held its inaugural "Australian Composers Competition" with the purpose of promoting "Creative Musical Art." It was widely considered a success and, encouraged by the enthusiastic response of Australian musical connoisseurs, held several more times in succession. Numerous laureates of this competition rose to considerable fame in Australia and abroad, such as Margaret Sutherland (1897–1984) and Clive Douglas, and thus was created the impression of Australian music riding on the crest of a wave of success.

Australian conductor Bernard Heinze (1894–1982) was an adherent to this seemingly indisputable opinion of impending national eminence, and, to further promote "native" music, he took advantage of an ABC wartime ban of German national music (e.g., Richard Strauss) to instead endorse "British" and "Australian" compositions. Many works were submitted for radio broadcasting and, despite the prevalent estimation that very few met any standard measure of performance quality, were aired on the ABC.

Perhaps galvanized by a sense of momentum in Australian art music, the ABC's first director of music, William James, proposed that the forthcoming Sydney and Melbourne orchestral programs each contain an "experimental" concert devoted entirely to Australian compositions. This self-assurance of Australia's inevitable prominence on the international musical stage, however, was not universally embraced and indeed had begun to wane in its superficial promise of a national cultural flourishing. Perhaps the most vocal representative of this phenomenon was Neville Cardus (1888–1975), a British music critic who holidayed in Australia for much of World War II. As Skinner describes,

> Despite fears that presenting a whole program of local work was tantamount to putting up a sign saying 'Beware: Australian compositions!,' the first concert went ahead with Heinze conducting the Sydney Symphony on 14 October 1941. The next morning, in the *Sydney Morning Herald*, the recently arrived Cardus attacked it as a 'deplorable mistake.' He could find nothing original at all in Hooper Brewster Jone's *Australia Felix*, Clive Douglas's *Symphonic Fantasia*, Robert Hughes's *Estivall*, or Miriam Hyde's *Fantasy Romance for Piano and Orchestra*, and dismissed with a mere mention works by Frank Hutchens and Alfred Hill, though he did admit finding a

'sincere note' in *The Breaking of the Drought* by Roy Agnew. But otherwise he heard nothing that was not 'mannered and embalmed thousands of miles away from Australia in heyday of Edward VII.'[3]

Though several additional attempts were made at such "Australian" programs, Heinze and James reluctantly conceded that they were largely unsatisfactory to the national public. Thus, they concluded that a more agreeable alternative was to occasionally interject an Australian composition in a program of standard European repertory; this policy has persisted ever since, a fact that can be gleaned from a perfunctory glance over contemporary Australian concert programs chosen at random. Indeed, the current website of the Sydney Symphony Orchestra boasts an impressive schedule laden with Bach, Handel, Mozart, Beethoven, Wagner, and countless other European immortals; yet, the notable lack of a distinguished Australian composer or musical work cannot be reconciled.

The Labor Government's Broadcasting Act of 1942 aimed to facilitate the insurmountable artistic goals for which Heinze and James then strived, however, and thus stipulated that a minimum of two and a half percent of music played on the ABC and commercial stations must be by Australian composers. After some deliberation and well-intentioned programming, Heinze admitted that there was still a shortage in meeting this already deplorable quota, despite using all suitable local work. (As Andrew Haveron, the current concertmaster for the Sydney Symphony Orchestra, so aptly expressed almost a century later, "if a composer cannot be premiered in his own country, then there is something seriously wrong."[4])

Perhaps such perceived inadequacy was not as much a result of Australian incompetence, however, as it was the inevitable byproduct of attempting to create a holistic musical culture with an ostensible lack of shared national characteristics. (Indeed, Sculthorpe would later bemoan the absence of Australian traditions and its detrimental effect on Australian composition.) The music of the 1941 Sydney concert proved to be a dual dissatisfaction: on one hand, the commissioned composers avoided the overwhelming risk that comes from entirely reinventing dogmatized traditions, and on the other, those same composers sought to portray a nation with distinct musical contributions. Unfortunately, such self-assertion cannot be achieved through fearfully clinging to culturally irrelevant compositional practices; the sole outcome is a tangible lack of commitment to either conservatism or radicalism, expressed merely as a hesitant oscillation between the two extremes.

Thus, Cardus returned to England in 1948 definitively declaring that "there are no Australian compositions."[5] There were, certainly,

Australian *composers*, yet he felt there was nothing to be heard that was "identifiably Australian." Cardus expressed his sentiment that everything written in Australia was little more than a "secondhand" imitation of European music, tainted by a sense of lethargy and dispassion that yielded an overall unpalatable quality.

While there is an element of truth to this statement, considerations of chauvinism may temper its harshness. The British likely perceived Australia as little more than an uncivilized land comprised of convicts; how could they possibly compare to the intellect, artistry, and power of the British Empire? What experiences could they possibly have but those derived from Britain? Why would they *want* to have experiences that are not directly connected to Britain?

Yet, for much of their history, Australians espoused this disparaging notion of the United Kingdom as an unquestionably superior culture. Firmly rooted in the psychology of the nation at the time was an

> essential divergence between the English and Australian attitude towards this country. Our weakness has been that we have accepted, without questioning, the English attitude, perpetuated in our literature up to the present day, the convict tradition, and accepted without protest the crude caricatures of the indigenous, but larrikin, "Bulletin" school, as representative portrayals of Australian life and standards. [. . . As] a people we have been passive in our attitude to culture. Our culture was imported from Europe (England mainly), and the flow has been continued unchecked ever since by any conscious, distinctively Australian contribution to the world stream. In all forms of expression—the press, radio, drama, cinema—we receive the opinions and impressions of overseas elements, but create nothing ourselves. [...] 'A nation culturally passive—culturally self-classified as second-rate—culturally dependent on another nation—is one which will exalt mediocrity and drive genius into silence or exile.'[6]

These varying attitudes, then, contextualized Australian sentiments of the period—while apparently contradictory to one another, they all betrayed the fundamental hesitation and self-doubt toward constructing a distinguishable "national" culture that, for an extensive period, crippled its growth. In its midst, few emerged to mediate what seemed to be the adamant silence of a convincing musical aesthetic.

Early Works

At the time of these developments, Sculthorpe was but a young boy, though he was undoubtedly aware, if only vaguely, of their implications. He had begun composing after his first piano lesson, around the age of seven or eight, but was feverishly discouraged by his father and severely admonished by his teacher; it seemed as though they were trying to protect him from the unmemorable, and perhaps even disfavored, career as an "Australian composer," if such a notion was yet in existence. His teacher even went so far as to assert that Sculthorpe should not pursue such vocation because "all the composers are dead!," although it is possible she simply meant that all *good* composers are dead (or are at least European).[7] The overwhelming lack of some recognizable form of a national music was stifling, particularly considering the already numerous "Australian" idioms in other artistic realms, and it seemed as though such a path was predestined to collapse from the weight of ever-accumulating anticipation. Musicologist Roger Covell would later comment on this period as one in which "all composers were deemed to be equally important—with the contrary result that many listeners outside their immediate circle of friends assumed that none of them was."[8] Sculthorpe was not to be deterred, however, and persisted in writing in secrecy under his bedsheets late at night. To him, composing was an intuitive response to music lessons: "I went to art lessons and learned how to draw and paint, and then it was time to go to music lessons, and I naturally thought I was supposed to write music." He even implies a degree of encouragement from his mother, who, "being a schoolteacher, taught us to be inventive, to create things."[9]

His *Juvenilia* compositions, written between the composer's age of twelve to fifteen (c.1941–1944), largely resemble the works of other fledgling musicians, utilizing standard forms (e.g., minuets, airs, preludes, marches, waltzes, nocturnes, fugues, variations, etc.) with evident French, Italian, and English influences. They are simple studies that, albeit not yet in full maturity, already suggested a prolific work ethic with the potential to develop into a unique compositional voice. Nonetheless, they are given scant attention by scholars and performers, although many of their manuscripts remain available in the Sculthorpe Collection of the National Library of Australia.

Initially, it appeared as though the dire predictions of failure from his father and teacher were to be fulfilled. Sculthorpe studied at the Melbourne Conservatorium of Music from 1946 to 1950 but was unable to earn a living as a composer, and consequently he returned to his native Tasmania. Somewhat dejectedly, he opened a "huntin', shootin', and fishin'" store with his brother, and, had it been slightly more profitable, might well have ended the discussion of any musical nationalistic ideals, were it not for Sculthorpe's insatiable desire to pursue composition. It is possible he realized that his lack of success was a result of a certain stagnation in his academic works, imbued with a lack of variety and relevance that the nation's negligible music education supported and even promoted; this, in turn, may have prompted his recognition of the absence of an "Australian" compositional idiom and stimulated his pursuit to formulate one.

In 1954, Sculthorpe composed his then-revolutionary *Piano Sonatina*.[10] It was performed at the International Society for Contemporary Music Festival in Baden-Baden in 1955; it was rejected, however, from the same ABC "Australian Composers Competition" heretofore discussed, on the premise that it was simply "too modern." Governmental institutions are not often predisposed to unconventional or outright disruptive works, and any successful alteration in their accepted aesthetic is but a cumulative result of countless minor changes over significant spans of time. Indeed, centralized bodies tend to uphold the archaic and solemn, rather than the innovative and exuberant. The *Sonatina*'s aggressive pitch clusters, static harmonic motion, continual reference to Aboriginal culture through terminology evocative of the "primitive," extreme percussiveness, and maddening repetition was unlike anything yet heard in Australia, astonishing listeners through a sudden subversion of what was deemed to be an appropriate expression of national life. The late musicologist, music critic, and composer Wilfrid Mellers wrote of the *Sonatina* that "its sounds and structures come out as aboriginal in that they function not by development, like a Western sonata, but by the juxtaposition of tersely delineated figures."[11] The continent was not a tame one, a fact which Sculthorpe understood and did not attempt to deny; why should his music be anything else but an honest encapsulation of these observations?

This contrast of wilderness against civilization has been present in the Australian continent since its colonization. Where there were foreign animals, exotic plants, and hazardous terrains, settlers imported rabbits and foxes for hunting, planted familiar vegetation, and constructed British houses; where there was no land suitable for long-term agricultural development, they imposed a complex system of derivative British ruralism; where there was an unforgiving landscape surmountable only by sheer eccentricity (it is not by accident that the platypus originated there), they sought to incorporate grounded British sensibilities, cultural values, and social systems. In part, this transplantation of the familiar is a natural human response to relocation and disruption. Yet, the incompatibility of the two perspectives stubbornly persisted in the Australian psyche, which Sculthorpe had now brought to the forefront of national musical discussion, if only subconsciously. On one end of the spectrum, composers were writing "unappetizing cold cuts of Europe rehashed by local 'composers' and passed off as their own";[12] on the other end was Sculthorpe, a solitary, revolutionary figure who had recognized the essential character of the Australian nation and displayed it in an entirely unapologetic manner. This attitude extended beyond his musical compositions and into numerous fantastical stories he would share; Ross Edwards, his student, once recounted:

> We learnt, for example, that he'd once made love to Elizabeth Taylor in her lavish hotel suite while her current husband had gone out to buy cigarettes. This is such stuff as myths are made on. Skeptical we may have been, but we were prepared at some level to suspend disbelief because we *needed* stories that embodied daring, virility and fertility—our own versions of Prometheus snatching fire from the gods or Zeus's seductions of mortal women. Always presented in an airy 'as you do' manner, Peter's tall stories, I'm convinced, were calculated to have a life beyond their first, predictable, impact. Perceiving this, my wife once said to him: 'Peter, you're such a clever man.' He just smiled and said, 'I know.'[13]

Yet it is precisely these "daring, [virile], and [fertile]" characteristics that distinguish Australia from antiquated Western cultures writ large, a perspective that Sculthorpe sought to project in his music and inspire in his students.

Sculthorpe's maturation point as an "Australian composer" had not yet been reached, however, and he went to study at Wadham College, Oxford on scholarship. He had already amassed a distinctive reputation, one which followed (and often preceded) him. Pianist, conductor, and music critic Curt Prerauer had decided that Peter Sculthorpe was "the only Australian composer who can be taken 100 per cent seriously"; Edmund Rubbra, his tutor in Oxford, greeted him in their first meeting as "Ah! . . . Australia's Bartók!";[14] and James Murdoch, the inaugural director of the Australian Music Centre, wrote in his survey *Australia's Contemporary Composers* that Sculthorpe had created a "tangible Australian idiom, and an unequivocal musical identity." Ironically, his studies in England were to positively contribute to his merit and professional standing in Australia, conferring upon him a degree of validation from his motherland: Sculthorpe had succeeded in "escaping" the confines of

Australia and completing an education sanctified by its relative longevity and proximity to the epicenter of civilization. In part, his choice of study was a practical response to the holistic lack of any standardized or otherwise organized musical education in Australia. Furthermore, Australia maintained strong sociocultural relations with Europe in general and England in particular (and continues to do so, albeit to a lesser extent), and the notion of such education as what Sculthorpe acquired was exalted in the likeness of a "Third World" country reverentially observing the unattainability of the "First World."

Notwithstanding the 1954 *Piano Sonatina*, it is uncertain whether Sculthorpe was yet thinking in a deliberately nationalistic manner. The concept was evidently present in his musical conscious, although the *Sonatina* may have just been a singularly violent reaction to the prevalent national soundscape of his time. If he was not actively striving for an "Australian" sound before his arrival in Oxford, however, it is unquestionable that the ambition was unequivocally lodged in his music thereafter. While he was studying under Egon Wellesz (a student of Arnold Schoenberg who assumed a pre-modern, if not entirely anti-Romantic, aesthetic), he formally met Wilfrid Mellers, whose wide literary interests encompassed many Australian writers and who recommended to Sculthorpe that he read D.H. Lawrence's *Kangaroo.*[15] This directly led to the composition of *Irkanda II* and his song-cycle *Sun* (1960), based on three poems by Lawrence and dedicated to Mellers, both of which are roughly identified as the inception of a convincing, albeit adolescent, "Australian" sound.

Then, unlike others before him, Sculthorpe returned to Australia before completing his studies. Several of his predecessors, such as Percy Grainger, had attempted to claim the title of "the first *real* Australian composer," but Sculthorpe deliberately sought to encapsulate the traditions of the nation's heritage through the Aboriginal peoples and their barren, expansive landscape, achieving this precisely through his physical presence within the continent. This decision necessitated a substantial degree of commitment and well-defined purpose, intermingled with a resilient optimism, as there was little practical prospect then for an aspiring composer in Australia in terms of fame, renown, or professional dignity. Someone with a realistic purview of an "Australian composer's" prospects would have strongly advised to the contrary of Sculthorpe's proclaimed ambitions (which, in fact, a number of individuals did). Sculthorpe was among the few who did not pay heed to such advice, however, and thus he ventured forward as an exception among his peers. Indeed, he confessed to a lifelong inclination for solitude bordering on anti-socialness, and therefore must not have been significantly upset by his deviation from established customs.

Another factor that encouraged his return to Australia was the ill health and subsequent death of his father. *Irkanda IV* (1961) was written in memory of this event, in lieu of any verbal eulogy, and foretold the melancholy that was to pervade his subsequent works.[16] Sculthorpe's program notes for the first performance of the piece, written in the third person, perhaps give a stronger indication of its purpose than any theoretical analyses could imbue:

> This work is a plain and straightforward expression of the composer's feelings upon the death of his father earlier this year. Although the music is quite characteristic in its austerity and in its economy of material, it is much less complex in its tonal organization than most of the composer's works. The one movement, predominantly slow, is made up of the alternation of a "refrain," heard at the outset, and developments of the intervals used in the refrain.[17]

He would later describe the work as a ritualistic lamentation, eschewing of modern dissonance and instead reliant on chant-like passages and musical symbolism; its high C, Sculthorpe would say, was a depiction of God himself, radiating through the music after a relentless progression of funereal passages juxtaposed against grotesque dances.[18] The first reviews of *Irkanda IV* called it "first-rate" and indicated that Sculthorpe might be "one of our few internationally recognized composers." Far more significantly, the work prompted a letter from critics Curt and Maria Prerauer, in which they requested to write an article about Sculthorpe and thus exerted what was to be an inestimable influence on his career. On hearing the recording of *Irkanda IV*, Carl Prerauer described it as a "masterwork" and "perhaps the first Australian music that can be called great without a mental qualification or query." He then authored an article asserting that Sculthorpe "is the first Australian composer to unite in his music all the elements that could constitute such an elusive thing as an Australian idiom." Felix Werder pointedly described it as a "truly Australian work."[19]

Sculthorpe, however, still had yet to firmly cement his fame and renown. John Gilfedder wrote in the *Advocate*, "a chauvinistically Australian weekly," that "Irkanda IV *sounds* Australian, yet personal . . . The next step (as Sculthorpe is well aware) will be to demonstrate that he can be as convincing with a large-scale multi-movement design and grander thematic material." While the subtle presence of Western tradition is not lost in this supposition—the unmitigated expansion of a form, coupled with its increased grandeur, reminds one of the evolutions of the sonata or the symphony—it nonetheless presented Sculthorpe with a new challenge he would need a few more years to meet.

Here is perhaps as suitable a place as any to conclude Sculthorpe's first period of composition. In addition to the glimpses of Aboriginal and otherwise non-Western musical influences heretofore discussed, much of his early music demonstrates the influence of Asian, Javanese, and Balinese aesthetics, largely owing to his belief that the future of Australia is inextricably connected to Asia as a result of their geographic proximity and cultural interchange. For example, Sculthorpe composed *Music for Japan* (1970), which "does not simulate or pay tribute to Japanese music; it serves instead as an essay in Australian sensibility (bound up with a mystical identification with landscape) for Japanese listeners." Thus, he simultaneously enshrouded European traditions through the use of Asian musical influences, while retaining its underlying associations by means of an elegiac atmosphere.

Excepting *Music for Japan* and his *Piano Sonatina,* however, his first pieces were not particularly "enterprising," experimental, or otherwise revolutionary in comparison to those of his contemporaries. He briefly explored the pervasive serial techniques of the time in his early years, but soon rejected them, instead favoring a "clarity and polish that identified him as a persuasive intermediary between the new wave of Australian composers and a generally conservative public." His early musical vocabulary is generally defined by

> an overall mood of sombre intensity articulated through strongly accented descending minor seconds and minor thirds; frequent and sometimes elaborate performance directions in Italian; occasional passages of spectral, stiffly jerking puppetry; short phrases; a frequent tone of smoldering unease; and the positioning of melodic phrases across regular or expected accents.[20]

Despite this apparent diversity, Sculthorpe's music maintained a consistency of style and manner that allowed it to be immediately identifiable to his listeners. One manner by which he achieved this was his creation of his "Woollahra chord," emulating the tradition of prior composers to invent harmonies that inadvertently become "signatures" within their pieces (e.g., Igor Stravinsky's "Petrushka chord," or Alexander Scriabin's "Mystic chord"). The "Woollahra chord" is comprised of a stack of thirds intersected by an augmented fourth, sometimes used in sequence at the tone or semitone, or otherwise made up of two pairs of major sevenths superimposed at the interval of a major third. Perhaps the most prominent example of this chord may be heard in the opening of his *Sonatina for Piano* (1954), where it appears with the pitches *G–B–F#–A#*.

The 1960s: Politics and Pivoting Points

In 1963, as a result of Prerauer's above-mentioned letters, Sculthorpe was appointed as a lecturer in the University of Sydney, a position he held for the remainder of his life.[21] As musicologist Suzanne Robinson indicates,

> Herein lie several of the factors which boosted Sculthorpe's career: the articulate commentary of the Prerauers and [Roger] Covell, Sculthorpe's immersion in university life (especially his relationship with stimulating junior composers) and, not least, his own canny ability to write music that "was innovative but comprehensible."[22]

Perhaps considering himself in an ideal position to initiate the advancement of an "elusive Australian idiom," Sculthorpe composed *The Fifth Continent,* a radiophonic work for speaker, orchestra, and recorded didgeridoo, interspersed with excerpts from D.H. Lawrence's *Kangaroo.* The five movements represent the Englishman's emotional journey through Australia, evolving from unmitigated fear to a form of reluctant love. Originally composed for the ABC's entry for the *Prix Italia* for radiophonic music, Sculthorpe later said the work was intended to make a "truly Australian statement."

Its overall construction is rather simple: at the start of each movement, a static element (e.g., a didgeridoo drone, tam-tam roll, or wind sound effect) provides the backing for the narration, followed by a musical sequence to illustrate the text. As with many of his other pieces, Sculthorpe collaged previously composed works: for example, the music for the second movement ("Outback") is an arrangement for string orchestra of the composer's *Irkanda IV* for solo violin, strings and percussion (1961), and the fourth movement ("Pacific") instrumentally adapts his setting of Lawrence's poem "Sun in Me" (1958), with virtually identical contours and musical motifs. These two movements represent Sculthorpe's emotive post-Mahlerian style; contrastingly, the third movement ("Small Town") uses what the composer referred to as his "light music" style, characterized by tonal music with elegantly crafted melodies and derived from earlier commercial music projects.

Rather than offering harmonic direction and patterns of tension and release, the music provides dramatic underscoring to the recited text, thus assuming a secondary role to the overarching plot. In the "Prologue," the harsh drumbeats and frantic music evoke the "primitive," dangerous, and unfamiliar landscape of "the newest country—young Australia." The "Outback" emphasizes the "untouched, unbreathed" atmosphere, underlaid by a didgeridoo and a melodically and dynamically "flat" string section; pungent dissonances and the seeming absence of any human presence throughout the narration are uninviting, and even the didgeridoo assumes an animalistic timbre, much like the growl of a disturbed beast. There are several rhythmic, almost dance-like, interpolations, but they quickly digress into a *danse macabre* between an isolated man and the unrestrained wilderness, accompanied by grotesque pretenses of melody on a violin.

Finally, in "Small Town," the main character encounters an amicable, somewhat quirky village. He is quickly confronted, however, with what is dramatically named "the void," a township memorial to fallen soldiers. The ensuing music is pastoral, melodic, and highly tonal, but subtly punctuated with foreboding elements of dissonance and whirling sound. An increasingly frantic bugle call emerges, encircled by an ominous nebula of sound. This call is, in fact, "The Last Post," a melody with particular meaning to Australians as a symbol of the first landing at Gallipoli on April 25, 1915 (i.e., Anzac Day). It is finally truncated by the sound of a canon, and the countrified music reprises.

The traveler arrives at the Pacific Ocean in the fourth movement, tranquil in the familiarity of the shore and "as alone and as absent and as present as an Aboriginal." The mysteriousness and ostensible absence of direction permeates, while their formidable undertones are accentuated through jagged accents and fragmented melodic lines. Percussion instruments, though occasionally militaristic in nature, again suggest the primitive character of the vast land, and the movement is concluded with a fleeting, almost imperceptible wailing sound that serves as a link to the "Epilogue."

In this final movement, the bush is described with a tender, almost reverential love originating from a deeply primal point of the main character, and delicate, cultivated beauty is juxtaposed against the vast wilderness. Graceful melodies meander above portentous bugle calls, dreadful church bells, and an intermittent didgeridoo drone, yet the protagonist peacefully admires the land "with a dusky, far-off call that he knew would go on calling for long ages before it got any adequate response from human beings."

The Fifth Continent, despite its ingenuity, has largely escaped scholarly attention and, where mentioned, remains as little more than a footnote. Sculthorpe's wholehearted attempt to create an "Australian" music was not yet taken seriously, and the work had an unenthused life before quickly dimming into relative obscurity. Here, he was faced not with utter failure, which at least offers one attention and publicity; rather, he encountered absolute disregard, a far worse outcome in its shroud of anonymity. Nonetheless, it is at points such as these that Sculthorpe demonstrated his resilience and persistence, as he continued to search for that which would define Australian music and culture.

In 1965, it seemed that Sculthorpe's quest had found success: for a commission from Bernard Heinze, he composed *Sun Music I.* Described as "something without rhythm, harmony or melody," it would come to represent the flourishing of an Australian idiom, the decisive and unwavering announcement of its arrival. It rendered any prior attempt toward nationalism an unconvincing manifestation of Australia, overridden by a poor self-definition and an otherwise lethargic attitude toward asserting the nation's individuality; with *Sun Music*, Sculthorpe gave free rein to the nation's latent potential with newfound momentum. Indeed, Neville Cardus—who, less than twenty years earlier, had returned to England espousing a dismissive opinion of the forlorn colony—wrote that Sculthorpe was set "to lay the foundation of an original and characteristic Australian music."

Most significantly, his *Sun Music* was a celebration of light. The work was, in a somewhat Beethovenian character, an uplifting representation of the Australian spirit and universal brotherhood unmarred by the unfortunate events that loomed over the composer's personal life. David Cairns, in a *Financial Times* review, described it as evocative of "the feeling of the sun as a vast, glaring, impersonal force in a country dominated by it."[23] Its timbre, color, microtonality, and shimmering harmonies created an atmosphere of a "static, incantatory, almost frighteningly inhuman kind. It is music of harsh colours, of a ferociously brilliant light which glistens and blazes, music which perhaps could only come out of a country in which heat, not cold is the enemy element."[24] Indeed, Sculthorpe regarded the sun as a life force, a creative mechanism that embodied several highly poetic themes and thus gave impetus to his music: the dualities of light and darkness, or life and death; sun worship in the pre-Christian cultures of Greece, Egypt, or Mexico; the Aboriginal Australian sun totems; and, more generally, the sun as central to mankind's destruction or salvation.

Imbued with references to Aboriginal, Balinese, Japanese, and East Asian cultures, *Sun Music* further sought to reflect Australia's geopolitical position, as well as Sculthorpe's own pantheistic outlook in "seeking the sacred in nature." Writ large, it represented a critical shift in the composer's own artistic philosophy, meandering away from the intimate and toward the universal: "the earlier strongly personal element of emotional subjectivity is replaced by a predominant element of ritualistic incantation," evoking a fundamentally spiritual experience of living within the ephemeral Australian environment.[25] Commercially, this work attracted the attention of Faber Music, and his subsequent contract with the publishing company would facilitate the widespread advertisement and distribution of his work. This, in turn, promoted the international recognition of Australian art music, no minor achievement on Sculthorpe's part. Though it was not his first "Australian" work, it was certainly the most successful from an aesthetic, cultural, and commercial perspective.

Sun Music also represented the fruition of a new idiom, emphasizing several themes which were to recur in most, if not all, of his later works. Among these are the representation of the environment and humankind's place within it; frequent harmonic plateaus that avoid the development sections typical of Western music and thus yield a ritualistic quality;[26] sliding string harmonics to suggest flocks of birds; an emotional pendulum between sorrow and consolation; drumming patterns inherited from Asia; echoes of Aboriginal melodies; and his above-mentioned "Woollahra chord." Indeed, the creation of this series was so pivotal in Sculthorpe's career that the title of his autobiography, *Sun Music: Journeys and Reflections from a Composer's Life* (1999), utilizes it as a point of departure. It is difficult to overstate the impact and influence that *Sun Music* exerted, both within Australia and across international borders, in terms of establishing a recognizable national voice. Referring to the opening of this chapter, in which it was stated that Sculthorpe had sufficiently delivered on the purpose of creating an Australian idiom by the early 1970s, our discussion could well be terminated at this point with reasonable satisfaction. *Sun Music*, however, is merely the beginning of the composer's immeasurable contribution to the cultural identity of the Australian nation.

Indeed, by his forty-fifth birthday in 1974, Sculthorpe had scarcely concluded but the first period of his binary compositional life. At the halfway point in his career, he had

> finally brought to conclusion most of the projects and public commissions whose long gestation had occupied him since the early 1960s. The period is characterised by such early, but still mostly locally recognised achievements, as the four works of the Irkanda series (1955–

> 61), the four orchestral Sun Musics (1965-69) that also formed the basis of the ballet Sun Music (1968), the String Quartets Nos 6–8 (1965–69), and the opera Rites of Passage (1973). Better known internationally is his music of the second period, including the orchestral Mangrove (1979), the Piano Concerto (1983), Earth Cry (1986), Kakadu (1988), the guitar concerto Nourlangie (1989), Cello Dreaming (1998), Great Sandy Island (1998), the choral-and orchestral Requiem (2004), and the later string quartets, Nos 10 (1983) to 17 (2007).[27]

It was also in his earlier years that he had begun to experiment with and formalize his compositional voice:

> In his mid-twenties, he began to feel that he had found a way; he began to tear music to the bone, using the device of repetition until perhaps it became boring—but the landscape at times was a little monotonous. He was consciously trying to do something about this Australian loneliness, about the horizontal feeling of Australia as opposed to European verticality.[28]

He had not yet, however, fully developed his artistic intentions, and thus had not achieved the maturation and profound consciousness of a separation with European tradition. It is evident that he recognized the physical and cultural isolation of the Australian nation, but he had yet to attain a complete catharsis and reconciliation with the resulting absence in its cultural identity.

Similarly, not all critics, especially those in London, were yet exalting Sculthorpe's reputation as a great Australian composer. The *London Times* remained skeptical; the *Observer* stated that his music was "full of far out sounds which just didn't *tell*"; Maria Prerauer unflatteringly compared some of his works with insipid film music; the *New York Times* critic Harold Schonberg regarded Sculthorpe's music as a kind of sideshow rampant with "nationalistic exoticism"; and Andrew Porter remarked that performances of his music were "lucky not to be laughed off stage."[29]

Such criticisms did not deter Sculthorpe, however, and he continued to compose with a vigor and constantly renewed ambition, as though seeking to reshape Australia's image and acoustical atmosphere with each work. Indeed, the opinions of those with no vested interest in the advancement of Australian art music exerted little influence on the popularity of Sculthorpe's compositions, and, as both Graeme Skinner and Deborah Hayes note, a complete catalogue of all performances of his work from this period is virtually impossible to compile.

Thus far, Sculthorpe's music displayed an ever-increasing prominence of Asian influences, partly resulting from his belief that Australian music should be

> more and more influenced by Asian music. Certainly, my own is, and the music of several other Australian composers. I think that all of Western music needs revitalization, and I'm convinced that Asian music—because of the different attitudes—can do this. And we're very lucky, because we're sitting in the box seat here. There's no doubt that our political, our economic future is bound up with Asia, and similarly the cultural interaction must be tremendous.[30]

Through the 1970s, however, these influences dwindled and were gradually replaced with Indigenous material. Certainly, they had been incorporated rather frequently in Sculthorpe's earlier works, but the concurrent advent of recordings and the relatively concentrated appearance of books on Aboriginal peoples galvanized his desire to imbue Indigenous motifs with an existence of their own in his music. Politically, the Indigenous civil rights movement was quite active at this time as well: in 1967, a landmark referendum was passed to grant Aboriginal Australians legal recognition as full citizens; in 1969, an Aboriginal delegation went to New York and presented a statement to the office of the UN Secretary-General; in 1972, the Department of Aboriginal Affairs was established; and throughout the early 1970s, inspired by parallel upheavals in the United States, Indigenous peoples held numerous sit-ins and protests across major urban centers. All these events occurred within the immediate political and cultural vicinity of Peter Sculthorpe and undoubtedly influenced his writing, which later inspired him to say that he was "always political" in his work.

Therefore, in 1972, Sculthorpe composed the opera *Rites of Passage*, replete with Aboriginal texts and poetry. It was described by musicologist David Matthews as

> the culmination of all Sculthorpe's musical and extra-musical thinking up until then. An enactment of an Aranda Aboriginal ritual of initiation, death and rebirth, it contains no parts for vocal soloists; the rites are performed by dancers, and between them a chorus sing chorales to words from Boethius's *The Consolations of Philosophy* which speak of the world bound together by divine love. *Rites of Passage* (which still has not been staged in [the United Kingdom]) needs an article to itself.[31]

Despite its artistic and cultural value, however, this work has been overlooked by the scholarly community, as in the case of *The Fifth Continent.* Yet, it is much more symbolic of Australia than may be suggested at first glance. *Rites of Passage* is not merely the musical reenactment of an isolated Aboriginal ceremony, but rather, a representation of the nation's musical history from birth through stagnation and then rejuvenation. It is also, perhaps, a miniature of Sculthorpe's development himself: an energetic initiation into a life as a composer, an ostensible death from musical torpor, and a sudden revitalization through a newfound purpose. Thus, Sculthorpe encapsulated the allegorical "rite of passage" through which the nation writ large needed to progress so as to construct its own identity.

Then, in 1986, Sculthorpe composed *Liszt in Australia,* later renamed *Djilile.* To commemorate the centenary of Liszt's death in 1886, renowned pianist Sonya Hanke commissioned and performed in Sydney and Budapest "An Australian Hexameron" (also referred to as "Hexameron 1986"). The work was a set of variations by six Australian composers on a theme of one of Liszt's Hungarian Rhapsodies, in imitation of a similar "hexameron" in which Liszt himself took part in 1837.[32] As Ross Edwards describes,

> Peter's contribution was *Djilile*, based on an Aboriginal melody from Arnhem Land and meaning 'whistling duck on billabong.'[33] Just what connection this had with Liszt beats me, but since the Liszt theme Sonya offered us was pretty corny, Peter may have chosen to ignore it altogether. On the other hand, come to think of it, there is a certain resemblance between the shape of the Liszt theme and the more subtle Aboriginal one. Peter went on to make many other versions of Djilile.[34]

In his original program notes, Sculthorpe indicates that he wrote the work as an adaptation of an Aboriginal melody, collected in northern Australia, for which he had a "special fondness": "I made this piano arrangement of it, with additional material, simply for my own pleasure, and perhaps for the pleasure of others."[35] He does not mention Sonya Hanke or the work's performances in Hungary.

Most scholarly mentions of *Djilile* refer to Sculthorpe's 1977 *Port of Essington* film scoring project, in which the Aboriginal melody was used to accompany scenes of tribal dancing.[36] Musicologist Jonathan Paget makes particular note of the melody's evolution (or regression) from presentation in "period costume," sounding quite like a Mendelssohn-esque parlor song, to a fierce musical trope symbolizing Aboriginality. Sculthorpe stated that "by the end of the film, the theme is completely transformed: it becomes *Djilile*, a tribal melody from Arnhem Land."[37] Here, again, the composer's obsession with Aboriginal culture and its associations with the Australian nation is evident, portrayed through anthropological recordings and a somewhat fabricated interpretation of their relevance to the Port of Essington settlement. The melody was then revived for Hanke's Australian adaptation of the 1837 *Hexameron*, presenting a unique subversion of the nation's relationship with European culture and a subtle testament to their own notions of identity and place.

Aboriginality and Environmentalism

Here, the bibliographical relaying of Sculthorpe's compositional activities must be briefly paused, in order to address several significant developments in the relationship between Indigenous and non-Indigenous Australian peoples. These changes were to have a substantial impact not only on the sociocultural ramifications of Sculthorpe's musical works, but on those of all composers who followed him.

Indeed, mounting tensions between these two cultural groups had become increasingly difficult to overlook. From the onset of European colonization in 1788, the Aboriginal peoples had endured a relentless subjugation and eradication of their traditional culture, manifested in myriad equally destructive forms. Introduction of previously unencountered diseases, genocide, civil warfare, enslavement, encroachment upon traditional territory, missionary settlements, the removal and relocation of native children to "civilized" institutions (often abusive orphanages), segregation, disproportionately high rates of incarceration, frequent medical malpractice, and the otherwise repeat denial of fundamental human dignity to Aboriginal peoples had fostered severe intergenerational trauma. Aboriginal peoples had only recently acquired legal recognition as "full" citizens of Australia, and their experiences within Australia were radically different from those of Sculthorpe or his contemporaries (many even refused to identify themselves as "Australians" altogether). Yet, the evocation of "Aboriginality," both musically and otherwise, had become lackadaisically synonymized with "Australianism." The hypocrisy of this national cognitive dissonance was not lost on various political activists throughout the second half of the twentieth century, and they unapologetically criticized the unethicality of such passive musical borrowings. Sculthorpe, as the predominant composer within the Australian "primitivist" musical aesthetic, was at the forefront of these concerns.

Within much of institutionalized Australian politics, however, Aboriginal preservation was largely an anthropological interest, rather than a legitimate campaign for political equality or integration. Sculthorpe likely shared their perspective of "armchair anthropology," rather than those of isolated civil and cultural rights groups, and thus he is not uncommonly criticized for his purely "academic" reliance on books, recordings, and other "colonial" mechanisms of cultural transmission, as opposed to any direct experience or contact with native peoples.[38] Nonetheless, Sculthorpe recognized the timely potency of Aboriginality in Australia's musical culture, as it had long been a pervasive element in the nation's tourism industry and, therefore, its popularized national "image."

Furthermore, the political movements of the 1970s and 1980s intended to advance the awareness and protection of both environmental and Aboriginal welfare. The two concerns were, in fact, inextricably related.[39] An unmitigated progression of natural disasters, such as cyclones, bushfires, landslides, unrestrained pollution, nuclear testing, a widening hole in the ozone layer as a result of chlorofluorocarbons, and widespread soil erosion, led to increasingly prominent "green movements" and protests throughout Australia, culminating in a governmental recognition of an environmental emergency. Simultaneously, an increasing consciousness of Indigenous culture and their sustainable land practices led to the popularity in public opinion for Aboriginal preservation.[40] These events facilitated a turning point in Sculthorpe's writing in 1988, as an explicit concern and advocacy for environmental, and perhaps Aboriginal, conservation became evident.[41] His orchestral work *Kakadu*, commissioned by Emanuel Papper as a birthday present for his wife, would reinvent Australia's cultural identity once more through the intricate incorporation of various acoustical symbols, thus exemplifying the distinctive qualities of the nation in a far more direct manner than Sculthorpe had accomplished previously.

About the work, he said:

> Since the Beethoven Variations of the same name, it is well-known that kakadu is the German word for cockatoo.[42] Certainly, there are cockatoos in my music, as well as many other kinds of birds. The work, however, takes its name from the Kakadu National Park in northern Australia. This enormous wilderness area stretches from coastal tidal plains to rugged mountain plateaux, and in it may be found the living culture of its Aboriginal inhabitants, dating back for fifty thousand years. Sadly, today there are only a few remaining speakers of kakadu or gagadju. The work, then, is concerned with my

> feelings about this place, its landscape, its change of seasons, its dry season and its wet, its cycle of life and death. In three parts, the outer sections are dance-like and energetic, sharing similar musical ideas. The central section is somewhat introspective, and is dominated by a *cor anglais* solo representing the voice of Emanuel Papper, who commissioned the work. Apart from this solo, the melodic material in Kakadu, as in much of my recent music, was suggested by the contours and rhythms of Aboriginal chant.[43]

Here, as in the general perception of the nation, Sculthorpe addresses the Aboriginal inhabitants as an extension of the Kakadu National Park itself, as attached to the landscape as are the flora and fauna. Yet, in doing so, he aligns himself with Henry Tate's sentiments that Aboriginality is somehow remote, detached, and "estranged from the psychology of the modern Australian." Indigenous culture is iconified as an experience of the Australian nation, rather than as a group actively experiencing Australia themselves, and therefore are as "inanimate" as their landscape.

The 1980s and 1990s: Commercialization and Disenchantment

In 1995, Sculthorpe composed *Anthem for Australia* for brass septet and percussion. In some respects, this work may have been a response to the lack of a "true" Australian national anthem—though Australia once shared Britain's anthem, *God Save the Queen,* it was replaced in 1984 with *Advance Australia Fair*, composed by Scottish-born Peter Dodds McCormick. McCormick spent much of his life in Australia, however, he was neither a particularly distinguished composer, nor was he especially dedicated to the musical advancement of Australia. *Advance Australia Fair* nonetheless enjoyed significant popularity since its composition circa 1878, and a 1977 plebiscite in Australia established it as the official anthem.[44] Given the lack of surviving commentary from Sculthorpe about these events, any hypothesizing about his sentiments likely amounts to mere conjecture. It is improbable, however, that he regarded the increasing clamor for superficially "Australian" music favorably.

The Australia Council for the Arts had, around this time, organized a competition for a new national anthem, for which participants were invited to submit separate lyric and music compositions. It was an utter failure, however: of the 2,500 lyric entries submitted, only six were considered suitable for consideration; all 1,300 music entries were rejected. (It seems that the perceived unsuitability of Australian music submissions is a tradition unto itself.) The National Anthem Referendum, then, was a hastily devised attempt to continue the pursuit of a new Australian "nationalism." The four songs represented ("God Save the Queen," "Song of Australia," "Advance Australia Fair," and "Waltzing Matilda") were all at least over a century old, however, and they somehow lacked the vigor and innovation so central to the nation's personality. Bearing testament to this is former National Party senator Sandy Macdonald's declaration that the selected national song should be abandoned "before we all go to sleep singing it."

Against this unfavorable testimony to Australia's musical capacity arose Sculthorpe's *Anthem*. It opens with a hesitant, jagged melodic line, punctuated by a trumpet soaring above with a fluid and dignified atmosphere. All instruments then coalesce into an endearing and largely harmonic progression reminiscent of a chorale, though the work is occasionally tinged with passages of melancholy, despair, and intense chromaticism. The final chords are tense, distraught, and foreboding, but culminate in a triumphant resounding of Australia's character. Indeed, the use of a brass ensemble and resonant percussion is reminiscent of Ancient Rome's imperial music intended to glorify both the state and its leaders, and the music maintains an atmosphere of dignity, presence, and optimism.

A year later, however, Sculthorpe chose to arrange McCormick's *Advance Australia Fair* for string orchestra, rendering his musical symbolism far more direct. The first enunciation of the melody is quite faithful to its model, but later repetitions feature reharmonizations, contrapuntal melodic lines that often take preeminence over the original melody, mournful chromaticism, an entirely altered original melody, and a distraught ending highlighted through exceptionally dissonant chords. Sorrow, grief, and anguish are as distinctive to Sculthorpe's musical language as *rubato* is to Frederic Chopin's, or diabolical virtuosity to Franz Liszt's; yet, its gradual domination of his national anthem suggests a disillusionment and somberness that is quite jarring. Indeed, Sculthorpe would later comment about his music that "there is much of [a melancholy air], because of the absence of traditions in this country. So, what do we have to write about? There's nature, life, love, and death. And of those, death tends to be a particularly moving subject."[45]

Perhaps such sentiments were a result of numerous political events through the 1980s, and even in the entire post-war period, that fueled the artificial "commercialization" of an Australian identity. Immigration programs promoted to populate the country led to the first influxes of immigrants since the 1850s gold rush arriving from somewhere other than Britain, thus destabilizing the contemporaneous understanding of Australia's "demographic." Simultaneously, Australia's connections with Britain were unravelling as the "end of the empire" prompted them to seek membership with the European Union in 1973, a decision that effectively alienated their geographically distant Pacific territories. As a result of the cultural and political vacuum that followed, a "new nationalism" among the elite emerged that focused on such things as the promotion of "Australian studies" (as opposed to exporting students to Europe and America), the advancement of Australian film, a new national anthem (from whence arose *Advance Australia Fair*), an Australian "republic," and a new flag.

Greg Melleuish, a professor in the School of Humanities and Social Sciences in the University of Wollongong, has stated:

> I would argue that there has been a failure by Australia and Australians, primarily at the elite level, to find an adequate new form of identity to replace the older one. This is particularly the case with the 'British' element of that identity. Having been cut loose from empire, they have failed over the past fifty years to carve out a place for themselves in the world. One example of this can be seen in terms of the changing Australian economy. In the 1950s Australia still largely 'rode on the sheep's back'.[46] There were then grandiose ideas of creating manufacturing industries and this was followed in the 1990s by the dream, promoted by Donald Horne (1989), that Australia would become the 'clever country'. In reality the economic well-being of the country has been maintained by the export of minerals, especially coal and iron ore, and the country is held hostage to world commodity markets.[47] Without the sale of commodities Australia may well have become a banana republic and lost its democratic character. In this sense, Australia in 2019 is not all that different to the Australia in 1949.[48]

These sociopolitical upheavals, though understated in their lack of any outward expression of violence or animosity, culminated in a period of an unnaturally constructed Australian identity that may have left Sculthorpe disillusioned with his parallel efforts in music. Perhaps he felt that his advancements in music had been disregarded by those who truly believed that there was no such thing as an "Australian identity," or he came to believe that his work was somehow devalued by the sudden influx of artists and politicians haphazardly concocting a lustrous national image saturated with stylized kangaroos and boomerangs. About this period, Sculthorpe commented:

> Australia lacks a common cause, and the self-interest of many has drained us of much of our energy. A bogus national identity and its commercialization has obscured the true breadth of our culture . . . We need to attune ourselves to this continent, to listen to the cry of the earth, as the Aborigines have done for many thousands of years.[49]

He therefore embraced a grave, environmentally inspired idiom permeated by themes of death, funeral rites, and ritual lamentation, yet simultaneously affirmative of his "belief in the possibility of future harmony on Earth," from the 1980s onwards. Furthermore, his work acquired a distinctly political purpose as a "call for justice for Aboriginal people," as seen in his *Requiem* (2004) for chorus, didgeridoo, and orchestra.[50] His sudden disdain for nationalism, however, leaves much ambiguity in the analysis of his subsequent compositions, particularly in consideration of his otherwise adamant insistence that he be considered a pivotal figure in establishing an Australian school of musical thought. Does his shift in ideology imply that his post-1980s work cannot be analyzed as "nationalistic"? Was this sentiment merely a temporary reaction to the "over-confident" sociocultural atmosphere of the 1980s, or did it indicate a greater realignment in artistic purpose? Owing to the general absence of documentation from Sculthorpe regarding this topic, these questions largely remain unresolved.

Such statements are not to suggest that his lifelong dedication to forging a national school of Australian musical thought was conclusively terminated before the turn of the twenty-first century. (Certainly, many of his later works continue to exalt the qualities and characteristics found in the more overtly nationalistic works.) Yet, it may be that the ideals he previously maintained were tarnished with a distaste that could not be wholly expunged, and thus Sculthorpe's 1996 *Advance Australia Fair* marks the conclusion of this discussion solely within the ramifications of this book.

Final Developments

Sculthorpe categorized his music into two broad categories: his orchestral works, which generally surround themes of "looking for the sacred in nature," and his solo and chamber works, which tend to be more melancholy pieces on intimate matters "to do with people."[51] Additionally, his works respond to national occasions: *Child of Australia* (1988) commemorates the bicentenary of the first European settlement in Australia in 1788; *Port Arthur* (1996), conversely, laments a mass killing at one of the most notorious prisons of the convict era. Inspired primarily by the landscape, the immigrants, and the Indigenous culture of the Australian outback, several defining characteristics of his works include: the use of traditional instruments, Australian Aboriginal scales, cyclic structures, chant-like melodies, obsessive repetition, quotations of Aboriginal and Torres Strait Island melodies or the composition of original melodies that reflected the general characteristics of those same Indigenous sources, imitation of bird sounds, and a synthesis of ancient and modern (i.e., European and Australian).

Notwithstanding his reputation as the most recognizably "Australian" musical figure in the generation after Percy Grainger (1882–1961), Sculthorpe was not the first composer to attempt the creation of an "Australian" identity in music. Yet for many, Sculthorpe came to be "representative of Australia as a whole," as his work consistently aspired to encapsulate a holistic national image, rather than merely borrow from several interesting elements within it. Indeed, on his 50th birthday, a colleague of Sculthorpe stated that he "has given Australia an identity in music. Because up to now we've been something of a poor relation of European music. But Peter's music is quite unescapably Australian in feeling." He was characterized by his desire to entirely separate himself from many "classical ways of thinking about music," as the harmonically driven theory, unambiguously tonal melodies, and conventional rhythmic structures did not adequately align with the vast, fragile, and static atmosphere of Australia's Outback landscape, which he associated with the Indigenous peoples and, thus, the nation writ large. In this departure from tradition, he "had created a tangible Australian idiom, and an unequivocal musical identity."

Peter Sculthorpe composed steadily until his passing in 2014 and contributed a substantial output of over 400 musical works. The pieces discussed here represent but a sliver of his contribution to Australian culture, forming a merely skeletal outline of Sculthorpe's musical legacy. They are but the most deliberate homages to Australia, the most unabashedly assertive of a national identity obscured by the stagnant perpetuation of cultures far-removed. Certainly, his numerous honors suggest his extensive impact on the country: he was named one of "Australia's 45 Icons" in 1999, selected as one of "Australia's Living Treasures," and awarded the Don Banks Music Award in 2007 for making "an outstanding and sustained contribution to music in Australia," among countless other accolades. His legacy, however, is not entombed in regalia, but rather is channeled through a still-evolving national identity. He solidified numerous aspects of Australia's emerging musical identity, such as a focused attention on the environment, Aboriginal traditions, the socio-political relations with Asian cultures, deviance from driving harmonic and melodic patterns of Western music, ritualism, introspection, and a tenacious individuality, which he transmitted to a significant body of admiring pupils who would adopt and develop his musical aims.

Sculthorpe is certainly not universally admired in Australia, nor is he an overly glorified national hero. Quite on the contrary, he is a subject of scholarly criticisms, and his work often sparks debate on the ethical ramifications of utilizing "Aboriginality" and Indigenous heritages. His music was a product of its political and cultural time, however, and Sculthorpe remained astutely aware of social developments despite his predisposition for solitude. From an anachronistically applied modern perspective, his tendency to ceaselessly reinvent—and perhaps even apotheosize himself—is questionable or even troubling, but such character traits are common among monumental figures throughout music's history. Sculthorpe's understated boldness in asserting Australia's cultural individuality and national heritage, particularly when his predecessors and contemporaries merely dismissed any potential for a "native" musical tradition, merits further research, as it established the cornerstone for the nation's still-evolving, but exceptionally dynamic modern soundscape.

A sole point of discussion that has remained unaddressed is a lingering potential that Sculthorpe may come to be acknowledged not as the *first* "Australian" composer, but rather, the *only* such figure. There are several reasons for this possibility: first, the National Library of Australia has accumulated a substantial collection of resources explicitly and exclusively related to Sculthorpe, an honor that is generally reserved for a central figure in a nation's cultural history; second, the increasing scholarship on Sculthorpe, without a parallel influx for other Australian composers, creates the erroneous impression that he is the only "nationalist" composer of note; third, his role as a transitional figure from European modernism to Australian individualism galvanized an ideological shift that has not yet been paralleled by another Australian composer; finally, his passing in 2014 establishes a temporal boundary of "tradition" and "detachment" that cannot yet be perceived in the living composers who followed him. Nonetheless, the belief that Sculthorpe is a singular, predominant figure is not conducive to the further flourishing of Australian scholarship and therefore should be avoided. Without understating or otherwise diminishing his cultural contributions, the music of currently active composers in Australia must be acknowledged as well. Furthermore, Sculthorpe's perception and treatment of certain themes, such as

Aboriginality, are rather politically outdated and thus do not accurately reflect the present state of the Australian psyche. To consider only his works would be to perpetuate an already archaic condition that demands rejuvenation and recontextualization, particularly through the works of those more attuned to contemporary philosophies and aesthetics.

CHAPTER SEVEN

"Sometimes I realize that the music I'm speaking has a broad accent"

Ross Edwards, b. 1943

Ross Edwards AM[1] (b.1943), recognized as "one of Australia's best known and most performed composers," has a prolific output in orchestral, chamber, choral, opera, film, and children's music. Born in Sydney, his first attempts at composition began at the age of thirteen, galvanized by a Sydney Symphony Orchestra performance of Beethoven's *Fifth Symphony* and Liszt's *First Piano Concerto*. He was enrolled in the Sydney Grammar School at the time, which did not offer a music program; driven by his newfound vocation, however, he entered the New South Wales Conservatorium to study oboe, piano, theory, and counterpoint, often foregoing his lunch hours to take additional lessons. In 1963, with the assistance of a Commonwealth Scholarship, Edwards enrolled in the University of Sydney; he soon became frustrated with their aesthetic emphasis on modernistic techniques, however, and left after only one year. This professional crisis was subsequently allayed with the encouragement of composers Peter Sculthorpe and Peter Maxwell Davis (1934–2016), and Edwards completed a Bachelor of Music degree at the University of Adelaide's Elder Conservatorium in 1969. During his vacations, he worked as an apprentice for Peter Sculthorpe. A scholarship from the Commonwealth then enabled him to pursue a Master of Music in London, after which he undertook a social hiatus to compose for a year and a half at a remote Yorkshire farmhouse. Edwards now holds higher doctorates from the Universities of Sydney and Adelaide.[2]

Compositional periods and influences

Edward's musical output will be considered in five general periods, each of which marks a significant shift in artistic philosophy.

Early student work

This period encompasses all compositional output during Edwards's years of training and education. Much as with Peter Sculthorpe, however, these works are rigidly academic and provide little indication of his subsequent musical language. Indeed, the earliest manifestations of Australian music education were exceptionally Euro-centric and produced idioms that were academically imitative rather than personally reflective, as indicated by Edwards's recollection of his studies in the University of Sydney:

> We were very boringly taking the European culture, whether it was the modernistic one, or the impressionistic one, or whatever you'd like to call it. In Sydney, we had someone who would get English people to come over for six months at a time and try to convert us to "their" style. There was one insufferable person who came, influenced everybody, and got everyone writing in the style of Stockhausen. And I thought 'Well, we don't need that! We need our own voice!'[3]

Perhaps expectedly, Edwards' earliest influences were modernist composers such as Stockhausen, Boulez, and Webern, as well as their Australian counterpart, Richard Meale, with whom Edwards studied in the University of Sydney.[4] Thus, his first writings were primarily serial, atonal, and inflexibly structured, reflecting the predominant avant-garde aesthetic of the time. Edwards continued to adhere to pre-compositional techniques throughout his Master's degree, albeit with less conviction and considerably less success. Significant examples of this period are *Monos I* for solo cello (1970) and *Monos II* for solo piano (1970), the latter of which would musically embody his disillusion with the modernist style through its frustrated convulsiveness and uncertain character. He would later describe these pieces as "a hollow exercise in futility," sustained by little more than the sheer rigidity of their internal structure; indeed, they are suffused by a "sense of parody," often marked by "stylistically inappropriate ending[s]" that seem "to peter out in [...] abandonment and flippancy."[5]

Despite his increasing distaste for, and frustration with, the compositional practices of the time, Edwards admits that he was nonetheless overwhelmed by an unanswerable desire

> first to find the voice for the sounds and music in his head, and then to articulate it on the page. He found it difficult to sleep because of it. At school, sitting in class, or going to school or the train, he was manipulating sound in his head. While it was always there, he couldn't

> properly characterize it, couldn't express it in a way that satisfied him.[6]

In an interview in 1992, Edwards would comment about this period,

> I think the turning-point in my early life as a composer took place in a dank Notting Hill basement towards the end of 1970. I was a postgraduate student in London and I existed only for my work, living on bread and cheese, black coffee, chain-smoking Gauloises, writing music compulsively for twelve-hour stretches and taking pills to sleep. I clearly found myself questioning the validity of this course of self-destruction and at the same time that of 'accredited' postwar European art music. What, ultimately, was the point of all those neurotic convulsions so meticulously ordered? Did they do anybody any good or were they just self-indulgent? So ended my 'angry young man' phase.[7]

His music of the period therefore duly absorbed the overarching sense of "claustrophobia" and artistic suppression that had defined both his studies and his personal life, and he relocated to a farmhouse in Yorkshire in search of "peace and quiet to get work done":

> Most unfortunately, however, this seemed to have a paralyzing effect—the landscape was so bleak. One thing that did happen during that period, however, was that I learnt to appreciate nature. I began gradually to acquire an external focus, and I found myself looking and listening. This helped to release me from the rather torpid inner world in my head that was dominated by my work.[8]

In 1972, after this hiatus in the English countryside, Edwards began to depart from the atonal, serial, and twelve-tone compositional techniques that characterized his earlier style and transitioned to a "minimalist" aesthetic. Deeply influenced by John Cage (1912–1992), Morton Feldman (1926–1987), and Toru Takemitsu (1930–1996),[9] his works *Mountain Village in a Clearing Mist* (1973) and *Antifon* (1973) represent this shift, described by composer Paul Stanhope as "having an absence of harmonic goals or climaxes, lack of sense of development as normally occurs in the European tradition, and emphasis on timbre."[10] Indeed, these seminal pieces constituted a transition that perhaps represented "a personal as well as a compositional pilgrimage for Edwards," denoting his concrete rejection of the "music as research" philosophy (introduced by Milton Babbitt) that had overcome Western "art" music and instigating his introspective search for the viscerally spiritual.[11] Bearing testament to this is his recollection of the developmental process that underlaid *Mountain Village in a Clearing Mist*:

> I made a point of jettisoning the various rules and niggling stylistic mannerisms I'd acquired over the years, allowing my creative process to flow unimpeded. This proved to be a liberating experience [...] In relinquishing a certain amount of control over my work—previously I'd aimed for total control—my subconscious mind reasserted itself and resumed its share of the work.[12]

The influence of the natural world

Edwards's shift toward minimalism and austerity coincided with his conclusive break from the then-waning Modernist movement, likely as a result of several interrelated factors. His disenchantment with what he considered to be the "stagnant" European art music of the time, coupled with his return to Australia to care for his terminally ill mother, contributed to a "period of silence"[13] from 1944–1977, during which he produced no music (with the exception of his *Five Little Piano Pieces* in 1976). Compounding these significant personal changes were his continued pedagogical obligations in the University of Sydney, a still-embryonic reevaluation and criticism of Western art music, and a readjustment of routine accompanying his recent marriage. Though he had once been obsessed with saving money to leave Australia, which he regarded as a "cultural desert," his return would paradoxically rejuvenate his then-inert compositional activity:

> I was in a very strange, trance-like state of mind, and I didn't quite know what I was doing musically. I wanted to find another language, something that was relevant to me, rather than what was perhaps expected of me at the time. Generally, the syntax of my musical language was very ossified, I suppose. It seemed to need a bomb under it—something had to go in order to let light in, and to let silence in.[14]

During this time, he meditatively immersed himself in the unfiltered ecological sounds emanating from the Brisbane Water National Park, a pristine natural preservation near his home. This, in turn, motivated his avoidance of other canonized and abstracted musical influences from Western cultures, which he would later recount:

> The summer days were swathed in the drones of cicadas with their mysteriously abrupt starts and stops and, at evening, the insects would

> start up. I was entranced by the insect chorus because it seemed to be on the verge of conveying some profound message which was ultimately elusive. All the temporal relationships in my music—the relative lengths of phrases and sections—are influenced by these ancient voices, whose near-symmetries and inconsistently varied repetitions often seem close to our inherited musical syntax. I don't doubt that, over the millennia, such voices have generated much of the world's music and it's not hard to detect their presence in various surviving folk and religious traditions.[15]

Though it may seem atypical to view this period as compositionally independent, particularly considering its absence of any significant musical work, it is designated as such due to his critical shift toward an artistic philosophy focusing on deep ecology, the reconnection of music with elemental forces, and the incorporation of birdsong and the patterns and drones of insects. These influences remained a pervasive element of his later works, as well—in his *String Quartet No. 4 "Ridley Gold"* (2019), for example, extended string techniques in the third movement ("Salute to Venus") mimic "exuberant Australian parrot shrieks."[16] Furthermore, it is during this period that Edwards developed his method of composition in which he "is not really in control—all I know is when something is working and feels spontaneous."[17] This transition represents a definite break from the total determinism of the pre-composed music that previously guided his musical style, and, on a national scale, signifies the Australian cynicism with "modernism" as it relates to musical nationalism (indeed, Edwards's modernist compositions were among the last vestiges of the tradition within Australia).

The Sacred Series

Simultaneous with his move to Pearl Beach, New South Wales, Edwards's "period of silence" was concluded with the completion of works *Shadow D-Zone* (1977), *Tower of Remoteness* (1978), and *Etymalong* (1984). They are notable in that they demonstrate a significant leap from the fierce complexity of his earlier works to an austere, meditative, and introspective atmosphere, incorporating elements of chant, the natural soundscape, and Zen philosophies. Generally, they derive from the acoustics of the Pearl Beach area, devoid of any harmony and instead structured through "just vertical combinations of sounds."[18] The term "sacred" is not intended to denote any religious or explicitly faith-based association, but rather, to suggest a state of mind akin to Buddhist meditation. Edwards himself applies this designation to any work that contains "long-held sonorities, silences, slow tempi, mostly quiet dynamics, repetitions of short gestures and subdued mood creating a quiet and contemplative atmosphere," or anything otherwise "designed to promote spiritual meditation."[19] "I've evolved a highly subjective method of topographical symbolism," he has written; "the art of composition has come to represent a ritualistic search for the life force underlying our sterile, material society."

Further distinguishing the works within his Sacred Series is his pervasive use of the piano, which is significant for two reasons: first, it is Edwards's primary instrument, thus facilitating an experimentation he otherwise may not have attempted on other instruments in his early stage of compositional revaluation; second, the inherently solitary nature of the piano affords an atmosphere of introspection, reflection, and meditation. The compositional structures of these pieces often utilize melodic and rhythmic "cells" at registral extremes, negating any symmetric phrasal continuity and instead creating a single, ceaseless evolution of sonorities. These ostensibly pulseless devices, constantly changing and unpredictable in nature (not unlike Percy Grainger's concept of "Free Music"), seek to come "quite close to our inherited syntax but eventually, with a quirkish twist, [retreat] into that mysterious world which passes all understanding."[20]

Maninya Style

Originating from a spontaneously conceived nonsense text that Edwards set to music in his *Maninya I* (1986),[21] this style, though still maintaining the underlying spiritual quietude of his previous period, is characterized by "rhythmic buoyancy and obsessive, chant-like repetition, faster tempos, tonal or modal harmonies, drone-based harmonic structure, and dance-based rhythms; it seeks to reintroduce corporeal energy and a sense of levity into 'serious' music."[22]

Such significant transition permitted Edwards to compose music that was not directed solely toward an academically inclined (or otherwise "progressive") audience. He commented,

> About 1980, recognizing my inability to work solely on a disembodied spiritual plane, but unwilling to relax the gnomic severity of the Sacred Series, I responded with enthusiasm to my own impulse to leap in a new direction and compose exuberant dance music.[23]

In this style, the repeated motivic cells first introduced in the *Sacred Series* are further explored, developed, and juxtaposed against one another in polyrhythmic and polymetric settings, thus lending the music a sense of extemporaneity and impulsiveness previously absent. Furthermore, there is a prevalence of modal harmonies, non-linear based harmonic structures, extreme repetition, rhythmic instability, elimination of decorative or otherwise musically superfluous elements, and even theatrical staging in large-scale works; much of the compositional material is supported by lengthy, static harmonies, then "combined with intricate patterns of pulsing rhythms" that imbue a "mesmeric quality [...] akin to the performance of an Indonesian *gamelan*."[24] As noted by Stanhope, an increased tendency to reuse material from his previous works is also evident; for example, his *Maninyas* violin concerto, commissioned by the Australian Broadcasting Commission (ABC), consisted of an amalgamation of earlier pieces such as *Maninya I* and *Maninya V*.[25]

Perhaps the most significant work of this period, however, was his 1982 *Piano Concerto*. Laden with "a history of controversy" (among its first reviews called it "the kind of piece that gives A major a bad name," a somewhat satirical comment given the *Concerto*'s pointed ignorance of any tonal implications), it is imbued with "exuberant dance rhythms, colourful instrumentation and flagrant tonality, once considered a provocative stylistic volte-face" by "orthodox modernists" of the late-twentieth century." It, fundamentally, aspires to express "the pure joy of living" that overcame Edwards as he transitioned away from the austerity of his previous period:[26]

> I'd got rid of what I had decided was a boring old avant-garde from Europe, and I was trying to find something that related to us, to me, and to Australia. And so at that point, I had really gone to an extreme with [the Sacred Series] pieces. They did work in the concert hall, but I sort of thought 'well, I can't keep doing this'. So, the shapes, the patterns, the general intent of the music I transferred to another style, and I think the first pieces I did with that was the infamous *Piano Concerto*. I just wanted to do something completely different; if you're going in one direction, I find, sometimes you want to run in the other direction, because you've done it too much. So, I admit I wanted to get up the nose of the boring people who were pushing European music as well, and I did that very successfully. [...]
>
> So, it reflected how I felt at the time. I was sick of listening to the minute details of an environment, and I wanted to embrace the whole thing—all its colour and its vibrancy, and so that's what I did, and people have gradually accepted it, even those sorts of people who write criticisms are less angry about it now. Some still are going. But

> then, having done that, I started to write music that was suitable for the concert hall and retained the spirit of what I'd been trying to do, which was trying to put people under, to mesmerise them, I was fascinated with what might happen. I'd been investigating all sorts of chant, and Sufi music, etcetera.[27]

Despite the ostensible familiarity produced by recycling previously composed works, Edwards tends to consistently subvert the expectations of both audience and performer. This is perhaps best demonstrated by his *Yarrageh: Nocturne for Percussion and Orchestra* (1989), commissioned by the ABC as a percussion concerto for Ian Cleworth. Rather than displaying a Lisztian temperament expected of a singular virtuoso, the percussionist merely acts as a mechanism to augment and vary the ephemeral temperaments of the orchestra; in the *Concerto*'s one movement, the soloist is granted neither physical nor artistic preeminence.[28] Indeed, the piece resembles Edwards's sacred style in its reflectiveness and stolidity and is thus inherently counter-intuitive to a standard concerto. Amplifying this are the various staging instructions incorporated into the score, some of which indicate that the lights are to be dimmed and only stand lights used by the orchestra; this atypical decision ultimately

> [seeks] to reveal to the listener the 'mysterious darkness' that underlies our ordinary consciousness. To do this it's necessary to 'turn off' the everyday world for a time by focusing attention and reducing distraction. This can be achieved by treating the music as a sort of contemplation object in which each single event is as important as every other: you don't have to think about where it's going or what kind of structure is being outlined—the present moment, ideally, should capture your full attention.
>
> I've applied similar techniques in writing this piece. I've avoided too much complexity and restricted myself to using just a few ideas, or motifs, which I thought were powerful enough to stand on their own and bear a considerable amount of repetition. The way in which these ideas have been distributed and combined is based on a method I've evolved over the years which is influenced by the sounds of the natural environment. [...] I suppose, then, it's reasonable to say that this work, along with much of my other music, represents an attempt to localise some esoteric oriental musical traditions. Much of *Yarrageh* was conceived as I walked through the Australian bush in early Spring. The title is an Aboriginal word which means 'the spirit of Spring'.[29]

Edwards argues that "this way of listening, much neglected in Western music of the past five hundred years, is standard practice within a variety of Oriental musical traditions, particularly those whose specific function is to enhance the contemplative faculties of the human mind." Thus, his evolving interest in Eastern cultures and their subliminally ritualistic aspects, as well as his further straying from any forthright emotional subjectivity that he perceives as having defined Western "art" music and culture, is evident through both the musical and the theatrical elements of *Yarrageh*.

It is likewise in this period that Edwards's musical language, once firmly rooted in the Australian Outback, begins to absorb influence from the Sufis and the African mbira, thus foreshadowing his subsequent eclecticism. These diverse styles, however, are unified by their communal reverence for the Earth and its natural elements.

Enyato Style

The *enyato*, a nonsense word intended to connote "contrast," is not as much an independent period as it is a definitive merging of his sacred and maninya styles. Comprising a collection of four pieces in two-movement form, the first of which is typically slow and introductory and the second lively and dance-like, it is intended to emphasize the commonalities between what are otherwise ostensibly unrelated styles.[30] Musicologist Philip Cooney refers to this set as "a fusion of opposites"; Edwards explained that they seemed "to be fusing European music, with my own, static, environmental music, as an integration of the two." Thus, they represent his "intuitive search for unity within diversity." Indeed, this period signifies a reconciliation with or acceptance of European music and tradition, yet recontextualized within a distinctly "Australian" framework.

Most significant about this period is his introduction of plainsong, either European or Aboriginal, which remains a constant presence in his subsequent works. Though the chant may be presented unadorned or accompanied only by a drone, Edwards often harmonizes them in a manner that retains their original character but redefines both their context and their symbolic intimations. Hymns, or hymn-like passages, are similarly introduced and treated in this period; particularly striking about their use, however, is their inherent rhythmic regularity that strongly contrasts the otherwise exuberant and irregular nature of surrounding sections. Furthermore, Edwards transitions from a narrow focus on any one particular instrument within a composition to the use of distilled fragments fleetingly adopted by a wide range of instruments in rapid succession.[31] Often, Edwards describes these contrasting dance-chants as an attempt to "suspend linear time and invoke present-centered consciousness, an obsessive, kaleidoscopic interplay of symbolically charged fragments—a sort of Australian dervish dance."

Mantra series[32]

This collection of pieces is, essentially, a culmination of his myriad previous compositional techniques, representing what may be considered an intrapersonal adaptation of post-modernism.[33] They are linked by their meditative qualities, thus referencing his "sacred" style, but present a significant shift in that the music is intended to serve a practical (i.e., "utilitarian") consequence, rather than merely to be limited to the scope of the concert hall. Such attitude is rather universal to the composers of the *Australiana* style: among the most significant objections to European art music is its "stale" atmosphere, existing for "its own sake" rather than serving a greater functional purpose. About this period, Edwards commented that "the term mantra reflects the nature of the music, which is 'repetitive,' it's a prayer of some kind of ritual. They are generally 'real' meditational objects—as opposed to Concert Hall pieces which have a meditational quality."[34]

Thus, Edwards's work began to discard the false aesthetic consciousness of his prior systems and acquire an acute functionality that, although still attuned with his individualistic musical idiom, served a dual purpose beyond the sanctions of institutionalized acoustical spaces; they rejected the mere pretense of utilitarianism and instead sought to encapsulate and embody its essential aims. This transition is best exemplified by his collaboration with Dr. Graham Williams, a meditation teacher in the Burmese and Tibetan traditions, which produced the album *The Joy of Being—Guided Meditation and Music with the Lifeflow Meditation Centre and Ross Edwards* (2008).

Since the turn of the 21st century, characteristics of his work generally exhibit the following traits: an austere and almost childlike simplicity, embellished Eastern pentatonicism, medieval Western modality, fragments of plainchant, occasional outbursts of expressionistic angst, complex textures that include the development of motives and Western counterpoint, Eastern heterophony, and a deep spiritual dimension with both Eastern and Western overtones. Furthermore, his music maintains a strong ecological focus, consistently referencing Mother Earth and maintaining the mysterious Australian bush as his central setting.

Subconscious Nationalism and the Future of (Australian) Art

Notwithstanding the plethora of influences from Peter Sculthorpe that Ross Edwards displays in his music, there exists a crucial overarching differentiation between their intentions of establishing a nationalistic "Australian" idiom: while the latter explicitly and consciously engaged in a lifelong pursuit to forge a musical voice for the country, Edwards rejects such purpose in his work, preferring instead to avoid the inevitable dogmatization concomitant to such activities and instead uncover that which "represented, well . . . me." Furthermore, Edwards does not deliberately and explicitly utilize Indigenous musical idioms, despite occasionally employing several of their traditional instruments (e.g., the didgeridoo, clapsticks, etc.). Nature and the environment, he asserts, remain "the supreme generative force" in his work; thus, any resulting overlap between his music and those of Aboriginal cultures can largely be ascribed as the unintentional result of utilizing the same source of inspiration.

Yet, it is impossible to separate his work from the unique qualities of his nation: he notes that many listeners abroad distinguish an exotic and, simply, "Australian" nature to his music. Edwards states: "Sometimes I realize that the language I'm speaking has a broad accent—I suppose I can feel a certain Australianness about it. It's not something nationalistic particularly; I'm more interested in a sense of place."[35] Though the notion of "place," from one perspective, is "ecological" in its ramifications, it necessarily implies relativity as well. Edwards composes discourse not merely on "place" in isolation, but rather, as it relates to and interacts with another. The acoustical depiction of specific environments renders his work not cosmopolitan, but national; not vaguely European, but inimitably Australian. "National," in this instance, certainly does not imply a concentrated effort to aggrandize one's own "place" to the detriment of another; Edwards merely comments on the inherent individuality of the Australian continent, circumventing its ostensibly "Western" origins and recalling its millennia of isolation, primeval activity, and innate eccentricity.

Paul Stanhope, a leading figure in contemporary Australian music, authored his Master of Arts (Honors) dissertation on the music of Ross Edwards, analyzing its ritualistic aspects as resulting from its qualities of angular, animated chant, repeated rhythmic cells, and elaborated drones. Beyond considerations of religiosity, however, particularly valuable in Stanhope's thesis is the emphasis on the possibility of the *subconscious permeation* of a given musical quality, style, or function. He suggests, for example, that "the nature of [Ross]

Edward's compositional process is so very intuitive," hence permitting the infiltration of influences "not immediately recognized" by the composer. Recognition of this assumption is critical, as it permits the argument that, inadvertently, Edwards has advanced the nationalistic musical idiom of Australia and explicated certain characteristics first proposed by Sculthorpe in his work. His music represents a style motivated by socio-cultural utilitarianism, permeated by a connection to place, and pivotal in developing a national soundscape unmistakably associated with its distinct heritage. Though he chooses to reject the inflexible stagnation inherent to the label "nationalistic," perhaps owing to his "recoiling against" the excessive burden of tradition imposed by European art music, Edwards is a central figure when tracing the gradual evolution of a recognizable national character in Australia.

Regarding the future of "Australian" art, Edwards contends that there must be more innovation in the presentation of music, postulating that traditional concert halls and performance practices will become increasingly outdated and irrelevant. Indeed, he advocates for what one may regard as an Australian *Gesamtkunstwerk*: music presented not in isolation, but in conjunction with the visual, symbolic, costuming, movement, and lighting arts that, when coordinated, facilitate a thorough realization of a work.

Among the greatest challenges in discussing Edwards's work, however, is that he remains among that unique category of composer who cannot be abstractedly theorized upon; his music must be presented within context. Arising from an extended period of reclusion and introspection, it ultimately determined a critical juncture within the nation's culture—Edwards could choose to remain within the modernist aesthetic of the time and thus further Australia's perceived attachment to the West, or he could entirely sever its influence and recontextualize the nation within a highly individualistic framework. In pursuing the latter, galvanized by his determination to expunge extraneous influences and gradually construct a personal idiom (a practice revolutionary in itself), there emerged a body of work that is distinctly individualistic, yet could only have arisen from a quintessentially Australian perseverance. Indeed, this philosophical reassessment appeared a matter of artistic survival—his "period of silence," instigated by his disenchantment with the social structures and artistic ideologies of the West, threatened to extinguish permanently his compositional activities if left unreconciled.

To demonstrate Edwards's "Australian" character within his music, therefore, below is presented an analysis of his *Sea Star Fantasy* (2015), a mature composition in his "Enyato" style.

Analysis of *Sea Star Fantasy* (2015) for solo piano as a representation of the Australiana idiom

In the introductory notes to the 2018 Hal Leonard Australia edition of *Sea Star Fantasy,* Ross Edwards writes:

> The two movements that make up Sea Star Fantasy are inspired by the plainsong *Ave Maris Stella* ("Hail Star of the Sea"), one of the most beautiful of the Marian hymns. From the Middle Ages to the present day, composers have seen fit to incorporate it into their own work, sometimes making it the basis of an entire composition. The Christian veneration of Mary as the Mother of God has ancient roots and counterparts in other religions. In my music, and in some ecological and ecofeminist movements, she has become established as a symbol of the universal Earth Mother, nurturer and protector of the environment. As in my double concerto, *Frog and Star Cycle* for saxophone and percussion, fragments of the plainsong are woven into the texture of the music. The first of the two movements is dreamlike and gently whimsical; the second, which begins as a sprightly dance, plunges into the heart of a tropical rainforest, alive with clamorous birds and brilliant colours, and reaching a passionate climax.
>
> *Sea Star Fantasy* was commissioned by John Porter as a special tribute to his friend and partner Ann Wesley-Smith. It was premiered as part of a piano recital given by Bernadette Harvey on 12 December 2015 in the West Recital Hall of the Sydney Conservatorium.[36]

Several significant pieces of information can be gleaned from this brief overview. First, its two-movement structure in contrasting styles clearly places it in the *Enyato* idiom, despite its date suggesting its categorization in the *Mantra* series (which is simply a free amalgamation of his various styles to date). In Aboriginal culture, with which Edwards assumes a passing association resulting from what he deems "the innate Aboriginality" of non-Indigenous peoples, time is cyclical and therefore permits such returns to previous "conditions."[37]

Second, its association with the *Ave Maris Stella* chant suggests a permeation of environmental, sacred, and ritualistic elements. A common chant from the eighth century onwards, *Ave Maris Stella* was often recited as a blessing of safe conduct for seafarers, thus espousing its allegorical translation of Mary as a "guiding star" on the way to Christ. It must be remembered, however, that Edwards's treatment of religion is not associated with any singular tradition or belief system. He has stated that "the Virgin Mary and her Asian counterparts such as the female bodhisattva Guan-Yin have become, for me, important symbols which are inseparable from the world ecological crisis in their role as nurturers and protectors of living things." The use of the Virgin Mary, therefore, is a sanctification of the natural world (i.e., an ecological symbol), rather than of the spiritual systems of those who reside within it (i.e., a Christian symbol); this representation is furthered by the subtle subversion of her name, in which "Star of the Sea" is transformed into "Sea Star" and thus obscures its deific associations.[38] Instead, the title evokes images of the Australian coast and, certainly, the coral life within the renowned Great Barrier Reef, which has garnered international attention with respect to global climate change.

Third, the 2015 concert to which Edwards refers was entitled *The Sonata Project: Bernadette Harvey*, which sought to explore the relevance of the traditional piano sonata genre in the twenty-first century and the "values, attitudes, and choices of modern composers."[39] It is therefore suggested that *Sea Star Fantasy* is shaped, however vaguely, by the ramifications of sonata form, an element which merits consideration in the overall analysis of the work. Given Edwards's predisposition to allude to historical music, it is possible that this work was modeled on the earliest recognizable "sonatas" in binary structure, paralleling his use of two contrasting movements. Perhaps it was considered from an even earlier perspective, in which "sonata" is simply considered a piece that "sounds" without any predefined form (deriving from the Italian word *sonare*); such attitude would allow the composer to focus on "sound" and the various mechanisms of its production, therefore bypassing the conventions (and restrictions) of artificial forms in favor of organic and flexible soundscapes. Conversely, Edwards may have chosen to wholly disregard the cultural implications of a "sonata" and instead explicitly defy it, likewise a commentary on the significance of Western forms within Australian music. It is from these considerations, then, that the *Sea Star Fantasy* can be analyzed as a quintessentially *Australiana* construct.

Religion, spirituality, and magic

Sea Star Fantasy was featured in the composer's 2018 album *Incantations: Chamber Music by Ross Edwards*. Its liner notes state: "Throughout a long and storied career, Ross has written music that celebrates Australia—its cultural diversity, its natural environment, and its connection to the vast and diverse Pacific Rim region."[40]

The use of the word "Incantations" in the title of the album suggests a direct association between the presented music and some element of mysticism, as an "incantation" is generally defined as a spell, charm, or enchantment that can be performed during ceremonial rituals or prayers and is intended to invoke the supernatural within "secular" forces. Music's primordial function as a response to, and often an attempted influence on, the events of the natural world permeates this work, thereby alluding to the "basic" religions of earlier societies in which practitioners sought to affect the spirits that animated the surrounding world. For instance, an expressive direction in the second movement, "*magical, starlit,*" evokes an ambiguous sensation of the mystic. Thus, Edwards's writing is ritualistic in its expressivity and functionality on a broad social level, much like the liturgical music of the medieval Christian Church.

In the second movement, the music frequently oscillates around the pitch classes "A" and "B", strongly resembling the reciting tone of a liturgical chant. Edwards's choice of pitch is not insignificant: many early chants, such as the *Collect*, *Pater noster*, and *Postcommunion* for Easter, consist of merely two notes, often centered around "A" or "G," with inflected notes one pitch below on "G" or "F." Thus, whether intentional or subconscious, the music alludes to sacralized traditions and themes of rejuvenation imbued through meditative undulations within repetitive melodic cells.

The natural environment

The melodic contour of the traditional *Ave Maris Stella* chant pervades the first movement; its rhythm is freely altered and varied, however, to create an elusive, quirky, and playful atmosphere conjuring an undisturbed natural soundscape. The melody ostensibly assumes a more metric form as the work progresses, and it soon acquires a regularity suggestive of a church bell sequence (indeed, the contour becomes almost exactly that of the famous *Westminster Chimes*); as though to avoid an unnatural or pedantic symmetry, however, Edwards quickly elaborates the rhythm once more. In conjunction with the rather ambiguous pulse is the remarkable freedom granted to the performer in regard to tempo—a general indication is given, but it is accompanied by "±" and "molto rubato," thus denying the listener any strict division of relative time.

Edwards further juxtaposes overlapping timbres, rhythms, textures, and melodic contours as though to suggest the interaction of countless independent species that are but vaguely aware of one another. A substantial range of the keyboard is utilized, although the individual elements themselves occupy minimal space; that is, vertical complexity assumes preeminence over horizontal. Yet each element is subject to unpredictably varied repetitions, mimicking the mesmerizing loops of nature (e.g., a sequence of waves breaking on a beach, or the rustling of leaves in gusts of wind), nebulously random in their minutiae but yielding a general impression of consistency. This is intensified by Edwards's predisposition for a variety of anachronistic and unusual meters such as 3/2, 5/4, 6/4, 3/8, 5/8, 7/8, and 5/16, facilitating a sense of asymmetry and irregularity, particularly when juxtaposed against more standard meters such as 3/4 and 4/4. Throughout, one senses that Edwards, rather than conforming the musical material to a predefined meter, sought to retroactively (and almost arbitrarily) apply meters that accommodated the caprices of the music.

Consideration and rejection of tradition

Although much of the *Australiana* idiom is premised on the abandonment of Euro-American classical traditions, there are several prominent aesthetic parallels with Western music in the *Sea Star Fantasy.*

In relation to its overall structure, the *Fantasy* substantially resembles the Baroque Doctrine of Affections, which is presupposed on the direct relationship of clarity through sectional contrast. Indeed, the first movement resembles an unmeasured prelude in the French tradition, while the second movement imitates a fugue in its rhythmically strict and contrapuntally intricate construction.

Yet, the motivic interplay is sonically Lisztian in that repeated cells are manipulated in various registers and occasionally modified with interpolated chromaticism, as though a diminutive version of his technique of thematic transformation. The rhythmic and timbral variation of the primary musical gestures permits a subtle and amorphous alteration of atmosphere—for example, innocently chiming *ostinati* introduced in the beginning of the work are later transfigured into ominous clusters of sound within the bass. Furthermore, the interpolation of the motivic cell in middle registers, encircled by dense figuration, resembles Liszt's renowned "three-handed effect," whereas the prominent virtuosic flourishes encompassing wide intervallic ranges are not unlike those in his *Hungarian Rhapsodies*, which Edwards has explicitly alluded to in other works.[41] Edwards draws more generally from Romantic characteristics in his exploitation of registral extremes, frequently oscillating between opposite regions of the keyboard without any transitional or connecting element; when immediately juxtaposed against one another, he defines these opposites as bell-like "archetypes," similar to Russian composer Sergei

Rachmaninoff's textural "bell" motifs.[42] These contrasts are heightened through his harmonic treatments, in which abrupt shifts between major and minor tonalities create dramatic acoustical coloration.

Writ large, the first movement strongly resembles Bartok's *night music* style in its evocation of spaciousness and loneliness, attention to sound portrayal over traditional harmony and melody, *ostinati* punctuated by curt motives, wide pitch ranges in glissandi and leaps, and the overlap and insertion of varying, but largely unrelated, melodic material. Bartok's music frequently imitates frog and cicada calls as well, both of which are heavily integrated into Edwards's compositional language.[43]

Despite his aversion to the aesthetic, Edwards seems to tangentially reference some of the constructive techniques encountered in avant-garde musics, likely owing to his exposure to these techniques throughout his educational years. For example, the aforementioned repetition and rhythmic manipulation of pitch classes "A" and "B" throughout the second movement is reminiscent of Hungarian composer Gyorgy Ligeti's *Musica ricercata*, "No. 1."

These are but a few of the influences heard in the *Sea Star Fantasy*, and thus they are hardly exhaustive. Adherence to tradition, however, is not as exceptional to the *Australiana* idiom as is its deviation from classical heritage. Most of the suggested references made in the *Fantasy* derive from what Edwards has called a "secularized abstraction," or a "phenomenon of desacralization, of taking things at surface value and overlooking or suppressing our awareness of their inherent mystery."[44] However diverse and stimulating as these musical allusions may be, their collective effect alone does not instill in the *Fantasy* its overall aim of restoring "our confident awareness and participation" in the sacred, defined by Edwards as something "imbued with the power of otherness, which is to be respected but not understood." His compositions seek "a sense of renewal and the return of some kind of cosmic spring which will help us view nature with a cleansed perception," implying an absolute absence of any tradition, rather than a subversion or rejection of any single one. What necessarily results from this approach, however, is an entirely new, "Australian" idiom.

Nonetheless, this statement raises the question of how to achieve an effect of "absence of any tradition"—from a practical standpoint, it is difficult to create something so abstract that it truly does not resemble anything else. His use of the five-line staff notation and its associated approximations of pitch, key, and meter are a derivation of Western music history. Edwards has repeatedly stated his interest in southeastern Asian cultures, in part a result of his apprenticeship with

Peter Sculthorpe; thus, his recurrent use of pentatonic and whole-tone scales used in the *Fantasy* suggests Japanese and Balinese aesthetics. Likewise, his pervasive use of drones refers to their "ultimate cultural source—the [Aboriginal] didjeridu."[45]

One approach to expunging evidence of Western cultures is to overtly defy their historical trajectories and conventions within one's own work. For example, the extensive use of drones is, in general, not very idiomatic for the piano, given the instrument's relatively rapid decay. Edwards's musical language is not as concerned with constraints of idiomatic writings, however, as it with the evocation of coloristic effects and qualities; indeed, he seeks to create novel techniques precisely by overstepping standard approaches to instrumental composition. He thus deviates significantly from Western practice, which has naturally favored the development of a progressively more idiomatic style as both the capabilities and the independence of any given instrument increases. Furthermore, the constraints of an instrument, though influenced to a great extent by their physical properties, are also impacted by the existing cultural assumptions of its role and thus may be approached from varying compositional perspectives. In his *Sea Star Fantasy*, Edwards does not treat writing for the piano merely as an abstract amalgamation of chords, virtuosic *passaggi*, and intricate counterpoint; rather, it is a dynamic manifestation of a numinous soundscape, complemented by drones, fragmented cells requiring dramatic differentiation, and dynamics in problematic extremes. (For example, his successive placement of *p*, *pp*, and *ppp* is rather difficult to realize on a piano, and indeed is scarcely perceptible to the listener; it is as though the music threatens to gradually extinguish itself through silence, before reemerging with flamboyance and unrestrained energy.)

Another aberration from tradition is Edwards's significant reliance on repetition of cells, albeit with almost indiscernible variations in pitch and rhythm. This practice lends the music a static quality and negates any sense of direction, climax, or resolution, compounded by the unvaried harmonic patterns stagnated by pervasive pedal tones. Such constant reuse and repetition of the musical material itself further imbues a ritualistic quality into the work, as specific elements are transformed into characteristic figures that, through their controlled reoccurrence, behave like rituals themselves.

"Radical eclipticism" within an Australian idiom

As demonstrated by the *Sea Star Fantasy*, Edwards has continued many of the musical conceptions presented by his mentor, Peter

Sculthorpe, such as the concentration on spirituality and chant, advocacy for the natural environment, and the rejection of Euro-American traditions through non-functional harmonic progressions and the intricate development of rhythmic and melodic cells. Though he does not espouse his categorization as a "nationalistic" composer, the nature of his writing certainly retains an "Australian" quality that is further to the aesthetic ideals of previous nonconformist figures, such as Sculthorpe; indeed, he eschews the superficially cosmopolitan nature of European modernism and instead composes music characterized by a "broad Australian accent."[46] On a much larger scale, the "nationalistic" movement within Australia resembles the common trajectory in music history of a temporary adherence to an internationalist or pluralistic compositional idiom, followed by a gradual national introspection that yields an identifiable "local" music. But a few examples of this expansive pendulum are the development of Italian madrigals, French chansons, and Spanish villancicos after a proliferation of the Franco-Flemish style at the start of the musical Renaissance; the reassertion of "French" and "Italian" opera styles, as well as the widespread independence movements and resulting nationalistic aesthetics in the mid-eighteenth century, after the predominance of the restrained and unaffected *style galant* throughout the Classical era; and the development of an *Americana* idiom after the neurotic, convulsive tendencies of modernism and serialism failed to establish a reliable presence in the United States. Such phenomena are often a result of vast political conglomerates that diminish regional differences (e.g., the Franco-Flemish style was a byproduct of the expansive Burgundian lands), whereas manifestations of "nationalism" represent a reevaluation or recontextualization of recognized folk cultures amidst a search for independence or identity. Though Australia is not actively striving to achieve an absolute separation from the Commonwealth, itself comprised of fifty-four tremendously diverse countries, composers such as Edwards recognize that it is necessary to establish a distinguishable voice and identity that reflects their experiences within the continent. It is simply no longer possible to transplant the social, cultural, and political elements from Britain into Australia, and thus the nation is presented with the relentless challenge of reinventing itself in a manner that is objectively relevant to the lives of its citizens. Uniting these ostensibly disparate philosophies is what Edwards terms "radical eclipticism" in his work, guided by the "long-established tradition of exploring and resolving disparity" in musical composition. This aim is manifested in his approach of "[appreciating] the benefits of human differences and [rebalancing] our relationship with nature," underpinned by the "strong, life-affirming" optimism of spontaneity and dance-like rhythms often central to survival throughout Australia's history.[47]

Specifically within Australian music, caution must be taken not to inadvertently superimpose Western preconceptions into their performance. The "classical" tradition has, for many centuries, been preoccupied with such concepts as the codification of time, calculated climaxes and resolutions, and linear dynamic gradations; yet, these constructs are often antithetical to the contemporary social structure of Australia and thus merely artificialize its musics. Furthermore, Edwards alludes to cultures that are inherently non-Western, albeit only metaphorically. For example, the interminable presence of drones in Edwards's *Sea Star Fantasy* refers to the acoustical qualities of the didgeridoo, whereas the emphasis on the natural environment invariably recalls the assertion of Aboriginal peoples that the land "always was, always will be" theirs.[48] Relentless repetition implies the cyclicity of time, punctuated merely by transitional passages and subtle alterations that perhaps suggest the numerous cultural upheavals and adjustments experienced by Aboriginal land-owning groups since colonization. Finally, an emphasis on modality and static strata of sound interrupted by episodes of frantic spontaneity, rather than an unyielding forward propulsion characteristic of Western harmonic theory, reminisces on the latent primordiality of man amidst the industrialization of contemporary society.

Utilization of a chant as the underlying structural unit of the work, expounded upon with somewhat hypnotic elaborations of minute melodic and rhythmic patterns, results in an atmosphere of meditation, reflection, and stillness, elements that are inherent to Edwards's compositional aesthetic. Furthermore, the avoidance of overt virtuosity shifts attention from the mechanical technique of the performer to the spiritual transcendence of both the performer and the audience, though there are occasional passages that demand great technical skill of the pianist.

The musical contour of the work itself is imitative of the Australian landscape, with considerable juxtaposition of the features of central versus coastal regions. For example, the flat, rugged terrain of the Outback, defined by accumulated sedimentation left largely undisturbed by any geologic or tectonic activity for vast periods of times, is represented by static strata of sound that coexist without directly influencing one another. The dynamic coastal cities, contrastingly, are represented by flamboyant passages and youthful energy. In turn, the immediacy in their contrasts metaphorizes on Edwards's dual life between metropolitan Sydney, where he held a position as a lecturing professor, and his generally peaceful compositional residence in the

Blue Mountains region, renowned for its dramatic cliffs, eucalyptus forests, waterfalls, and quaint villages. Such extremes are quite characteristic for Australia writ large, despite the popular preconception that the continent is solely comprised of a perpetual Outback with merely isolated pockets of civilization, and thus these differences influence the variability within Edwards's musical language.

Certainly, the *Fantasy* is a manifestation of Australia's national character in its quirky atmosphere, subtle subversion of entrenched Western traditions, understated humor, and exceptional diversity. Despite its numerous extraneous influences, it represents an "interior monologue that could only have been composed by [Edwards]"[49] as a miniature of his experience within the nation. It is not an assertion of national superiority or unmitigated chauvinism, as one typically associates with the term "nationalism"; it simply represents a distinctive musical idiom in a region still elucidating its cultural identity and artistic relevance in a broader social and geopolitical framework. Indeed, Philip Cooney best summarized Edwards's contribution to Australian musical culture thus:

> In Australia, his music has helped to break down the resistance to contemporary music amongst local audiences and helped to disprove any lingering notion that the work of Australian composers is somehow inferior to the music from other times and other continents. He has achieved his goal of restoring both spontaneity and the power of healing to music, both within the concert hall and the wider community.[50]

Though Sculthorpe certainly established a foundation of "Australian" music that Edwards further developed, Edwards himself made tangible the various manifestations of the nation's cultural identity. The ever-increasing popularity of his music has dispelled the notion that the continent has not produced any artistic works of note, and he continues to compose with an unfailing vigor that represents both himself and the Australian experience. Certainly, his reserved personal manner belies his fierce individualism, and he has developed an inimitable musical style that is both exceptionally convincing and immediately recognizable within and beyond Australia.

CHAPTER EIGHT

"An optimistic, personal geography"

Paul Stanhope, b. 1969

Paul Stanhope (b. 1969) is an Australian composer, conductor, and Associate Professor at the Sydney Conservatorium of Music (The University of Sydney), whose music "springs from a personal response to a wide variety of events and experiences" surrounding "geography," symbolism, and Indigenous Australian culture.[1] His work "has, at its heart, a contemplation of the complexity of the human condition and a desire to make a positive contribution to human understanding and engagement, which speaks across national and cultural divides."[2]

Stanhope studied composition at the University of Wollongong, under Andrew Ford and Andrew Schultz, and at the University of Sydney, under Peter Sculthorpe. Additionally, he spent a relatively brief period at the University of York, which, under Wilfrid Mellers (with whom Peter Sculthorpe had become acquainted during his studies in England), had a tradition of inviting and promoting Australian composers. Stanhope completed a Master of Arts (Honors) degree at the University of Wollongong in 1994, with a thesis centered on the "aspects of ritual" found within Ross Edwards's music; in 1999, he was awarded a Ph.D. in composition from the University of Sydney, for which he submitted a portfolio of works and analytical commentary entitled "A personal geography." Then, as a recipient of a Charles Mackerras Scholarship, Stanhope departed in 2000 for postdoctoral study at the Guildhall School of Music in London; in 2001, he also received the Peggy Glanville-Hicks Fellowship in support of his work.[3]

Several early, though significant, musical projects during his academic studies would come to define his subsequent artistic development. In the early 1990s, for example, Stanhope transcribed the *Mularra* clan-songs ("manikay")[4] of Rembarrnga as part of a fieldwork project at the University of Sydney, later developing two early series of solo and chamber instrumental works that alluded to these Indigenous Australian chants.[5] A few years later, his composition *Night Prelude* (1997) would invite Graeme Skinner's interesting description of the music as "an Australian's response to the unusual experience of a Northern English winter,"[6] marked by a profound experimentation with post-Webern techniques of restraint, integration, and subtle exploration. Finally, in the early 2000s, Stanhope composed a *Fantasia* based on an early twentieth-century English hymn, which embraced a "quiet radicalism" and drew "only tangentially, and occasionally ironically, on the mood and style of its model"; it is largely permeated by pentatonicism, atypical rhythmic figuration, and a varying textural palette that exploits the diverse timbres of orchestral forces. Writ large, such experimentation is quite representative of Australia's musical development, as it permits influence from myriad cultures, idioms, and styles while simultaneously contextualizing their commentaries within a nationally relevant framework.

Though already laden with an impressive array of accolades upon his return to Australia, Stanhope describes the period after his studies as "a moment of crisis, wondering if I would have to reevaluate things"—opportunities had "dried up," and, indeed, prospects for young artists appeared bleak.[7] (This may have resulted, in part, from the contraction of the artistic sector after a subtraction of available funding through the Australia Council for the Arts during the conservative Howard Government era, in operation from 1996–2007;[8] thus, this segment of the economy was in the midst of a restructuring toward private philanthropy.) The apparent stagnation in his career was not to last long, however: in 2004, Stanhope was the first Australian to be awarded the prestigious Toru Takemitsu Composition Prize, which quickly established him as a preeminent cultural figure both domestically and abroad.

Other recognitions soon followed. In 2010, Stanhope was the featured composer for Musica Viva, Australia's oldest independent professional performing arts organization; in 2011, he was awarded two APRA/Australian Music Centre Awards for "Instrumental Work of the Year" (followed by "Orchestral Work of the Year" in 2018); two substantial orchestral projects composed throughout 2013 and 2014 were supported by a Sidney Myer Creative Fellowship, of which he was the first Australian recipient; and in 2018, his piano trio "Pulses" was premiered by eight competing ensembles in the Melbourne International Chamber Music Competition. This list is scarcely exhaustive, and one would indeed be challenged to offer a "brief" summary of Stanhope's contributions to the international musical community. Nonetheless, it is a point of departure when considering the development of an "Australian" musical infrastructure, education, and idiom.

Australian Musical Identity

Stanhope closely follows the musical traditions established by Peter Sculthorpe and Ross Edwards, owing to his frequent and extensive contact with both figures:

> Peter Sculthorpe heard some of my music at a very fledgling stage and said, "keep going." Those two words from someone as influential as Peter meant an awful lot. Later I studied with him and it was a fascinating process. I've also had tremendous support from Ross Edwards—never strictly a teacher but more a friend and mentor and someone I've looked up to over the years.[9]

A number of Stanhope's recent compositions explore the rich heritage of Aboriginal culture and seek to interweave it, through a thorough and respectful permissions process, with Western musical traditions, most aptly demonstrated in *Jandamarra: Sing for the Country* (2014) with a libretto by Steve Hawke.[10] In 2008, Hawke, alongside members of the Bunuba community, had written a stage play based on Jandamarra's life; following a commission from the Sydney Symphony Orchestra in 2014, Stanhope and Hawke turned to adapt aspects of this dramatization in collaboration and consultation with Bunuba elders. Emerging from their partnership is a dramatic cantata set in the imposing landscape of the central Kimberly, which outlines the life of Jandamarra (c. 1870–1897), a young Bunuba resistance hero, and illustrates a genocidal conflict amidst the incursion of white immigrants onto traditional land.[11] Jandamarra is a blemished hero: though he was once quite committed to the moralities of his Bunuba heritage, his initiation is interrupted by a raid of European settlers, and he is imprisoned in Derby.[12] As young adult, he collaborates with the white police force as a "tracker" under Bill Richardson, an unsuccessful local prospector who was hired as a civilian officer. In alliance with Richardson, Jandamarra rounded up and imprisoned Aboriginal peoples, thus galvanizing Bunuba elders to submit themselves to arrest and, as portrayed in the cantata, "sing" him back home. Though Jandamarra is an exiled member of his community, he is convinced to defect from his post by shooting Richardson and, therefore, liberate the Bunuba people. A civil war follows, in which the Bunuba community sought to maintain its autonomy from the non-Indigenous settlement that had assumed administration of the region. Although they ultimately reclaimed their land,[13] their emancipation necessitated sacrifice: in a hecatomb laden with ritualistic symbolism, Jandamarra is assassinated by another tracker, Mingo Mick, who was recruited by the West Kimberly police command. This event, in turn, paradoxically unites the Indigenous and non-Indigenous peoples, as they acknowledge their communal losses of life and—not unlike a Greek tragedy or a Shakespearian drama—transcend their cultural differences to recognize their shared humanity.[14]

Particularly unique about the creation of this work is Stanhope and Hawke's commitment to thorough and consistent consultation with the Bunuba people, realized through the adoption of collaborative composition, periodic consultations, procedures to ensure the explicit and informed consent of all participants, and the active commissioning of Bunuba community elders as story-tellers, musicians, dancers, and actors. Their partnership was further formalized with a joint copyright over *Jandamarra*, shared between Stanhope and Bunuba Cultural Enterprises.[15] Respect for Aboriginal agency and their intellectual jurisdiction remained the utmost priority for Stanhope and Hawke, exemplifying an approach that ultimately produced a validating and empowering work with regard to Indigenous heritage, as well as a culturally and artistically effective experience for Australian audiences; thus, the piece is dualistic in its political incorporation of Aboriginal heritage and its considerations of the Australian "geography." Notwithstanding any overt or intentional objectives for the continuation of Australian "nationalism," Stanhope and Hawke perpetuate a continuing dialogue on the intersectionality of the nation's evolving cultural identity through such complex and enriching musics.

Jandamarra: Sing for the Country is divided into twelve sections, some of which are discrete movements, while others are merely connecting interludes that propel the narrative developments.

Themes and Connection to Nationalist Idiom

Youth, innocence, and coming of age

An open and optimistic atmosphere permeates the beginning of the work, depicted by the independent melodic contours in ascending perfect intervals of Jandamarra, the protagonist of Aboriginal heritage, and Lindsay, his close companion and son of white settlers. In a symbolic extrapolation of these two characters, the mixed-race Gondwana Choir performs a succession of pure, iridescent harmonies in a high register.[16] These concurrent musical gestures often occur at the end of phrases, implying a sense of youthful admiration of the world, and are then amplified by whole tone and semitone two-note groupings in galloping rhythmic figures, signifying the freedom and energy with which the two boys traverse the expansive Australian landscape. The young Jandamarra, in a poised assertion of his coming of age under the Bunuba tribal law, declares that he "will be a man"; the music deftly amalgamates the ascending intervallic patterns and animated rhythms as a transitional device between his youth and adulthood. Additionally, the use of perfect fifths throughout connecting melodic phrases indicates motifs of optimism and "purity."

Events of corruption, disturbance, and interference with the supernatural world that punctuate such idealistic sentiments as the two boys mature are suggested through capacious orchestral crescendos, imposing low brass and tremulous string figures, and ominous intervallic patterns. The primary narrative device changes from the youth choir, characterized by its harmonious and resonant timbre, to a solo baritone, marked by darker sonorities and dramatic coloristic effects, occurring synchronously with the temporal shift from young Jandamarra to his elder counterpart. Such developments are represented by apprehensive quintuplet figures, mostly performed by the brass instruments, that underscore dynamic scenes foreshadowing impending calamity. Minor second intervals from the prior galloping theme are transformed into threatening harmonic tone clusters, thus subverting notions of innocence into careless naivety. Thematically, the expansion of this whole-tone and semi-tone interchange produces an octatonic scale, which becomes a significant unifying device throughout the entire work and serves as a transitional element between tonal and atonal figurations.[17] More generally, these shifts between consonance and dissonance correlate with events of order and anarchy, respectively.

At its next appearance, this octatonic "leitmotif" reinforces a particularly tense moment in the movement "The Choice," in which the chained Bunuba peoples sing in defiance of Richardson (symbolizing their collective resistance against Australia's colonial system), thus urging Jandamarra to decide upon his loyalty and formalize his allegiance through action. Its layered repetition has a maddening effect, gradually intensifying as though representing Dionysian intoxication and ultimately motivating Richardson to drink himself into a state of unconsciousness; this, in turn, offers Jandamarra the opportunity to actualize his pivotal decision to shoot Richardson and emancipate his people. Expansions of these motifs are presented in their most dramatic, harrowing form after Jandamarra is shot in Tunnel Creek, in an extended passage for brass with a rolling timpani drone.

In stark contrast with these notions of evil and corruption, each of the aforementioned events is immediately followed by moments of repose, contemplation, purification, and renewed vitality. The very musical gestures that once symbolized youthful innocence and inquisitiveness transform into purgative mechanisms, restoring balance and neutrality amidst chaos; reflective silence interrupted by perfect intervals, ascending lines, unobtrusive orchestration, and an airy choir restore reverence for, and submission to, the natural world.

After such extensive metamorphosis and development, the whole tone-semitone motif heretofore associated with scenes of danger and dread is once again transformed in the "Dirrai Lament," a melody composed by Bunuba woman Molly Jalakbiya and incorporated as a symbol of Jandamarra's death. Its initial connection to tragedy is maintained through the use of an extremely low vocal register and static drone, much like the timpani in the earlier excerpts; rather than menace, however, its range illustrates the grief and dismay of profound loss caused by the preceding events.[18] Melodically, the descending minor triad and ponderous repetition of a single note, colored by the second scale degree in E minor, indicate exhaustion, despair, and pensiveness; the outer contour of a perfect fifth, however, foreshadows cleansing, regeneration, and unification. Furthermore, the use of "pure" perfect intervals implicitly recalls the melodic patterns of Jandamarra and Lindsay performed at the opening of the cantata and thus reflects on the transience of youthful innocence. Thus, Stanhope's layering of the Bunuba *Dirrai Lament*, Jandamarra's leitmotifs, and fragments from the work's prelude ("The Land is Full of Spirits") ultimately converge to unite the multifaceted elements and themes heretofore presented in the cantata.

The recitation of the *Lament* is also employed as a symbolic unifying device. Prior to this moment in the cantata, Jandamarra's and Lindsay's mothers stood on opposite ends of the stage; they both commented on events as they transpired and maintained an equal function for the duration of the performance, yet they remained physically and psychologically separated by their speciously insurmountable cultural differences. The *Lament* unifies them at the end of the work, however, to mourn the loss of their children and acknowledge their shared experiences of love and grief.[19]

Synthesis of Aboriginal and Western musical elements

Regarding the themes and messages of the work, Stanhope suggests that "it is a truth-telling piece, and non-Aboriginal people will find some of those aspects confronting. It's one tiny little piece in an enormous puzzle [of conciliation]."[20] The plot is of utmost importance, and the music is constructed around the roles of the soloists, narrators, and choirs. Indeed, Stanhope likened its dramaticism to that of "a colossal Greek tragedy" in its exploration of fate, catastrophe, and the supernatural, as well as its utilization of a choir as a narrative mechanism.[21]

The orchestral music primarily underscores and provides responses to the various plot developments, as opposed to dictating or preemptively motivating its evolution; thus, the Western musical forces are reactive, rather than directive. A vast palette of coloristic effects is employed to evoke the story's setting, ranging from tone colors typical of the twentieth century (e.g., *col legno, sul pont*, string harmonics, and brass mutes) to a didgeridoo and unusual breath effects from the woodwinds. Drones and drone-based harmonies permeate the soundscape, alternated with dramatic, rather than tonal-centric, chordal progressions. Stanhope further manipulates polytonality, polyrhythms, changing time signatures, and *ostinati* to evoke various psychological, emotional, and aesthetic states. These dynamic, imposing Western forces are then balanced by Indigenous language, traditional dance, and music, performed by members of the Bunuba community. Regarding the use of Bunuba language, a community elder declared that it "gives an identity or foundation to all people; it links you to the ground and country. Speaking our language helps you understand country and culture in a better way. This is how our story stays alive; it is part of our lives."[22]

The aggregate effect of these compositional elements achieves two aims: first, it provides for a faithful retelling of the Jandamarra story from a Bunuba perspective; second, it shifts the focus of the audience from the sonic to the kinetic parameters of the work. Thus, the plot remains tangible, explicit, and direct, rather than abstract and permissive to varying interpretations of the listener. Ultimately, the sequence of events serves as the formal structure of the work, orienting the observer in an otherwise unfamiliar sonic landscape and permitting absolute clarity.

Centering Aboriginal cultural material and community experiences achieves a dual aim of rectifying cultural infringements of colonists throughout Australia's history: indeed, Stanhope notes that "for many years, composers have included or appropriated Indigenous material into their music and either made a mess of it, or not realised they were committing a theft."[23] Thus, he and Hawke were careful to construct *Jandamarra* around the music, language, and traditions presented by the Bunuba community, conceding absolute autonomy and integrity to their heritage and custodianship of the material.

Religion and spirituality

Stanhope defines this work as "somewhere between a cantata and an oratorio—although the subject of the piece is not a traditional religious work, it does respond to elements of Bunuba spirituality."[24] Cantata-like elements certainly unify the otherwise diverse and expansive piece: for example, the *Junba* song cycle is employed as a narrative thread, much like a Lutheran chorale structurally fortifies Bach's cantatas.[25] In consideration of intercultural musical guidelines, however, songs of the *Junba* are never directly transplanted into the Western forces; instead, echoes and premonitions of its musical contours are applied to suggest musical unity.

Through its placement in three pivotal moments of the plot's development, the *Junba* song defines and augments the structure of the work. Its first appearance is in the "Requiem for Lindsay," after Lindsay's "soul" is taken by the Rainbow Serpent: while the children's choir sings fragments of plainsong-like melody from the Latin Requiem Mass, the Bunuba singers chant the "Winjiwi" verse from the *Junba*; the similarity and juxtaposition of vocal styles evokes the co-existing profundities of these two sacred musics, while simultaneously reinforcing the tensions between the two cultures through the layering of two seemingly conflicting texts.

Its second appearance is during "The Choice," in which the *Junba* acts as a "magic song." Its ultimate purpose is to "sing" Jandamarra back home, revealing to him the corruption into which he has been lured by the non-Indigenous settlers (much in the manner of Satan's acts of temptation within the Christian religion) while simultaneously purifying him of its internalized presence. Paradoxically, the song's cleansing of Jandamarra dually serves as a symbol of defiance against the imposed colonization of the West, as its tenacious repetition is used to exasperate and psychologically "intoxicate" Richardson. Indeed, as Stanhope described:

> Much of the story of Jandamarra, as told in its original stage play, has to do with singing; the power of song to spur people into action or to console and heal. The threads of traditional Kimberley music which we are very fortunate to have permission to use—including verses from the Yilimbirri Junba which references the Jandamarra story—add to the rich texture of the story-telling. The weaving together of the earthy Kimberley singing, the power of dance and the telling of this narrative through song and the majesty of the orchestra brings to life the landscape, the terror of conflict and the triumph of survival.[26]

In its third (and final) appearance, Jandamarra is depicted by the narrator as "singing and dancing, dancing and dreaming" to the land through an allusion to the *Junba*'s melodic contour. Such states suggest spiritual transcendence or hypnotization, much as in the manner of a shaman entering a trance.

Beyond the literal allusions to Bunuba spirituality and mythology (e.g., the first line of the work asserts that their "land is full of spirits"), Stanhope incorporates elements of ritual and spiritual geography with recourse to Australian Indigenous chants, such as in the *Wangga* performed immediately after the Prelude.[27] Repetition, rhythmic augmentation and diminution, and various mechanisms of elaboration suggest states of hypnotism that echo some of the elements of *Junba* and *Wangga* songs and dances performed as part of the cantata, intended to portray Jandamarra as a "Jalgangurru" (i.e., a cultured man of spiritual power).

Though it is utilized in myriad settings, chant is considered an inherently spiritual practice due to its effectively universal presence in world religions. Its neuro-physical effects, both on the performer and the listener, are extensively documented in the scientific literature; among the most common, however, are the slowing of the brain's activity, increased association with the physical and temporal elements of one's immediate surroundings, and the promotion of a sense of a belonging with those engaged in the collective production of sound. Similarly to the unification of the separated white and Aboriginal mothers through a shared performance of the "Dirrai Lament," the use of chant in *Jandamarra* facilitates the secondary aim of the work in that it actively unifies the performers and passively engages their listeners, both of whom comprise fundamentally disparate cultures, yet share an overlapping history.

The aforementioned Rainbow Serpent is, in itself, a reference to the sacred. Rainbow Serpents are a common element in the spiritual traditions of many Aboriginal cultures, often symbolizing the multifaceted creation of the Australian landscape; specifically within Bunuba culture, however, the arcane snake spirit is traditionally referred to as "Yilimbirri Unggud" and serves to represent the spring that is the centrifuge of Jandamarra's fall and renewal. Yilimbirri's musical leitmotif is not so much a fixed theme, therefore, as it is an ambiguous texture, suggesting the somewhat ethereal nature of the snake spirit. It is first heard through gyrating chromatic figures performed by combinations of low woodwinds, such as the bass clarinet, bassoon, and contrabassoon, and is often accompanied by cymbals and metal sticks. Subsequently, when Yilimbirri is awakened as a result of Lindsay's inattentive upheaval of "bush law," the previously mysterious chromatic lines are more fiercely orchestrated for low winds, strings, trombones, and tuba.

From a greater narrative perspective, Jandamarra was considered more than a warrior; he was a leader of his people and "a man bestowed with great spiritual powers from the timeless law of [the Bunuba] country, who could disappear, transform into a bird, and shield himself from deadly weapons."[28] Thus, the work is centered around a quasi-shamanistic figure and thereby assumes an atmosphere of an ancient myth, further resembling its previous comparison to a Greek legend.

Sense of place and connection to land

About his work, Stanhope states:

> My music presents the listener with an optimistic, personal geography . . . whether this is a reaction to the elemental aspects of the universe or the throbbing energy of the inner city. It's a part of a process of producing symbols which try to make sense of that which goes on around me.[29]

Jandamarra is, above all, a work intrinsically related to place. Stanhope utilizes the "nationalistic" sonic aesthetic preconceived by Peter Sculthorpe and Ross Edwards, such as timbral movement detached from Western harmonic theory, Aboriginal instruments and idioms, and integrated elements of ritual; yet this is not as much a conscious assertion of an abstract "nationalism" as it is a narrative organically derived from Australia's history, culture, and environment. An important distinction between the work of Sculthorpe and Stanhope, however, is their approach and contextualization of Aboriginal heritage within a larger framework—while much of Sculthorpe's music employs Indigeneity as "ornamentation" detached from its specific cultural setting, Stanhope aims to holistically integrate Indigenous history and imagery through partnership, co-ownership, and respectful practice with its custodians. Thus, his work demonstrates a politically and culturally updated practice that rejects the (often harmful) colonial and post-colonial mechanisms of his predecessors in incorporating Aboriginality within an "Australian" idiom. Among the most direct manifestations of this notion is in the final movement, "This is Our Home," a celebratory epilogue that seems to fit with Stanhope's assertion of optimism, commemorating land, kinship, belonging, and survival: though its text is in the Bunuba language, reinforcing the Aboriginal peoples' position as the First

Peoples of Australia, it is neither divisive nor territorial in character. Rather, it is performed by all choirs and the orchestra, asserting the coexistence and solidarity of the two cultures despite their extensive post-colonial legacy of conflict.

While Australia's "nationalist" idiom is still in a quite tentative stage, Stanhope's work *Jandamarra: Sing for the Country* lucidly exhibits certain themes that are central to its incipient soundscape: coming of age amidst individual uncertainty, ritualism and spirituality, a reverent connection to the physical land, and the coexistence of white and Aboriginal culture. Indeed, Jandamarra may be considered a metaphorical representation of Australia itself: his tumultuous transitions from naivety and innocence to maturity and self-assertion are perhaps emblematic of the nation's complex sociopolitical history, while his straddling of "white" and "Aboriginal" culture represents Australia's hesitant oscillation between Western and native ideals. Furthermore, *Jandamarra* consciously strives to fulfill a political function as a "truth-telling" piece and is revolutionary in that it focuses entirely on the experiences of Aboriginal peoples.

Requiem (2020)

Another recent work of Stanhope's that furthers the themes of "healing, mortality, hope, ritual, and powerful connection to country" evident in *Jandamarra*—namely, his *Requiem* (2020) for chamber choir and soloists, winds, percussion, and harp—likewise merits discussion. Composed over a period of twenty years (its first iterations appearing in 1999, when Stanhope was still a student), it is emblematic of his desire to create an "ongoing conversation between old and new" that is recurrent in many of his compositions.

The Western tradition of composing a Requiem Mass in commemoration of a deceased individual is quite extensive, with the earliest surviving polyphonic setting dating from the mid-fifteenth century (Johannes Ockeghem's *Requiem*). Numerous composers have since set the texts standardized by the Council of Trent (1545–1563), including Wolfgang Amadeus Mozart (1791), Hector Berlioz (1837), Giuseppe Verdi (1874), Gabriel Fauré (1890), and Benjamin Britten (1962); Peter Sculthorpe, too, composed a full choral *Requiem* in 2004, into which he notably incorporated the didgeridoo (about the work, Sculthorpe stated: "It seems to me, the way the world is going, we need all the Requiems we can get.").[30] Owing to the gradual expansion of its form, the enlargement of its ensemble to incorporate a substantial number of accompanying instruments, and the free alteration of its texts, it eventually assumed a role as "art," or concert, music and was no longer confined within the realms of liturgical funeral ceremony. Thus, both the functional and the philosophical implications of the genre were removed from their original context, absolving the Requiem from any strict association as a remembrance of the dead (and as an imposing reminder of the Lord's Judgement); Stanhope's setting, as in much of Australian music, instead transforms its import into an ode of renewal and a celebration of life. Within the context of this expansive heritage, Stanhope sought "to disrupt the ancient narrative," asserting that "[in] every age, composers have repurposed or personalised the narrative and themes of the requiem, and it is certainly the case with mine"; "I can't imagine a purely European set of texts or a straight liturgical requiem actually being appropriate anymore!"[31]

Among his most radical alterations to the Requiem tradition was his treatment of the text, a particularly significant decision when considering the immutability of the standardized liturgy throughout history. Influenced by Johannes Brahms's German translations in his *Ein deutsches Requiem* (1868), Britten's addition of English poetry to his *War Requiem*, and Fauré's exclusion of the ominous "Dies Irae" movement, Stanhope juxtaposed (and often superimposed) the writings of Emily Dickinson, Mary Elizabeth Frye, Neela Nath Das, and Indigenous Australian Oodgeroo Noonuccal against the traditional Latin text.[32] Remarkably, however, he is perhaps the first composer to render these extraneous elements not merely tropes, but replacements to the original text; in doing so, he reclaims the control the Church sought to impose throughout its centuries of dominance in the West and offers a distinctly personal, subjective rendering of the sacred narrative. Ultimately, these two cultures create audible focal divisions: "as you listen to a piece with dual texts, you immediately understand the English clearly enough, but you don't necessarily comprehend the Latin. That automatically brings out a foreground and background." Furthermore, a "text divide" exists in that

> all the English texts are by female poets, which wasn't a deliberate decision; I arrived there subconsciously. The requiem form, amorphous as it is, really does come out of the patriarchal system of the Catholic Church and its liturgy, so I left out the whole sequence, the *Dies Irae* and so on, to dilute that somewhat. In the end, the Latin church texts are still associated with that patriarchal and, in some ways, dictatorial institution, especially if you know any of the church history—it's pretty terrible at times. So, the question is: how do we approach that in this day and age? How do we cope with the history

> of oppression? I guess my idea was to try and find antidotes to balance the associations of those texts.[33]

Certainly, such recontextualization of what Stanhope asserts to be an otherwise archaic tradition prompts consideration as to what a Requiem must now represent, and on whose narratives it must direct its attention. Perhaps appropriately, Stanhope sought to address the post-colonial relationship between Indigenous and non-Indigenous peoples within Australia, stating:

> The question to myself was, what does it mean to die on a country which has been dispossessed from its original inhabitants? What can we learn from this ancient and ongoing culture that we can respectfully apply in this context? Although these are some specific aims, I think the observations made by Oodgeroo [in her poetry] are universal in that they apply to the human condition and I hope some of this emerges in the music.

The juxtaposition Stanhope thus presents in his Requiem is multifaceted and poignant. By uniting the solemn, expressly dictated heritage of the West with the diverse, oral traditions of Indigenous Australian culture, he comments on their contrasting attitudes toward life, death, mourning, and spirituality; parallelly, their bodies of texts and their settings often conflict with one another, each seeking to be preeminent within the ensemble. The traditional Latin prose is frequently framed within historical techniques, such as canonic polyphony reminiscent of Ockeghem and monodic plainchant of the early Church, whereas the non-liturgical poetry is offered soaring melodic lines with atypical embellishments and ornamentation, glistening harmonies, and unusual instrumental timbres.

Themes of Aboriginal death rituals are dealt with most directly in the second movement of the *Requiem*, centered around *Tree Grave,* a poem by Oodgeroo Noonuccal that vividly describes the emotions consequent to a traditional mortuary procession. The deceased body is wrapped in bark and carried to a lagoon, where it is buried in a hollow tree;[34] in Aboriginal spirituality (particularly in Arnhem Land), the soul then transcends through the tree into the realm of the dead, which Noonuccal terms "The Shadow Land." Rather than merely retelling traditional belief, however, Noonuccal emphasizes the sensitive experience of the living in response to profound loss, detailing the "wailing" of their "wild death croon" as they bore the corpse to its final resting place, as well as their "wandering" and "turning" thoughts amidst a labyrinthine forest that persist long after the burial ceremony has concluded. Stanhope complements this ponderous movement through the suggestion of slow processional music and reflective instrumental interludes, and he heightens the singularity of the poem's narration through the use of a soprano soloist. Meandering melodic lines and continuous interchange among the instruments suggest the warped shadows one might anticipate from "wandering fires" navigating through "haunted swamp-oaks"; their relentless, subtly varied repetitions evoke the tumultuous emotions scarcely restrained by the deliberate pace of the music's evolution. Unusually high pitch ranges or melismatic interjections place emphasis on words imbued with visceral anguish, such as "bark" ("in bark we bound him"), "weeping," "thoughts" ("but our thoughts are turning"), "night," "afraid," and "ghostly," conjuring a sense of the supernatural while reminding of the inconsolable suffering of those who remain on earth. Images of wailing, evoked through two-note slurs (i.e., "sigh" figures), glissandi, intricate ornamentation, and dissonant intervals (e.g., tritones) appear not only to represent the "wild death croon" of the mourners, but the cries of the departed souls inhabiting the Lagoon through which they are passing as well. The dead, which Aboriginal cultures regard with both immense reverence and great fear, plead with the living and perhaps lament the Indigenous suffering caused by European colonization; occasional instrumental interjections augment these torturous images through dissonant, piercing shrieks.

Similarly to Sculthorpe's own *Requiem*,[35] Stanhope addressed concerns of environmentalism, conservation, and climate change, as well as their relationship to remote settlements (many of which are densely inhabited by Aboriginal peoples) in his third movement "Kyrie/Rain of Merciful Cloud." About the music, he wrote that "Australia's most devastating drought in years had still not broken when I wrote this movement, and the stoic yet desperate cries of rural communities wore heavily on my mind."[36] The section opens with the punctuated, despairing pleas of "Kyrie eleison" ("Lord, have mercy"), emphasized through dissonant harmonies and extended vocal techniques; following a brief interlude reminiscent of monodic plainchant, however, Indian poet Neela Nath Das's text "Mercy" suffuses as though dispelling earthly suffering, ultimately climaxing at the line "the rain of merciful cloud." Indeed, the emergence of a novel English text appears to release the constrictive bounds of a stagnated, imposing tradition such as that suggested by the archaic ceremonial text, in turn suggesting the necessity to reevaluate the social and cultural systems underlying post-colonial Australia. Emphasizing these vocal and textural shifts are a harp and metal percussion, which, at the end of the movement, imitate the sounds of precipitation falling upon a dried earth. Likewise, these instruments imbue a sense of mysticism, ritual, and spiritual replenishment into the performance, suggesting the generalized "magic" of the earth replenishing itself after upheaval.

In the fourth movement, simply entitled "Song," Stanhope presents a highly philosophical reflection on the inherently dualistic nature of love. Oodgeroo Noonuccal's poignant poetry offers a constant juxtaposition of light and shadow—she asserts that "love is linked with pain" and cautions the listener "not to evade Love's companion Sorrow," depicting an understated cynicism typical in the aftermath of death. The instrumental setting is initially quite sparse, supplemented by a disjunct and fragmented vocal melody, together suggesting the hollowness of emotion that accompanies the shock of great loss and the struggle to cohesively articulate one's thoughts. In the last stanza of the song, however, the text "grief is not in vain" signifies a shift toward solace, musically reflected by richer scoring, lush harmonies, and vocal melodies that are both lyrical and intervalically graceful. In a culmination of emotion, all instruments perform bitonal clashing phrases laden with a final, overwhelming sense of anguish; yet they are soon subdued, as though conceding to their fate and resiliently recomposing themselves.

Through the first five movements of *Requiem*, the overarching impression is of subtle, yet detached, juxtapositions between Indigenous and European themes: movements of solely Latin text, such as the "Introit" and Sanctus," interchange with Aboriginal perspectives of death within their dispossessed country, as in "Tree Grave" and "Song"; it is only in the third movement ("Kyrie/Rain of Merciful Cloud") that European and non-European traditions merge as a result of their shared experience of indiscriminate environmental calamity. Yet even then, colonial and Indigenous Australian ideologies do not explicitly interact. In the sixth movement ("Agnus Dei/Do not stand at my Grave and Weep"), however, Stanhope appears to quench notions of division through a communal search for peace, healing, and renewal. Contrasting the Latin text from the Requiem Mass with Mary Elizabeth Frye's funerary poem, the dramatic pacing of the two narratives move in parallel with one another and occasionally merge in climactic exclamations (e.g., "dona nobis pacem," translated as "grant us peace," and "I am not there, I did not die"). "It is as though the mourning hymn of the Agnus Dei is in conversation with a voice from beyond the grave, decrying that in death the individual becomes the universal: the winds that blow, the sunlight on ripened grain, the soft stars and circling birds of flight."[37] Though the Latin text is often set in polyphonic textures referring to early music practices, the distinctly non-Western ornamentation, unconventional harmonic motion, and expansive vocal ranges within the choir reconcile its historical Catholic origins with the more immediate, compelling surface of Frye's poem, offering solace in its assurance that one is not enchained by their grave after death, but is instead omnipresent in the subtle "glints" of the seemingly commonplace in nature. It is at this moment in the *Requiem* that the genre's "objective" elements are superseded by its "subjective" responses, thus intimating the possibility of assuaging—and eventually remediating—the extensive legacy of confrontation between Aboriginal and non-Aboriginal peoples.

Immediately following this reaffirming movement, however, is "Dawn Wail for the Dead," a lamentation that "captures the remembrance of ancestry and the concurrent recognition of this heritage as part of everyday existence." Conflicting emotions of grief, represented through "wails" and allusions to "the Dark Place," are presented against the hopeful kindling of "fires," "laughter," and a "new day calling"; metaphorically, it contrasts the "unreconciled elements in Australia between non-Indigenous people and the original, continuing owners of this land" against the renewed potential for conciliation and harmony between these fundamentally disparate cultures.[38] Further representing these emotional pendulums are stark contrasts between tonal and bitonal harmonies, demonstrating the extensive legacy of conflict and tension that have long defined the sociopolitical relations between these two groups. Repeated melodic intervals of (predominantly minor) seconds suggest the unsteady, reluctant steps of one burdened by exceptional grief; simultaneously, constantly descending melodic lines in both the instrumental and vocal lines imply inconsolable sobbing. Particularly striking about this movement, however, is that its extreme variations of sentiment (reflected, for example, in the immense range of the vocal setting) are controlled by an overarching impression of composure and restraint. Little variation in dynamics is present, and emotions themselves are offered in a pragmatic manner. Melancholy pervades the music, but it is largely settled and reflective. The movement closes with a somber, ritualistic horn solo that imitates the final vocal melody, demarcating the last remembrances of the deceased before the living return to "life," "laughter," and a "new day."

"II. Tree Grave," "IV. Song," and "VI. Dawn Wail for the Dead," taken together, comprise a subplot within the overarching dramatic continuity of *Requiem*. The three songs were initially composed for an independent song cycle (*Songs of the Shadowland*), completed in 2001, and seek to depict the "devastation at the loss of loved ones," the "deep hurt caused by the onslaught of European colonization," and the "moments of optimism" set in relief against "the backdrop of sadness" that has defined Aboriginal culture since the late eighteenth century.[39] Metaphorically representing these complex, and often contradictory, emotions are the Indigenous mortuary rite and the sequence of reactions expressed by those executing the ritual, evolving from desolate anguish to acceptance to, finally, a return to the mundanity of the commonplace and unremarkable. This narrative is reinforced and heightened by the other movements within the work that, albeit ostensibly unrelated, express parallel themes of loss, pleading, the search for comfort, a renewal of hope, and optimism for the future. Indeed, the pluralism afforded through the variety of selected texts reflects the diverse, heterogenous nature of Australian society itself. Writ large, the parable of the embedded song cycle communicates a perspective of the nation's history frequently ignored—namely, its legacy of conflict with (and brutal subjugation of) Aboriginal culture, followed by the gradual attempts of the Federal Government to redress the trauma of its Indigenous peoples. Furthermore, the inclusion of these songs within *Requiem* "continues [Stanhope's] long personal quest to find a genuine connection to place through music," recontextualizing the tropes of an otherwise archaic Catholic tradition within a dynamic nation that is similarly grappling with the implications of its colonial past.

Commenting on the completion of this narrative arc is the "Lux Aeterna" movement, characterized by a highly dualistic music predicated upon juxtaposition, austerity, and apparent simplicity. The opening text "lux" ("light") is set in harmonic intervals of minor ninths between the altos and sopranos, an interval whose exceptional dissonance arises from its proximity to absolute consonance (i.e., an octave) and evokes tension and irresolution. Likewise, the shimmering quality produced by the faint dynamics, static motion, and high register suggests a sudden, brilliant infiltration of luminousness. As the other voices enter to complete the initially sparse texture, there emerges an extreme registral differentiation between the bass and soprano that perhaps connotes the earthly grave, a perpetual reminder to the living of the passing of a loved one, as compared to cross-cultural perceptions of "heaven," a spiritual realm that offers solace and comfort in its promise of eternal peace. Much of the movement is ridden with pungent dissonances and unstable rhythmic patterns, imbuing an overarching sense of anxiety and concern for the "afterlife" that is perhaps inescapable in its uncertainty; after a series of developmental episodes, however, the music dissolves into a consoling hymn-like section that coincides with the text "in aeternum, quia pius es" ("in eternity, for You are good and kind"). Directly contrasting the preceding compositional techniques, defined by their modernity and experimentalism, is the more conservative setting of the hymn-like passage, marked by few passing instances of dissonance (often manifested in intervallic suspensions) and a traditional treatment of modal harmony. It is as though the music seeks simultaneously to cast light on Australia's problematic history and to offer hope for a peaceful future, imploring the mercy of a universal deity; indeed, one is reminded of Biblical passages centered around motifs of repentance and compassion, such as Chronicles 7:14: "If my people, who are called by my name, will humble themselves and pray and seek my face and turn from their wicked ways, then I will hear from heaven, and I will forgive their sin and heal their land." Jarring dissonances soon return, however, reminding the living that they must continue to confront the reality of the earthly world and acknowledge the malevolence prevalent among human beings. Extrapolating these narratives suggests an allegorical representation of the Australian nation itself, in that it reminds of their colonial heritage and its impact on Indigenous cultures (presented from an Aboriginal perspective throughout the preceding song cycle), their present efforts to acknowledge and rectify its consequences, and their necessity to actively reconstruct an Australian identity that ethically embraces its First Peoples. In an uplifting and celebratory conclusion of *Requiem* is the finale entitled "In paradisum/Hope is the Thing with Feathers," which seeks to "[move] beyond commemoration and onto life renewing," thus both acknowledging Australia's past and embracing its future.[40]

The premiere of *Requiem* was met with great public acclaim: musicologist Peter McCallum stated that it "is a major contribution to Australian choral music and deserves not only the standing ovation given it at the end but wide dissemination,"[41] whereas Alex Siegers wrote that it "exuded a sound which I can only describe as uniquely Australian."[42] Stanhope himself acknowledges the historical implications of composing a Requiem Mass, both within the Western tradition writ large and its Australian derivatives, yet he is not encumbered by the expectations of standard practice or traditional functionality; rather, he sought to experiment with (and often interrupt) the "template" of the "old Catholic narrative," stating:

> There was no mysterious masked figure with a bag of silver. And I'm pretty sure none of my rivals tried to poison me. And unlike Mozart with his Requiem, although it took me a while, I did at least manage to complete mine. Mozart of course is incomparable. But I've wondered of late whether composers are spooked by his conviction

> that he was writing his own funeral music or just whether it's the size of the undertaking—a new Requiem is a comparatively rare beast.[43]

It is perhaps indicative of Stanhope's compositional output that the two analyzed works within this chapter are both ambitious, multi-movement structures that emphasize concepts of identity within place, Indigeneity, and reckoning with post-colonial heritage. Furthermore, both utilize choirs as a central ensemble and narrative device, likely resulting from his extensive experience both as a chorister in his youth and a professional choral director throughout Australia (e.g., with the Sydney Chamber Choir from 2006–2015, which premiered *Requiem* in 2021). Through both his familiarity with the capacities of this musical force and his attention to the programmatic continuity of his music, Stanhope's compositional voice is defined by his experimentation with the various technical and coloristic elements of a choral ensemble to achieve atypical effects. For example, he describes his approach to sonorities and voice leading as a "pyramid structure," in which

> there are larger intervals at the bottom and smaller intervals at the top. It's a pretty tried and true method, but it's also interesting to find ways to disturb that. When you can strip the choir back to say, two or three vocal sections, or a small group of soloists from the larger group, you have more of an opportunity to explore different colours out of that pyramid structure, so you don't necessarily need the tenors and basses to be spread so far apart. I like mucking around with tonal chords and false relations, so you set up tonal chords that then bleed out of that tonality and into another one, creating crunches that in a voice leading sense are intuitive to the singer. It works the opposite way as well—sometimes crunchy chords resolve to bright tonalities. Suddenly, overtones start snapping together and you get loud chords. If you want a loud chord, you need to run them in certain parts of the voice, and the partials need to ring together, otherwise they don't work. They need aspects of consonance to actually work, but there are ways of mucking around with that consonance to add depth and to experiment with texture.[44]

Stanhope's music thus represents a highly unique juxtaposition of tradition and innovation, in which aesthetic trends throughout the history of music are elaborated upon within an individualistic, progressive framework. Perhaps most effective in his compositional approach is his eschewal of both absolute radicalism and absolute moderation—throughout, consonance complements dissonance, light complements dark, modernization complements custom, and various narratives complement one another. Indeed, the programmatic elements of his music exemplify this dualistic nature of his work, in that they are both profoundly universal and intrinsically Australian in character.

CHAPTER NINE

Compendium of Characteristics that Denote or Identify the "Australiana" Idiom

A style, then, is not a fashion and, far from being planned, calculated and willed, is rarely recognized until it has shaped every art product of a period, and a long period at that. Even we, with all our accumulated experience and piercing self-consciousness, have no idea of what to future ages may seem to have been the style of our own day. We know our fashions only, [. . . which] follow one another so swiftly that they leave no precise impress on the mind, except of newness and ever more newness. Yet it is probable that posterity will discover that we had a style. [. . . It] is more doubtful whether contemporaries were aware of it, and we must not assume that its artists deliberately thought it out. More likely they yawned, stretched, stumbled, tumbled into it, finding, as is the case so clamorously to-day, eulogists to sing their praises.

BERNARD BERENSON[1]

Musical *Australiana*, though still in a developmental stage, may be identified by several distinct recurring themes catalogued below. While this list is scarcely exhaustive, it aims to encompass the most widely encountered influences for Australian composers throughout the nation's history; conversely, not every composer explicitly utilizes each presented element.

The Natural Environment and Its Native Flora and Fauna

Among the most prominent motifs within Australian music are allusions to the natural environment, such as through the imitation of bird calls, insects, or nocturnal creatures; evocations of the landscape or topographical features; motivic representations of symbolic Earth figures; and, in recent years, reactions to the changing climate as observed through bushfires, catastrophic natural disasters, rising sea levels, or the eradication of significant geographic locations. Perhaps as a reflection of Australia's vast physical distances, both within itself and between other nations, motifs of remoteness, isolation, loneliness, and introspection are also quite prevalent.

In colonial and post-colonial works, the environment was often revered as an impassable (and thus unattainable) paradise, laden with exotic flora and fauna; indeed, it was almost portrayed as an "erotic feminine," in lieu of any anthropomorphic subjects so often encountered in traditional Western works (e.g., Oriental women). Within this framework, the landscape represented both the pastoral and the adventurous; by romanticizing it within a musical framework, composers could embrace the dual cultural perspective of Euro-American nostalgia for pre-industrialized sceneries and an Australian resilience necessary for survival in the Outback. Furthermore, many early national composers exalted the rhythmic, melodic, and harmonic qualities of native Australian birds, and thus they often constructed works with transcribed calls or songs as foundational "cells." Concurrently with the increasing advocacy for environmental preservation in the late twentieth century, however, these representations of the environment and its flora and fauna were no longer abstracted and idealized, but rather reified through acute political aims. For example, Peter Sculthorpe considered his work an embodiment of the Australian landscape, through which he could advocate for its conservation. In this regard, he felt that his music was consciously political, in that it had always concerned "the preservation of the environment and more recently, climate change."[2] Sculthorpe frequently used a recurring semitone motive (pitch sequence *G–A –G*) throughout his music as an ecological *leitmotif* of the Earth,[3] derived from his belief that Kepler discovered the sequence in an attempt to calculate the "harmony of the spheres."[4]

Similarly, Ross Edwards has offered numerous analyses of his own works and the motivic and thematic threads he subconsciously (or deliberately) intersperses throughout them, in which he suggests a pervasive eco-musicological focus within composition. Rhythmic interplay or counterpoint "recalls the intersecting voices of insects and frogs"; drones (or sustained pedals) are associated with the "unpredictable starts and stops" of the cicada chorus, as well as the didgeridoo; birdsong evokes "wildness, freshness, joy, etc."; Earth Mothers, such as the Virgin Mary and her Asian counterparts, symbolize "the world ecological crisis." He further states that he "has created a distinctive sound world aligned with principles of deep ecology while seeking to reconnect music with elemental forces."[5] Fundamentally, Edwards considers his works, particularly those with

Aboriginal elements (e.g., the didgeridoo), a "unification of earth-based musics," thus allowing for a seamless merging of Indigenous and non-Indigenous cultures.

Albeit more implicitly, Stanhope, too, has sought to represent concepts of geography, place, and environmentalism in his work. For example, pieces that seek to center experiences of Indigeneity are often predicated on the acknowledgement that Aboriginal peoples are the traditional custodians of the natural land; destruction or unnatural alterations to the environment, in turn, indicate disrespect to their creator spirits and invite unwelcoming consequences for all who reside within the nation. Other compositions, such as the third movement of his *Requiem* ("Kyrie/Rain of Merciful Cloud," 2020), explicitly confront the devastating effects of climate change on the continent. His music is intrinsically connected to the Australian environment and thus holistically represents the experience of adapting, surviving, or perishing in a seemingly hostile environment, both from perspectives of its Indigenous peoples, dispossessed of their ancestral lands, and of European colonists, striving to unsustainably exploit its resources.

Indigeneity and Aboriginal Musical Cultures

Inextricably linked to the environment is the representation of Aboriginal peoples and cultures, as they are considered the First Peoples and custodians of the Australian lands.[6] Thus, composers incorporate Aboriginal myths, Dreamtime stories,[7] and sacred rituals; historical accounts of encounters with colonists; Indigenous instruments, such as the didgeridoo or clapsticks, or a conscious imitation of their acoustical qualities through Western instruments; texts comprised of Aboriginal languages, or imitative nonsense words and syllables; or co-performance practices with Indigenous musicians, actors, or communities.

Though Aboriginal musics were of interest to the first settlers as novel, exotic, or simply unusual elements of a foreign territory, little methodical or sustained interest is evident for over a century after the Tasmanian "Black War" (1824–1831). Exempting the occasional satirizing of Aboriginal peoples in "bush ballades" or other "folk" musics, Australian music sought to avoid the inconvenient presence of these land-owning groups, instead maintaining that the sole attribute of interest on the continent was its inimitable environment. Indeed, it was not until the systematic documentation of Aboriginal tribal musics in the early twentieth century that European enchantment (or obsession) arose, largely stimulated by new developments in mechanical equipment and culminating in works such as John Antill's *Corroboree* (1946) and Peter Sculthorpe's *Piano Sonatina* (1954). Scholars Roger Covell and Gordon Kerry acknowledge, however, this somewhat fantastical source of influence (e.g., amateur ethnography or "armchair anthropology") as dated and anachronistic, since "Australian composers deriving from European and North American traditions had no more in common with Aboriginal music than they had with the music of any other non-European indigenous people," and thus could claim little justifiable motivation to incorporate Indigeneity in their works.[8] Indeed, the early use of Aboriginal culture is regarded as a fanaticism within a "primitivist" aesthetic (i.e., the emphasis on "undeveloped" or "crude" "folk" cultures as indicators of authenticity),[9] an element present in numerous nationalistic idioms across temporal and geographical boundaries.

In a nebulously critical extension of this framework, musicologist Rachel Campbell argues that Peter Sculthorpe's method of developing a national musical idiom is closely modeled after that of Bela Bartok, is heavily dominated by a "primitivist" aesthetic, and excessively emphasizes "Aboriginal" inspirations without any legitimate basis in cultural research or preservation.[10] More subtly, she scorns Sculthorpe's "notorious" inclination for "exaggeration" and his underlying inconsistency in altering (or denying) the source of influence in his works, both characteristics driven by a fervent attempt to usurp any active Aboriginal participation in artistic creation and, therefore, to be singularly "instrumental in the forming of an Australian school of musical thought." Thus, Campbell portrays Sculthorpe as having achieved little more than an aura of determined inauthenticity throughout his compositions. She further states that, despite Sculthorpe's insistence on referencing Indigenous heritage to create a national music derived from "folk-primitivism," his interaction with Aboriginal culture was limited to "books and articles" that yielded, at best, a superficially academic understanding.[11]

Campbell additionally identifies fundamental characteristics of Sculthorpe's work which were to constitute "his" national idiom, such as a high presence of harmonic dissonance, static pitch clusters, extreme limitation in pitch ranges (resembling a chant or incantation), syncopated rhythms, percussive passages, marked articulations, and expressive texts intended to evoke a sense of the "primitive" (e.g., *Savage, Burlesque, Gruff, Brutal, Alert,* etc.). Thus, she challenges the validity and appropriateness of Sculthorpe's use of Aboriginality, implying that it is a lackadaisical approach to force its synonymity with being "truly," primordially "Australian."[12]

Notwithstanding such criticisms, however, the incorporation of Aboriginal culture in Australian music appears almost intuitive. If "nationalism" is a discourse on "unique peoples," Aboriginality must surely be the most straightforward response. Does this nonetheless constitute a superficial exploitation of their culture? While musicologist Jonathan Paget addresses several concerns and potential controversies over the manner through which Sculthorpe utilized Aboriginal melodies, particularly in the context of Australian colonialism, he generally asserts that Sculthorpe's music displays a genuine admiration and respect for Indigenous culture and places "Aboriginal music in the spotlight, creating greater public awareness of [its] richness."[13] Indeed, he inventively subverts this fundamental question, proposing instead that the way Sculthorpe "actively allow[ed] Indigenous music to shape and influence his style could be construed as a reversal of colonial power structures." His primary emphasis is on Sculthorpe's "recycling" of the Kakadu songlines,[14] the contextualization of Aboriginal melodies within either a Japanese or a Balinese idiom,[15] and the frequent recurrence of the environment as a source of inspiration.[16] Tangentially, Paget alludes to Sculthorpe's "identification with Aboriginality"[17] as a potential consideration for his fervent citation of Indigenous culture, though Paget ultimately asserts that "his choice of Indigenous melodies [simply] *confirms* pre-existing aspects of his own style."[18] Such incorporation could, depending on the ultimate intent of the composer, then be considered an important case study in understanding the processes of selection, filtration, assimilation, and reconciliation of multicultural influences within a framework of Western classical music.

Indeed, Aboriginality may even be elevated from a dubious or, at best, passive assimilation to that of considerable intercultural collaboration and reconciliation—for example, Paul Stanhope's landmark composition *Jandamarra: Sing for the Country* was hailed as "a work of major cultural significance" in Australia, largely for its representation of Aboriginality within the context of colonial violence. Throughout the compositional process, Stanhope's "first priority was to tell the story" laden with European infringement onto traditional lands, extensive subjugation of native culture, and relentless aggression against Aboriginal peoples; thus, the roles of the soloists, narrators, and choirs are paramount (predominantly performed by Bunuba community members), which the Western orchestra then merely supports and colors.[19] In doing so, Stanhope reframes Aboriginality within an Indigenous perspective and cedes control of a narrative long dictated by ambitions of the colonizers, rather than the experiences of the colonized.

In a presentation for the Australian National University's Conference on Belonging, Ross Edwards was invited to speak on the question: "How have non-Indigenous Australians rationalized, argued, thought through or been baffled by the issue of forming affections to, living in and belonging to, a place and a country from which the Indigenous people have been largely dispossessed?" His response may be considered as philosophically intermediary between Sculthorpe and Stanhope: though eschewing the purely academic use of native musics, he states that his music retains an "incipient Aboriginality" as a result of its strong sense of place and belonging. Explicit references across the two seemingly antithetical cultures are largely absent throughout Edwards's work; instead, he argues that Indigenous and non-Indigenous musics draw inspiration from the same fundamental source: the Australian landscape's near-symmetries, inconsistently varied repetitions, mysteriously abrupt start and stops, sense of timelessness, and absence of demarcated musical climaxes and resolutions.[20]

Asia and the Pacific

Australian composers frequently utilize extraneous cultures across Asia and the Pacific, evoking these regions through the prominent use of modal and symmetrical scales, native instruments, musical structures, and timbres or textures that mimic the aesthetic qualities of traditional art (e.g., brush-painting).[21] Sculthorpe was a significant, if not the central, impetus for this shift in aesthetic attention, proclaiming that he "would like to see the future of Australian music more and more influenced by Asian music"; prior to his advocacy for their use—and notwithstanding a brief period in the mid-nineteenth century, when a high percentage of Asian immigrants arrived in pursuit of gold and thus influenced, however tangentially, folk musics—policies such as "White Australia" discouraged an attitude of productive intercultural relationships. Though influences from the Asiatic and Pacific regions are scarce prior to Sculthorpe and his contemporaries, his vast pedagogical influences persuaded composers of the following generations to freely experiment with their instruments, philosophies, and materials throughout their music.

Edwards, for example, sought inspiration from Asian cultures soon after rejecting European modernism; regarding his *Mountain Village in a Clearing Mist* (1973), he stated:

> I just wanted to use the title of a Chinese brush painting, because the whole philosophy of Chinese calligraphy was what I was about. Trying to get at something absolutely essential, with the utmost economy of means. It somehow had to be related to my own environment, and particularly, the Australian bush.[22]

Philosophies centered around Eastern religions and ideologies (e.g., Zen Buddhism) would continue to pervade Edwards's later works and define their austerity, simplicity, and reservedness; indeed, he would come to regard his "Sacred Series" as "sonic contemplation objects" comparable to the "honkyoku" repertoire of the Japanese "shakuhachi."[23] Works such as *Shadow D-Zone* (1978) confirm these references to East Asian traditions in their use of gongs, tam-tams, or other similar instruments intended to "shroud [...] a feeling of tonality or equal temperament."

Literature and Visual Arts

Extramusical influences extend further to prominent literary figures. Australian poets, such as Les Murray, Judith Wright, John Kinsella, Oodgeroo Noonuccal, James McAuley, Christopher Brennan, John Shaw Nielson, and Vincent Buckley, among others, are frequently featured in song cycles, choral works, and other vocal compositions. English writings are also capitalized upon, such as those from Donne, Shakespeare, Hart Crane, Yeats, Emily Dickinson, and D.H. Lawrence; they are typically drawn from historical or globally popular sources (e.g., Shakespeare) or otherwise allude to an experience with the Australian continent or peoples (e.g., D.H. Lawrence's *Kangaroo*). To a lesser extent, foreign texts of French, Chinese, or Japanese writers, either in their original language or in English translation, are found in Australian works, as well as Medieval literature (e.g., Hildegard of Bingen or Julian of Norwich). Composers often reference or imitate favored visual artists, as well: for example, the Sculthorpian schema of drones, slow harmonic rhythm, and locally busy foregrounds has its equivalent in the landscapes of Australian painter and printmaker Fred Williams OBE (1927–1982), who aimed to reimagine compositional space so as to accommodate the overwhelmingly flat and continuous Australian environment.

Ritualism, Spirituality, and Magic

Music of the *Australiana* idiom further displays pervasive elements of ritualism, spirituality, and magic, achieved through a variety of mechanisms such as: chant or chant-like passages, often underlaid by drones or static, non-functional harmonies; direct reenactments or suggestions of rituals, whether Aboriginal or otherwise; reference to various Christian saints and prayers; reference to East Asian religious customs or figures; composition specifically for meditative or spiritually engaging purposes; and the redefinition and recontextualization of what is generally considered to be held "sacred" or "secular" in Western cultures. There are also references to early, often sacred, musics, such as Gregorian chants, hymns, and antiphons. This evaluation of the sacred is further amplified by the tendency to incorporate subliminal religious allegory. Among the most obvious examples of such symbolism is the pervasive use of bipartite or tripartite structures, or a permutation of either structure (i.e., a reference to East Asian dualisms, such as Taoist *yin* and *yang* and Zoroastrian *spenta mainyu* and *angra mainyu*, or the Christian Holy Trinity),[24] both within an individual work and as an organizational mechanism for a larger cycle. Although binary and ternary forms are among the most commonplace of Western music and thus appear relatively unremarkable, Australian "nationalist" composers do not seek to retain the formal structures utilized throughout the compositional canon; thus, their organizational mechanisms assume an inherently figurative nature, representative of the composers' ideology concerning the surrounding world. For example, many binary structures of traditional Western music do not necessarily incorporate drama or significant contrast between sections, such as Baroque dances that move among tonal centers but otherwise develop a single motif or sentiment; in *Australiana*, however, sections are distinguished by their dramatic and textural contrast and are symbolic of environmental or psychological dualisms pervasive in the nation.

In collaboration with the Canberra International Music Festival, Ross Edwards delivered a lecture on the juxtaposition of "sacred" and "secular" in a post-modernist compositional environment, asserting that "one of the functions of art must surely be to restore our confident awareness and participation" in responding to the sacred. Somewhat straying from the overarching theme, Edwards opines that many young Australian composers of the post-war generation rejected the European art traditions "that had seemingly let them down," instead bravely striking out "into the unknown in search of sanity"; here, it may be assumed that he is referring to a newfound exploration of their true "home." Furthermore, he alludes to such themes as the mysteriousness of the present moment, the timelessness of eternity, closeness to the Earth, coloration with material from Southeast Asia, and the incorporation of European plainchant that has been modified to reflect the Australian soundscape.[25] All such motifs carry a distinctly sacrosanct connotation, implying a reverential suspension in the Australian environment and its generative qualities.

Edwards, ultimately, asserts that his music is an attempt to facilitate transformation and healing "through spiritual connectedness with the Earth," largely by juxtaposing "European and Aboriginal" philosophies; he thus seeks to reinstate the "universal function" of music as an agent of ritual and healing.[26] Perhaps the most important thematic consideration of this presentation is Edwards's emphasis on music as a mechanism for restoration and reconciliation. Indeed, as the dynamic tension between Indigenous and non-Indigenous peoples is among the greatest structural faults in Australian national identity, such themes appear quite frequently in those composers who may be deemed "nationalistic."

Another principal element in Edwards's analysis of his compositional output is its rejection of "accredited" Western systems of art as "stale, irrelevant, and crudely inflexible." Since Australia is a relatively young nation, it is significantly less burdened by accumulated tradition; indeed, it is a creative, bold, and dynamic landscape with much space for experimentation, a perspective that is generally accepted by modern Australian composers. Edwards, despite his insistence that he does not consider himself a nationalistic composer,[27] subtly draws attention to such connections to place when analyzing his *Maninya*[28] style:

> To me, it's come to mean 'dance/chant,' and more specifically, *Australian* dance/chant. It has the essential characteristics of most chants from around the world except that it follows insect rather than speech rhythms, and it's not concerned about elucidating a text, but rather, pointing directly to the unfathomable mystery of existence.[29]

Furthermore, he has frequently composed music specifically for the purpose of meditation. Dr. Graham Williams, a friend from Edwards's student days and director of the Lifeflow Meditation Center in Adelaide, is seeking to develop a "uniquely Australian form of meditation" and perceived that "all of Edwards's music possessed a quality that naturally induced a meditative state."[30]

Building upon this assumption with a more definitively religious analysis, Paul Stanhope's Master's thesis delineates the aspects of ritualism and utilitarianism present in Edwards's works. Stanhope asserts that the majority of Edward's music written after 1970 is permeated, albeit subconsciously, by aspects of a ritual; simultaneously, they consciously reject European art traditions, defined as "the doctrine of music for its own sake," and "give music a sense of place by relating it to the sounds of the Australian bush." Finally, Stanhope traces Sculthorpe's significant influences within Edward's music, thus emphasizing the continuation of musical language pioneered by his teacher and mentor.[31]

Music Beyond the Concert Hall

Within the philosophical and aesthetic ideologies of nationalistic Australian composers, there is an explicit aim to recontextualize the purpose of music within performance. "Music for music's sake" is often dismissed, and compositions incorporate theatricality and dramatic elements to enhance the sensory experience of the listener. This effect is achieved through directions for atypical lighting, costumes (even for stationary performers), eclectic arrangements of performers, acting or a physical depiction of a narrative, and the inclusion of narrators or central speakers. Further to this multidisciplinary approach are the explicitly functional musical aims of many works: music is written to support some concurrent dramatic action (e.g., theater or dance), facilitate meditation and introspection on the part of the listener, or otherwise be treated in a manner free from the traditional constraints of a concert hall or restrictive performance venue. Among the most explicit examples of this are Ross Edwards's album *The Joy of Being: Guided Meditations and Music* (2008), created in conjunction with the Lifeflow Meditation Centre in Adelaide, and Paul Stanhope's *The Magic Island* (2012), composed for the Royal Children's Hospital in Melbourne. The latter work specifically sought to "provide a positive environment for children recovering in hospital," offering a fantastical escape from its sterile, and often unnerving, atmosphere: "*The Magic Island* imagines a place beyond the walls of a hospital ward—an Island of hope, playfulness and optimism."[32]

Such ideals of utilitarianism likewise assume a practical justification—for example, Ross Edwards has stated:

> I suppose it's almost the Protestant work ethic in me, it says that if I'm being funded to write this music, it's quite wrong that it's played in front of twenty-seven people who applaud slightly and then forget it.

> Therefore, I would like [my music] to have a very wide use, and in fact the whole concept of 'art music' to me is very suspect.

Thus, his composition of music intended as an aid to meditation is an attempt to imbue functionality, purpose, and longevity into his work:

> This function of music [...] has been recognized and valued throughout the ages, and it's naturally associated with things like meditation and yoga. But it's been neglected for a long time in the Western world—especially since the rise of concert halls and the decline of the great tradition of European church music [...]
>
> What I've been trying to do over the past twenty years, is re-explore the potential of this kind of music, and to give it a sense of place by relating it to the sounds of the Australian bush—especially the sound patterns made by insects, which, if you listen long enough, can lead you into a timeless domain where the concerns of self and society are temporarily suspended.

Though the extent to which Edwards pursues this aim of extra-musical functionality is perhaps not shared by all Australian composers, their music is nonetheless marked by a desire to exude more than merely "aesthetically pleasing or intellectually interesting" qualities. For example, Sculthorpe's later works were distinctly conservational in intent, in that they sought to inspire a sense of urgency into the public perception of the intensifying ecological crisis; Stanhope, similarly, expresses political and cultural concerns of post-colonial relations between Indigenous and non-Indigenous peoples and thus advocates for critical reevaluations of Australia's history.

Rejection of Western Theory

Throughout *Australiana*, there is a significant rejection of canonized Western theory and harmony (i.e., "verticality," or the emphasis on the motion from one harmony to another and the resulting schema of "tension" and "release") and a concentration on overlapping "strata" of dissimilar, yet synchronous, sounds (i.e., "horizontality"). Oscillations between tonic and dominant harmonies, which inherently generate expectations within the listener for an eventual "resolution," are often replaced by tonic and subdominant harmonies, and composers frequently circumvent the use of the dominant altogether. In Western harmonic analyses, subdominant harmonies serve an ambiguously dualistic role, in that their function is predicated on what follows them. Thus, they are truly only "subdominants" when shadowed by a dominant harmony; otherwise, they are merely extensions of the tonic. In *Australiana*, this compositional mechanism deemphasizes the experience of time as one organized by periods of tension and repose, and its music often seems to exist "outside of time." Self-contained groups of material, repeated figurations, and harmony that avoids strong differentiation all contrive to create a sense of time without beginning or end. Indeed, Ross Edwards has described his works as entering into an intuitive, nocturnal state of consciousness "in which linear, or clock time is suspended, and listeners are invited to turn their attention inwards in present-centered contemplation." Many of these attitudes and perceptions arose throughout Australian composition as an intuitive result of their rejecting Western socio-cultural and musical ideologies, and thus derive from a reevaluation of locality, temporality, and identity; for example, musicologist Deborah Crisp wrote that:

> Many composers have found that Asian music provided a starting point for the development of their language, and most commonly, it was the Asian concept of time which seemed to hold the most promise. European music is based on the division of time, tension becoming an important element in the essential forward movement of a work which implies development and resolution. Harmonic resolution, in the European sense, is unknown in Asian and Australian Aboriginal music. The division of time is unrelated to harmonic tension; time exists in its own right as a superstructure containing smaller, more detailed melodic and rhythmic patterns. Many composers felt that this concept of time in music was more appropriate to the vast, monotonous distances of Australia, and many seem to have arrived at an understanding of Aboriginal culture through the music of Asia.[33]

Such manipulations of time are particularly ubiquitous in Edwards's music: perhaps relating to the seemingly perpetual history of Aboriginal peoples on the Australian continent, his music seeks to equate "nature" with "a sense of the eternal":

> I liked the idea of a piece not starting anywhere, but having started, you would have opened a 'window' and there was music coming in. And that's why many of [the Sacred Series] pieces begin as though they have already been playing and then they stop abruptly as though someone shut a window, so you've got a great slice of eternity.

Indeed, this fleeting sense of an unattainable perpetuity, one which is inherently counterintuitive to the goal-oriented nature of Western society (and, duly, its music), is often encountered throughout Australian compositions, recontextualizing their perceptions of time, space, and development within a nationally relevant sonic aesthetic.

Despite the immense diversity inherent to the music of *Australiana,* it is fundamentally identified by several recurring themes: allusions to the natural environment, suggestions of Aboriginality, influences from Asian and Pacific cultures, spirituality and religiosity, the recontextualization of European "art music" and its performative function, and the rejection of Western music theory and compositional structures. Additional extramusical material is derived from Australia's colonial relationship between non-Indigenous settlers and Aboriginal peoples and its evolution thereof, as well as the literary and visual contributions from contemporaneous artistic movements.

The *Australiana* idiom, eclectic and experimental in character, has largely been defined by the dynamic sociocultural developments throughout the history of "the Land Down Under." Fostered by the fierce independence, adventurous predispositions, and understated humorousness of the nation writ large, its musical developments of the last century reflect individualistic narratives representative of exceptional diversity. It is hard to overstate the innovative energy underlying Australia's culture, perpetually inspiring compositions of evolving aesthetic values and ideologies

Perhaps more abstractedly, Australian music distinguishes itself from other Western compositions in its vivacity and animation—it is imbued with the unmitigated exultation of being alive, energized by the nation's inclination to discover and reinvent itself each day. It rejects the convulsive nihilism of European modernism, the relentless reevaluation of man's relevance, and the scientific impulse to turn the subjective into the impartial; instead, Australian music embraces the exuberance of humankind's sheer existence, unbridled by philosophical convolutions or pseudointellectual conundrums. This characteristic is present even in music of mourning or sorrow: death is not considered the terminal point in a linear progression of time, but rather, an opportunity for rejuvenation, renewal, and reconstruction.

Though Australian composers continue to search for the musical characteristics that holistically reflect their experiences, the overarching concerns surrounding nationalism have "now given way to the insight that all music composed in Australia can be described as Australian, regardless of the influences it shows"—in essence, an acceptance and validation of subconscious nationalism among those Australian composers who remain uncertain of their still-fluctuating cultural identity.

CHAPTER TEN

Final Questions

Does Australia have a culture distinct from Britain, given their lingering political attachment to the Commonwealth?

Although it is a rather intuitive assumption that immigrants transmit their native culture to their children, such trend is not a sustainable model for a lasting national identity beyond the physical borders of a country; in fact, associations to a "motherland" largely fade by the "second-generation immigrant."[1] Thus, Australia's attachment to the Commonwealth is better understood as a mere formality, sustained for reasons of practicality, rather than as a decisive element of their national identity. Indeed, several factors explain Australia's abstaining to declare itself an independent republic: first, a formal change would not substantially improve the livelihood of an "ordinary Australian" and thus is not a pressing national concern; second, discourses on the theme of republicanism largely focus on what Australia *doesn't* want to be, rather than around productive questions of their relationships with "the country, the land, one another, and the position of Indigenous Australians"; third, Australians do not predicate their identity on a formalized constitution or any single institutionalized structure; and, fourth, Queen Elizabeth has become a familiar, even amicable, element of Australians' lives, and therefore is retained as a matronly symbol of the nation.[2]

Australian culture, however, is certainly distinct from that of Britain and the Commonwealth. Their natural environment, Indigenous cultures, unique flora and fauna, national character, and specificities of the English language are vastly different from their mother country. More significantly, their experiences, both mundane and geopolitical, are detached from those of Britain and Europe, and the musical developments discussed throughout this book organically arose from these natural discrepancies. Otherwise, British musical institutions and traditions would have continued to flourish without an overarching sentiment of estrangement and disenchantment—indeed, the very premise of nationalistic movements is that a culture is sufficiently distinct to separate itself from the "dominant" aesthetic.

It is also important to recall that Australian culture underwent several "political" changes in its musical aesthetic. Its earliest manifestations were colonialist in nature, exhibiting the influence of another, more "powerful" nation. Subsequently, it became patriotic, suggesting a voluntary belonging to and equality with another nation; it is now developing its nationalistic idiom, in which it asserts a detachment from the perceived uniformity of the Commonwealth. This trend is further illustrated by ongoing debates concerning the replacement of the current national anthem, *Advance Australia Fair*, as popular opinion largely maintains that "it is just terrible—no one likes it."[3] Composed by the Scottish-born Peter Dodds McCormick in 1878, it bears such little relevance to the soundscape of Australia that petitions to entirely discard it are becoming increasingly widespread.

Additionally, a discussion with Natalie Williams, a mid-career composer with a "dual life in the United States and Australia," raises a significant consideration regarding the national character that influences the Australian political and cultural atmosphere:

> When I first came to the States for my doctorate degree, I saw for the first time a group of people who were proud of who they were. It made sense to me why Americans would never leave America—they know who they are, they're a complete country, they've got everything they need, and they don't need to go 'outside.' In Australia, we are uncomfortable in taking pride in who we are as a culture. That is an American thing. Down here, that approach is seen as negative and boastful. As in, 'why would you boast about where you come from?'
>
> Displays of patriotism are looked down upon as "tall poppy syndrome." That has stuck from our heritage as European convicts, since everyone who came here was from a low socioeconomic status and thus wanted to remain equal.
>
> Any celebration of who we are and what makes us unique is discouraged. We will be fine if we separate tomorrow from the Commonwealth, but we are still not overtly nationalist. Australians try to hide themselves; when Sculthorpe went to England, he was embarrassed to be an Australian. That is something I don't see changing soon.[4]

Indeed, the absence of much scholarly discussion of Australian music may be explained, at least in part, by the country's inherent unwillingness to "boast" or "flaunt" its national culture. Though it may be argued that this mannerism undermines any musical nationalism (how can they be nationalist if they don't assert themselves as a nation?), it merely subverts a supposedly extravagant movement into one that is understated, subdued, and modest. It does not, however, subtract from the individuality and uniqueness of its music.

Are the selected composers the only representatives of the Australian nationalist idiom?

No. Peter Sculthorpe is generally recognized as the first to definitively initiate the formation of a consciously nationalistic musical identity, and thus he is represented as a "pivotal" figure between colonial and contemporary national expressions. Ross Edwards was Sculthorpe's student, and, in turn, both Edwards and Sculthorpe mentored Paul Stanhope. These three figures therefore represent a traceable lineage of Australian "nationalism," whether intentional or inadvertent, and cumulatively represent a foundation from which an Australian musical identity may emerge.

Yet, there are many composers who deserve further investigation but are not presented within the scope of this book, owing to constraints of both time and space. A few of these are Peggy Glanville-Hicks (1912–1990), Malcom Williamson (1938–2003),[5] Anne Boyd (b. 1946), George Lentz (b. 1968), David Young (b. 1969), and William Barton (b. 1981).[6] This is far from a comprehensive list, given that Australia's musical nationalism has yet to fully develop.

Is it ethical for non-Indigenous Australian composers to interweave Aboriginal musical cultures in their music? If so, in what manner?

While the question of intercultural ethics is among the central issues concerning the *Australiana* idiom, it is unfortunately one that the author is unable to answer. Many scholars have fiercely debated the propriety of Sculthorpe's fervent use of Aboriginality as a mechanism for "Australianism," and, from a modern perspective, there is much that may be seen as lacking in his approach. But a few examples are the absence of any cultural "permissions" from Indigenous communities, his merely academic interaction with Aboriginal musics, the seemingly haphazard manner in which he chose native words and imposed self-defined connotations to them, and the direct quotation of many traditional melodies, all of which have tarred the contemporary reception of his work. Other scholars prefer to leave questions of permissions, ethics, and collaboration to the respective Indigenous communities with which a given project is concerned, as they are the traditional custodians of their musical cultures and thus have the most authority with regard to their interpretation and distribution. Some composers simply avoid incorporating Indigenous musics altogether, due to their uncertainty regarding the most ethical manner in which to approach obtaining permissions and retelling narratives that are not their own. At another end of the ideological spectrum, individuals such as Henry Tate (and, later, Richard Taruskin) have argued that the "modern Australian" has little to do with Aboriginal culture overall, asserting that the latter is too "estranged" from the psychology of the nation to be an effective nationalistic device.

Thus, the ethical questions surrounding this topic are complex and ephemeral in nature—the "correct" answer is often a product of the time in which it was given. Numerous organizations, both private and governmental, have since been established that seek to protect the artistic and intellectual property of Aboriginal communities, many of which offer guidelines on the proper procedures for communication and collaboration between Indigenous and non-Indigenous musicians.[7] Furthermore, it is important to consider the purpose with which a composer unites the two cultures within a work. In contrast to Peter Sculthorpe's use of Aboriginality as ornamentation or local "coloring," for example, Paul Stanhope's *Jandamarra* is designed to be a "truth-telling" work, with distinct political and artistic aims that were mutually agreed upon with the Bunuba community as the piece was constructed.

Therefore, no single answer or perspective can truly encompass the vast spectrum of non-Indigenous and Indigenous relations. In some respects, the two cultures merely occupy the same continent, yet share few tangible similarities. In others, however, their histories have significant and dramatic intersections which need not be easily dismissed. Their inhabitance of the same land is perhaps inconsequential on a minute scale; yet, this sharing necessitates a communal, and perhaps reluctant, forging of the same environment, history, and collective social responsibility.

Concurrently, the notion of Indigenous music existing only through non-Indigenous composers is fallacious. Numerous Aboriginal composers are widely recognized for their substantial contributions to Australian musical culture: for example, Deborah Cheetham composed the opera *Pecan Summer* in commemoration of the Cummeragunja walk-off and described it as "an opera for the twenty-first century, a contemporary opera for Indigenous Australians, a story for all Australians";[8] William Barton, despite minimal formal education in music, performed his *Kalkadungu's Journey* in Westminster Abbey for Queen Elizabeth II and the Royal Family, in commemoration of Commonwealth Day 2019.[9]

The ethical considerations of this cross-cultural fertilization arise, in part, from the enduring power structures between Indigenous and non-Indigenous peoples. Since James Cook's "terra nullius" declaration in 1770, many decades of Aboriginal subjugation, enslavement, and intentional destruction of traditional culture left bitterness and distrust between the two cultures, compounded by delayed governmental responses at mitigating these intercultural conflicts.[10] Thus, the incorporation of Indigenous musics in the works of non-Indigenous composers frequently rouses suspicions of theft and imposed colonialism and therefore are subject to numerous processes of consent for use. In recent years, it has been accepted that a non-Indigenous composer can do no more than merely suggest or evoke, rather than directly quote, Aboriginal musical material.[11]

An additional layer to the creation of such "classical" musics by Aboriginal musicians likewise exists. While non-Indigenous composers have often incorporated native cultures in an attempt to impose a sense of "Australianism," Indigenous peoples likely regard the performance of their traditional musics as a discourse on the celebration of their culture and the simultaneous mourning of post-colonial disturbances. The act of composition is a commemoration of their cultural resilience and enduring presence (thus their maxim "always was, always will be"), whereas the performative aspect of their work is a corporeal embodiment of their "collective consciousness." Thus, the same physio-acoustic framework is utilized for jubilation, grief, cultural continuity, and communal reverence. Writ large, their music has both restorative qualities for the cultural and psychological well-being of Aboriginal peoples, while simultaneously advocating for a reconstructive approach to Australian society.

Aboriginality is but one aspect of Australian culture, however, and does not assume a central position in what may be argued to be the "egalitarian" music of the nation. Ross Edwards states that the singular connection between his own music and those of Indigenous peoples is their common source of inspiration—namely, the natural environment and all sounds emanating from it. The Aboriginal perception of "Australia" is vastly different from that of non-Indigenous peoples, and therefore it is difficult to convincingly merge them in a work that communicates a single, "national" experience unified in a "nationalistic" idiom. Notwithstanding the touristic association of Aboriginal peoples with Australia, composers, musicians, and performing artists must individually evaluate the depth and authenticity of this professed relationship in the presentation of identifiable music.

Through what framework can Australian "national" music be understood?

Should Australian "national" music be analyzed through Western traditions, since this is the foundation for virtually all its composers, or rather through ethnographical perspectives, as it draws heavily from Aboriginal, Asian, and other non-Western structures?

Generally, the music of Australian nationalist composers cannot be strictly or solely analyzed in terms of traditional Western harmony, melody, and structure, as they eschew such preconceived devices of expression in favor of more ambiguous and adaptable frameworks. Certainly, they borrow many elements from Western culture, such as the system of notation, instrumentation, standard performance venues, hybrid or derivative musical forms, and compositional techniques, among numerous others. The two primary mechanisms with which Western music is analyzed, however, are lacking as structural units in Australian classical compositions: counterpoint, generally in regard to pre-eighteenth-century music, and harmony, almost exclusively in post-eighteenth-century music. Though their music undoubtedly incorporates superficial instances of both counterpoint and harmony, neither the underlying structure of their works nor the composers' approach toward these elements align with typical Western usages. Rather, the music is structured around rhythmic and melodic "cells" that are developed and manipulated; "horizontal" strata of sound that, albeit ostensibly contrapuntal, lack the strict adherence to vertical intervallic relationships; evocative or imitative qualities of sounds; and a functional, rather than purely aesthetic, approach to composition.

Further to this ambiguity is the frequent use of ethnographic recordings, anthropological resources, and even independently conducted research projects for the purpose of composing a culturally "authentic" work;[12] this is compounded by the pervasiveness of non-Western musical cultures (e.g., Japanese, Balinese, and Aboriginal) within the music of Australian composers. Thus, any thorough analysis must take into consideration both an ethnographic and a Western musicological perspective.

In part, the eclecticism and diversity of Australian music is a result of the demographic profile of the nation itself. Indeed, much of the population has origins in somewhere outside of Australia, resulting in a highly pluralistic outlook that is counterintuitive to a vision of a single, isolationist country. Diversity is therefore a tradition unto itself in the nation's music, defining its course of development after the aesthetic constraints of serialism had relaxed:

> Perhaps the approach of 'we are similar in our diversity' best characterises the path (and tradition) of Australian music that stems from this era. Composers establish their own unique styles and approaches, competing for commissions and opportunities alongside each other but while working in a plethora of styles. [...] The '50s and '60s informed what we do today, but Oz is a sounding board for what happens in the rest of the world, about 20 years behind. There is a fragrance of Australian-ness in the works of most Australian composers; attributes which are still being studied and codified; and on which we perhaps don't yet all agree. It is easier to suggest that this era was the beginning of a tradition of diversity, rather than a chronological tradition in itself.[13]

Recently, however, there has been a greater initiative toward looking "inwards" at the native cultures and abundant natural resources, thus stimulating a more prevalent focus on Indigenous, rather than Asian or European, cultures.[14] Given the vast array of musical influences, an exceptionally diverse population that has yet to conglomerate itself under a single label of "Australian," and a relentless uncertainty of what it is that constitutes an "Australian" sound, it is difficult to conclusively determine whether the musical processes within the country are a result of an internationalist attitude, or are instead a unique byproduct of the nation.

Does the Australiana idiom consist of an absolute eschewal of Western tradition?

Though *Australiana* does not entirely reject Euro-American traditions, there is debate as to the degree of its independence from such aesthetics. Peter Sculthorpe and Ross Edwards, both of whom studied in Europe in their formative years, expressed an unequivocal disenchantment with European "art music" and sought to turn away from it, at least for a significant period of time; it was considered stagnant and largely irrelevant to the political and cultural experiences of the Australian nation. Paul Stanhope, however, has not expressed such outright distaste for European traditions. He is a representative of the following generation of composers, born into existing Australian musical institutions that, albeit still comparatively limited, mediate the need to undertake studies abroad;[15] thus, the "cultural cringe" that was experienced by Sculthorpe and Edwards had largely dissipated by the time Stanhope conclusively initiated his compositional career.

Stanhope's discussion of his *String Quartet II* (2009), provides further commentary on his interactions with the "cultural weight of tradition":

> There are references to structural elements, or ideas of the formal elements from the eighteenth and nineteenth century that find their way into this piece, although in a reinvented form. For example, in the third movement, there's a set of variations; the fourth movement is called a "scherzo"; the second movement is a very condensed sonata form with a prelude at the beginning, such as Haydn might use. These elements draw from tradition, but they are knitted together in a continuous fabric [...] to give a different experience [to the listener].[16]

Despite the overarching presence of Old-World European tradition, Paul Stanhope consciously strove to express what he felt was the "Australian experience" implicit in the work. *String Quartet II* was a commissioned work for the Czech Pavel Haas Quartet; thus, Stanhope felt that it must, in some way, be a tribute to the Czech composer after which the group is named:

> [Pavel Haas] met a very tragic and horrible death in the Nazi concentration camps during World War II. But instead of writing what would inevitably be a rather somber piece, I decided to focus on the idea of the Australian experience of this. We didn't experience in Australia a tyranny like they did in Europe in the middle of the century, but instead many people fled the horrors of Europe and started a new life in Australia—*that* is the Australian experience. Of having the background in Europe, of all that great appreciation for culture and ideas and weight, and then transplanting that into a new context.

There are some, however, who argue that Australian nationalism was a byproduct of European musical movements, rather than an organic innovation confined to the reconsidered experiences of composers. Musicologist Michael Hooper specifically discusses the period from 1960–1975 as one dominated by a subliminal nationalistic aesthetic, influenced by European modernism and newly emerging political relations with Southeast Asia. Its music was built on "difference, difficulty, and argument," a time of critical self-defining that rejected stereotyped notions of Australia as a land of "sunbathing, drinking coffee, and dangerous wildlife"; he juxtaposes this against nationalism of "stable questions and fixed positions" from 1988, which was marked by a fervor and commercialism incited by the bicentenary of Australia's colonization. The central argument of his book, *Australian Music and Modernism, 1960–1975* (2019), is that this fifteen-year period coincided with the first self-conscious perpetuation of musical modernism in Australia. Though instances of Australian "modernist" composers were evident prior to 1960, such as Percy Grainger, he asserts that there was no cohesion of a single movement of "art music" that can be subjected to proper analysis and discussion.[17] Hooper, therefore, contends that the ongoing tendency to use "nationalism" as a mechanism to produce a coherent narrative is misguided, as such preconceptions of all active composers "working seamlessly towards a central ideal" simply did not exist prior to the late twentieth century.[18]

Notwithstanding the ambiguity surrounding the "inception" of Australian nationalist music, there has certainly been an active discussion among Australian composers as to its definition and purpose within the nation's culture. It is scarcely possible to find a conscious, collective effort toward the realization of a preconceived aesthetic end such as that suggested by Hooper; even less so in a country uncertain in its own identity relative to itself and other nations. Further complicating this realization is the doubt about the degree of overlap between Australian "nationalistic music" (which largely rejects the "art music" of the West) and Euro-American traditions. For example, Ross Edwards has described some of his music as akin to minimalism (e.g., *Tower of Remoteness*), and Peter Sculthorpe once recalled his disappointment upon learning that the impressionistic techniques he incorporated in his early works were not his own innovations. Even conscious uses of serialism were subject to "local" adaptations, such as in the manipulation of matrixes to mimic organically derived shapes. Thus, there is still considerable room for discussion on this topic.

Is the "cultural cringe" still ubiquitous today?

The "cultural cringe," stimulated and upheld by the dominance of atonalism throughout the twentieth century, achieved its zenith in the 1970s and 1980s. Indeed, prominent musicologists of the time were publicly embroiled in arguments about the relative merits of "modernism," and composition students felt as though they could not hope for a fulfilling career if their work did not stylistically conform to the ambiguous ideals of this movement.[19] Through the late 1990s, however, the perception that one could "either be a modernist or an outcast" had begun to wane. Peter Sculthorpe was among the few composers who, at the time, drew attention to the vast wealth of native cultures and natural landscapes in Australia as a source of musical influence; yet he was also representative of a larger shift, in that those who were embracing nationalism were simultaneously transcending modernism, or at least reinventing and subverting its dicta in their compositions.

Presently, Australian compositional focus is on plurality, experimentation, and individuality, as constituents are beginning to recognize and engage with their national identity, though their self-image is neither fully formed nor universally agreed upon.

What is the impact of Australia's vast geographical distances on its distribution and recognition abroad?

Though it is challenging to quantify a linear relationship between Australia's substantial geographical isolation from other nations and the commercial success of its music, it is not unreasonable to assume that its separation from the sociopolitical mainstream of the Western world minimizes the accessibility and recognition of its musics. Contemporary Australia is undoubtedly a derivation of Western society, owing to its colonization by and associations with the Commonwealth, yet its geopolitical relationships more closely interpolate it within East Asian traditions. Thus, there is a significant cognitive dissonance in the psychology of the nation that perhaps inhibits the distribution of its music across Europe and America.

Conversely, the perceived detachment of American, and perhaps European, existence from that of Australia stifles the impulse to investigate or incorporate their musical contributions into the canonized artistic discourses within educational and cultural institutions. Though the international public is aware that such a thing as "Australia" exists, common knowledge scarcely extends much further; indeed, the nation remains an impassable emblem of the "exotic." Its apparent reservation on the international stage, though an extrapolation of their national character, limits the global dissemination and popular awareness of their creative works. Such attitudes extend even to the treatment of a composer's own music—Ross Edwards, for example, has stated that he often does not attend the premieres of his own works (particularly those outside Australia) owing to his somewhat introverted inclinations, preferring instead to learn of their reception from the accounts of his friends and colleagues.[20]

These characteristic concerns of distance and isolation are pervasive within Australia as well. Indeed "few of the landscapes that feature in Australian music are actually inhabited by the people who write the music, or for whom it is written," whereas the highly urbanized centers are but narrowly featured.[21] Though, in the 1960s and 1970s, the impending bicentennial of James Cook's arrival in Australia spurred an abundance of themes surrounding exploration and voyaging, the nation's composers until recently maintained a merely passing association with the remote locations they sought to represent.

The cumulative effect of these phenomena has certainly impacted the dissemination of Australia's music abroad, as well as the nation's general lack of canonization relative to the widespread perception of Europe as the origination point of modern civilization. It is not possible, nor is it within the scope of this book, to approximate a quantification of Australia's inherent "tyranny of distance" as it relates to the international dissemination of its composers' musical output.[22] It must suffice to assert merely that there *is* a significant impact. Such concerns of distance and isolation are not easily mitigated by the vast technological advancements of the modern era; it is subconsciously, yet stubbornly, engrained within the psyche of those within and outside Australia.

What are possible areas of future research regarding "Australian" music?

Though some suggestions are implied above, it is perhaps necessary to restate them in a more systematic and organized manner. Analysis of additional composers who contribute to the *Australiana* idiom is certainly merited. Thus, a more holistic and contextualized representation of the nation's musical developments and aesthetics may be constructed. Furthermore, a greater discussion on the ethical ramifications of transplanting Aboriginal culture within the works of non-Indigenous composers is necessary, with emphasis on the various opinions and sentiments of Aboriginal musicians and community members themselves. Questions regarding cross-cultural interchange have not yet been fully examined or codified, thus fostering uncertainty and hesitation in producing works that consider, or even tangentially reference, the turbulent history between colonists and Indigenous peoples. Another interesting perspective may be an analysis of the utilization of Western musics by Aboriginal peoples to negotiate cultural trauma and social reconstruction; more specifically, the adaptation of extrinsic performance devices to communally process grief and instigate national conciliation and understanding. In turn, such processes may be perceived as a subversion of non-

Indigenous adaptations of Aboriginal musics to perpetuate a "national" sound.

Another unanswered consideration is the proportion of national versus international influences. Is Australian music an amalgamation of a cosmopolitan, intercultural outlook, or is it "nationally" shaped by the demographically diverse constitution of the population? Is it inherent to the nation's character to regard their music as self-enclosed? Conversely, an interesting point of consideration is the delineation of Australia's geographical isolation on its musical dispersion and cultural relevance to the broader world. Does its extreme isolation impact its marketability and significance to foreigners?

Finally, it is worth analyzing the effects of Australia's enduring attachment, both politically and culturally, to the British Commonwealth, particularly amidst the changing landscape of the European Union. As the United Kingdom continues to witness the impacts of the 2016 "Brexit" decision, its larger political conglomeration undoubtedly experiences repercussions and aesthetic shifts. Specifically within Australia, the music must reflect the dual isolation from the United Kingdom and, on a more imposing scale, the European Union. In this isolation, Australian musicians must delineate an idiom that embodies their incipient identity and cultural independence.

CHAPTER ELEVEN

Overview of the Aesthetic Periods of Australia's Musical Nationalism

English Folk Song—Colonization to Mid-Nineteenth Century

At the onset of colonization, convicts and free settlers transplanted musics from their native countries as a mechanism of adjustment and entertainment. Their performances of songs and dances largely retained their original structures and were not influenced by contacts with Aboriginal peoples; neither were they impacted by the radically different nature of the Australian continent as compared to their homelands. Much of this music was transmitted orally and comprised the folklore of the initial immigrants, and thus no single composer or work can accurately signify its breadth or sociocultural function.

Salon music, too, was a manifestation of this phenomenon, albeit arriving subsequently with the immigration of wealthy, "cultured" individuals. Preferences for these forms of pleasant, light-hearted musics stimulated, in turn, the importation of fortepianos, organs, and easily portable instruments such as guitars and violins. Representatives of this style include Isaac Nathan and Frederick Ellard, both of whom composed works with elements of "refined" dance (as opposed to the unrestrained and energetic nature of convict dances) and social pleasantries (e.g., Ellard's collection of works in homage to various "ladies" of high society).

"Australian" Folk Song—Bush Ballads of the Late Nineteenth and Early Twentieth Centuries

Toward the late nineteenth century, with the gradual increase of "native" workers (e.g., swagmen, bushrangers, and sheep shearers), there emerged an attempt to formulate a distinctly "Australian" folklore as manifested in "bush ballads." Figures such as Banjo Peterson and Henry Lawson excelled in embodying the notions of "mateship," egalitarianism, and anti-authoritarianism, utilizing strophic rhyme structures to narrate colloquially Australian epics of strife and perseverance within the "bush." Many of these sentiments originated in the convict traditions of the nation, in which the innate equality and collective oppression of their social tier fostered a sense of camaraderie and mutual aid.

The popularity of the ballads owes in part to their adaptations of English folk songs already well known to the "battler" class of society, and the rapidity with which they disseminated across the population garnered their praise as "authentic expressions of the national spirit." Some criticisms derided their largely romanticized depiction of the "bush" and their caricatures of Aboriginal peoples; nonetheless, the stock characters and their qualities sacralized within this body of song remain an integral feature of the Australian nation and its constituents' sense of identity.

English Pastoralism—Early to Mid-Twentieth Century

A conscious awareness of "Australianness" began to permeate the nation's "art" music in the early twentieth century, which had heretofore predominantly consisted of "salon" compositions, military band performances, and liturgical works derived, or entirely transplanted, from European religious traditions. Though the music was largely indistinguishable from concurrent British compositions in the pastoral style, composers nonetheless strove to programmatically depict what they felt were central elements of Australia—namely, its natural landscape and the flora and fauna within it. Fritz Hart's symphonic work *The Bush* (1923) and Henry Tate's two compositions included within his 1924 book *Australian Musical Possibilities* (*Morning in the Gully* and *The Australian Thrush*) are quintessential representations of this period, in that they explicitly reference the Australian environment as a quaint, lush, and unassuming region of much mystery and tempered beauty. A later example of this style is Peter Sculthorpe's fourth *String Quartet* (1947–1950), subtitled "Recollections of Holidays spent in a Country Village in Tasmania" and with aesthetic precedence in such composes as Frederick Delius and Ralph Vaughan Williams; its first movement is intended to evoke the Tasmanian wilderness, its second is simply entitled "Pastorale," and its third ("Country Dance") aims to juxtapose the untamed land against the quaint town indicated in the work's title.

This period of Australian "nationalist" music, however, overtly excludes any mention of Aboriginal peoples, instead representing the "bush" as a pristine environment entirely devoid of human presence. Such decision was largely a result of the sentiment that Indigenous culture was (paradoxically) exotic, and thus composers maintained that it was too far removed from the conscious of the "modern Australian" to effectively promote a sense of national identity.

"Australian" Modernist-Primitivism—circa 1946–1965

A departure from the conservative British pastoralism of the prior era facilitated the emergence of a modernist-primitivism aesthetic, largely paralleling its occurrence in Europe and abroad (e.g., as observed through Stravinsky's 1913 *Rite of Spring* or Varese's 1927 *Ameriques*). Indeed, for much of Australia's history, the musical developments within the country were predicated on aesthetic shifts in the Western world, and thus it may well appear that their "nationalism" was little more than their attempting to remain modern in a global environment otherwise unconcerned with Australia's existence. (Ironically, Australia's vast distance from Occidental regions inherently prohibited its composers from imitating Euro-American aesthetics during their zenith, and thus they consistently remained merely reactive, rather than contemporaneous.) Yet national composers did not seek strictly to mimic their Western counterparts. Rather, their modernist outbursts emerged as a natural reaction to their awareness of their isolation in the post-war era, their singularity as a nation, and the overtly hostile atmosphere of their natural environment. Indeed,

> cultural historian John Williams characterized 'Australian reactions to modernism 1913–39' as those of a 'quarantined culture' responding to the recent traumas of nationhood (1901) and war (60,000 deaths, 150,000 other casualties) by turning in upon itself and nurturing deep nostalgia for its pre-modern past.[1]

It was further to assert the "masculinity" of the nation and its constituents, as "young Australian men appeared to lose interest in the making of music, art, and literature" that was not abrasive and assertive, as though any other idiom "had become effete and feminized."[2]

Furthermore, their "modernism" resulted not necessarily from structured matrixes, intricate tone rows, or totalistic serial techniques (indeed, composers often subverted the accepted practices of Expressionism), but more generally from impression and intention.

Harsh dissonances, uncontrolled ferocity, and a sensation of fear and disenchantment permeate works of this era; it is likewise in this period that Aboriginality is reintroduced into Australian music, albeit through a framework of primitivism that segregated Indigenous peoples from "civilized" society. Those who utilized the traditional pre-compositional techniques associated with serialism likewise did so in markedly different manners than their European and American counterparts, such as through the manipulation of tone rows derived not from a standard matrix, but from the superimposed drawing of organic shapes (e.g., spirals) onto their matrixes to yield repetition, asymmetry, and occasional fragments of tonality.

Among the most prominent compositions within this aesthetic are John Antill's *Corroboree* (1946), Clive Douglas's *"Jubilee" Symphony* (1951), and Peter Sculthorpe's *Piano Sonatina* (1954). Interestingly, Sculthorpe serves as a pivotal transitional figure between this period and the next, bridging the two philosophies and "relativizing" Australian nationalism for contemporary audiences. He, as well as his student Ross Edwards (both of whom experimented with these techniques in their earliest works, albeit in a strained academic manner), would serve as the last tenuous vestiges of the already waning serialism.

Rejection of European Aesthetics and the Search for an "Australian" Voice—c. 1965 to Present

After a period of experimentation with primitivism and serialism, Australian composers who sought a distinctive musical idiom for the nation had grown disenchanted by the confines of these aesthetics. Indeed, "modernism" had become so prevalent within—and, supposedly, so necessary for—Australia's concert music that compositional creativity was wholly stifled; stylistic independence, experimentation, and individuality had become subservient to the dominant ideology that modernistic approaches to music were the only "correct" ones. Within this stage, later termed the "cultural cringe," emerged three successive generations of pivotal composers, including Peter Sculthorpe, Ross Edwards, and Paul Stanhope.

Intimations of this aesthetic shift were present prior to 1965, of course, but it was not until Sculthorpe's revolutionary work for orchestra, *Sun Music I*, that Australian composition acquired a culturally and commercially successful standing within the global musical canon. Though many works throughout Australia's history temporarily laid claim to a "discovery" of a national idiom, none did so quite as effectively as Sculthorpe's *Sun Music* series. The primary difference was namely in its internationalization, acquiring acceptance from those "beacons of civilization" (e.g., England) that had long dictated the preferences within Australia's educational and professional musical realms.

The idiom introduced by Sculthorpe, and later developed by his students Edwards and Stanhope, embraced minimalism, austerity, profound ritualism and reverence for the sacred, and Asian and Pacific musical cultures; in doing so, it rejected Western theoretical systems and their concepts of "art" music, both in a state of arrested development. Aboriginality was likewise embraced in a marginally more humane manner, however, its treatment varied across each generation as a reflection of the changing notions of Indigenous peoples and their relevance within Australian society. While Sculthorpe abandoned the pretense of savagery and primitivism present in prior works, his understanding of Indigeneity remained limited to ethnographic recordings, musical transcriptions, and field reports; thus, his music represents these peoples as neither autonomous nor entirely human. Rather, they are perceived as elements of the landscape itself, inanimate and dated curiosities whose sole purpose is to evoke a sense of "Australianness." Amidst environmentalist and social rights movements throughout the late twentieth century, however, the perception of the national public understood Aboriginal peoples as active custodians of the natural landscape; this shift is duly reflected in Edwards's music. Though he states that Aboriginal cultures are never explicitly referenced within his works, he utilizes their soundscapes as mechanisms to depict the natural environment. Thus, his music embraces an eco-musicological approach that temperedly and implicitly recognizes Indigenous peoples. Paul Stanhope's music, however, is radically different from both Sculthorpe's and Edwards's in its unequivocal declaration of Aboriginality and acknowledgement of the tense post-colonial relationship between Indigenous and non-Indigenous peoples. His music is partially shaped by the contemporary advocacy for Aboriginal protection and cultural restoration, and he therefore represents these diverse peoples as an integral—and fundamentally human—element of the nation.

Having undertaken his studies in the era after the "cultural cringe," Stanhope exhibits no explicit desire to reject Western systems as expressed by Sculthorpe and Edwards, and his music largely reconciles "Australian" with "Western" influences. Indeed, his music often utilizes Western structures and references canonical figures of music's history. What results, however, are works that are unambiguously "Australian" in character, sentiment, and heritage, foregoing the perceptible awkwardness of "nationalist" music in earlier periods of their history.

"Australianness" as a compositional aesthetic, albeit a terminologically laden concept, is continuously adapting and truly represents an organic and nuanced process that, after many years of colonization, is now reaching maturity. Perhaps most intriguing about its development is the distinct individuality amongst its various composers—each retains a unique and unmistakable identity within their music, yet the overall impression of their repertoire is undeniably "Australian" in nature. It is thus difficult to impose a dogmatic uniformity as to what constitutes an "Australian" aesthetic, and, indeed, it is unfair to attempt such a definition. The nation is inherently pluralistic, diverse, and experimental, and so too must be their music.

Timeline of Major Events Throughout Australia's History

Circa 50,000–70,000 BC
Aboriginal peoples migrate to the Australian continent.

1770 Captain James Cook, aboard the HMS *Endeavour*, explores the east coast of Australia and names it New South Wales.

1788 Great Britain establishes a penal colony in Sydney Cove (New South Wales).

1790 Surgeon George Boucher Worgan imports the first piano to Australia.

1824–1831
Tasmanian "Black War." Incited by the incursion of European colonists and their agricultural livestock onto traditional land, it remains among the deadliest wars in Australia's history by *per capita* and is the subject of ongoing historical dispute for its classification as an act of genocide against Aboriginal peoples.[1]

1825 Van Diemen's Land (modern Tasmania) becomes a colony.

1830 The colony of Western Australia is established.

1836 The colony of South Australia is established, to which convicts were never sent.

1851 The colony of Victoria is founded.
Gold is discovered in New South Wales, prompting a sudden influx of immigrants and thus transforming the convict colonies into more progressive cities inhabited predominantly by free citizens.

1854 Frederick Ellard composes his *Australian Bird Waltz*, considered the first published musical work to structurally incorporate Australian bird calls.

1859 The colony of Queensland is established.

1868 Great Britain ceases the deportation of convicts to Australia. Between 1788 and 1868, approximately 160,000 convicts had been sent to Australia.

1879 The first degree in music is awarded in Australia, conferred by the University of Melbourne.

1887 Francis Ormond endows Melbourne University's Chair of Music position, first filled by George William Louis Marshall-Hall in 1890.

1890 A.B. "Banjo" Peterson publishes *Old Bush Songs,* a collection of colonial ballads.

1891 G.W.L Marshall-Hall begins his appointment as the Ormond Professor of Music at the University of Melbourne.

1901 The six colonies federate into the Commonwealth of Australia. Suggestions for federation are documented from as early as 1842 and councils were held several times over the next few years, however, the idea repeatedly failed to achieve ratification. It was not until the late 1880s that a serious and sustained movement for Federation arose, roused in part by an increasing nationalism amongst Australians, improved communication systems throughout the colonies, and similar federation movements throughout the world (e.g., in the United States and Canada). After several more unsuccessful councils, the final (and decisive) push toward unification came from the Commonwealth, as its political leaders sought to consolidate their Australasian territories and thus counter the expanding colonial activities of the German and French in the Pacific. A number of concerns, debates, and oppositionist movements arose in response to the proposed federation of the colonies, and many territories (particularly the smaller ones) staunchly refused membership for fears of imbalanced power distribution and economic disadvantages. Though these ongoing arguments significantly delayed the official merger of the colonies, *The Commonwealth of Australia Constitution Act (UK)* was passed on July 5, 1900 and given Royal Assent by Queen Victoria on July 9, 1900. It was proclaimed on January 1, 1901 in Centennial Park, Sydney, and the Australian national flag was adopted.

Perhaps expectedly, federation galvanized the production of "nationalistic" art. Around each significant anniversary (e.g., jubilee, centennial, etc.), an increased concentration of music on "Australian" themes is evident in the work of active composers, even if they were otherwise not particularly patriotically inclined.

1902 Women are granted the right to vote through the Franchise Act.

c. 1905 "Stolen Generations," or "Stolen Children," policies begin. The Stolen Generations were the children of Australian Aboriginal and Torres Strait Islander lineage who were removed from their families by both Australian government agencies and church missions and placed under the care of officially appointed guardians or institutions. The overarching aim of this practice was to assimilate Aboriginal peoples into Australian (i.e., "white") society; Auber Octavius Neville, the "Chief Protector of Aborigines" during much of this period, even advocated for the successive "breeding out of colour" by "marrying white" over several generations. With the abolishment of the Aborigines Welfare Board in 1969, all states repealed legislation that permitted the forcible removal of children under the pretense of "protection." It is difficult to conclusively identify when these practices were effectually ceased, however, as some extant documentation reports the continued removal of children through the 1970s. As a result of their severance from traditionally sacred lands, native cultures, and familial clans, Aboriginal peoples developed severe intergenerational trauma and a distrust of Western social structures, thus further problematizing non-Indigenous appropriation of their heritage.

1912–1913

Considered a pivotal year in music history, 1912 is generally accepted as symbolizing the dissolution of eighteenth-century tonality that had heretofore dictated compositional construction. Around this time, three significant works were written that conclusively challenged and subverted traditional norms of tonality and form: Claude Debussy's *Prelude to the Afternoon of a Faun* (1912), Igor Stravinsky's *Rite of Spring* (1913), and Arnold Schoenberg's song cycle *Pierrot Lunaire* (1912). Strongly contrasting these progressive compositions was Percy Grainger's idyllically pastoral *Colonial Song* (1912).

1914–1918

Australia fights in World War I. 330,000 Australians serve; 60,000 are killed and 165,000 are wounded. During this war, Australian soldiers were engaged in the disastrously unsuccessful Gallipoli Campaign. Exceptionally poor conditions, insufficient preparation, and the resultant high number of casualties on the part of the British Empire resulted in the reasonably prevalent view amongst

	Australians that the English acted with both carelessness and incompetence toward their constituents. Thus, the Gallipoli campaign has come to symbolize for Australians both an important milestone as an independent entity in global affairs and as the beginning of a national consciousness and identity. The date of the initial landing (April 25) is now commemorated as a public holiday (Anzac Day) in Australia, during which thousands of people gather at memorials and honor the patriotism, bravery, and sacrifice of those who lost their lives in the war.
1915	Sydney Conservatorium of Music is founded.
	A.E. Floyd begins his appointment at St. Paul's Cathedral in Melbourne, Australia.
1917	Opening of the Trans-Australian railway. At the time of Federation, Perth (the capital of Western Australia) was isolated from the remaining Australian states by a vast and inhospitable desert terrain, accessible only by an uncomfortable sea voyage and connected with a single telegraph line. Thus, one of the incentives offered to Western Australians to join the new Commonwealth was the promise of a federally funded railway that would adjoin it with the rest of the continent. The railway includes the longest stretch of straight track in the world (297 miles), and former Australian astronaut Andy Thomas has noted that the line is identifiable from space because of its unnatural straightness: "It's a very fine line, it's like someone has drawn a very fine pencil line across the desert."
1923	First public radio station opens in Australia.
	Fritz Hart composes his symphonic suite *The Bush*.
1924	Henry Tate publishes his collection of essays entitled *Australian Musical Possibilities*.
1927	Federal parliament moves from Melbourne to Canberra.
1929	Peter Sculthorpe is born.
1930s	The "Jindyworobak" movement in literature, led primarily by poet Rex Ingamells, emerges and gains popularity.
1932	Australian Broadcasting Commission established.
	The Sydney Symphony Orchestra is established by the Australian Broadcasting Commission.
1933	Inaugural "Australian Composers Competition" is held by the Australian Broadcasting Commission.
1938	Percy Grainger endows the Grainger Museum in Melbourne, Australia.

1939–1945
World War II. The Australian Air Force is active in Britain; its navy operates in the Mediterranean; soldiers are stationed in North Africa and the Pacific.

1942 Labor Government's Broadcasting Act created, stipulating that a minimum of two and a half percent of music played on the ABC and commercial stations must be by Australian composers.

1943 Ross Edwards is born.

1944 A.E. Floyd begins his weekly "Music Lovers' Hour" broadcasts.

1946 John Antill composes *Corroboree.*

1951 Jubilee of Australian federation. The "1951 Commonwealth Jubilee Composer's Competition" is presented by the Australian Broadcasting Commission on behalf of the Commonwealth Government.
Clive Douglas composes his *"Jubilee" Symphony.*

1954 Peter Sculthorpe composes his *Piano Sonatina.*

1963 The Musicological Society of Australia is established.

1965 Peter Sculthorpe composes *Sun Music I.*

1967 Constitutional referendum grants citizenship to Aboriginal peoples and Torres Strait Islanders.

1969 Paul Stanhope is born.

1972 "White Australia" immigration policy is abandoned. This policy was institutionalized after the Federation of Australia and the Immigration Restriction Act of 1901, with the aim of maintaining the country as "an outpost of the British race." The desire to prevent the immigration of people of non-European ethnic origin, especially Asians and Pacific Islanders, however, originated in the tense competition in the gold fields between European and Asian miners during the mid-nineteenth century gold rush. After 1972, successive governments implemented policies that would make racially based selection criteria unlawful when evaluating immigrants.

1973 After fourteen years of construction and an actual cost almost fifteen times greater than originally budgeted, the Sydney Opera House is completed. (In the 1980s, the Opera was met with the additional, unforeseen cost of installing a net above the orchestra pit following a performance featuring live chickens, one of which walked off the stage and landed on top of a cellist.)

1986 The Australia Act of 1986 is signed, granting full independence from the United Kingdom. The Act prevents the United Kingdom from legislating with effect in Australia, for the United Kingdom to be involved in Australian government, and for an appeal from any Australian court to be heard in a British court. In effect, it renders Australia a "sovereign, independent, and federal nation"; it is still a member of the Commonwealth of Nations, however.

1993 Aboriginal land rights are recognized.

2008 Prime Minister Rudd apologizes to the Stolen Generations.

2014 Peter Sculthorpe passes away.

The Sydney Symphony Orchestra premieres Paul Stanhope's work *Jandamarra: Sing for the Country.*

2021 The Sydney Chamber Choir premieres Paul Stanhope's work *A New Requiem* (2020).

Notes

Preface

1 A didgeridoo is a cylindrical wind instrument made from the naturally hollowed-out trunk of a eucalyptus tree; it produces a continuous drone comprised of a fundamental pitch and an overtone heard an interval of a tenth above.

2 Emil Chudnovsky, interview with Andrew Haveron, Kirov Academy "The Classical Music Podcast Ep. 2," podcast audio, June 23, 2020. https://www.youtube.com/watch?v=eu4JVyeLU8s&t=5833s.

ONE

Terra Australis Nondum Cognita: Colonization

1 Edward Brooke-Hitching, *The Phantom Atlas: The Greatest Myths, Lies and Blunders on Maps* (San Francisco: Chronicle Books, 2018), 225.

2 Walter Ghim, "Vita . . . Gerardi Mercatoris Rupelmundani," *Gerardi Mercatoris Atlas sive Cosmographice Meditationes de Fabrica Mundi et Fabricate Figura* (Amsterdam: 1606), 12.

3 Fowell is likely referring to an arrangement of airs from English composer William Shield's (1748–1829) opera *Rosina*, performed in Covent Garden (1782), either in a print or a manuscript copy.

4 James Beattie, *Essays on Poetry and Music as they Affect the Mind* (Edinburgh: Creech, 1776), 174.

5 John Whiteoak and Aline Scott-Maxwell (eds.), *Currency Companion to Music and Dance in Australia* (Strawberry Hills: Currency House, 2003), 5.

6 Tootaha, mentioned on approximately fifty occasions throughout Cook's journal, was identified as a Chief of an unidentified native tribe.

7 James Cook, *Captain Cook's Journal during the First Voyage round the World* (Frankfurt: Outlook, 2018), 132.

8 Cook, 176.

9 Cook, 292.

10 For example, many missionary settlements sought to teach hymns and other Western musics to young Aboriginal children. While the songs were often quickly learned and mastered (despite their unfamiliar lyrics and Western musical characteristics), they were then adapted by Indigenous communities within a context of native performance and ceremony. Thus, while Western interference altered Aboriginal culture, it consistently failed to wholly eradicate it. See: Catherine J. Ellis, "Developments in Music Education Among Aboriginals in Central and South Australia,"

in *Aboriginal Australian Music*, ed. Jennifer Isaacs (Sydney: Aboriginal Artists Agency, 1979), 32–33.

11 Composers of the nineteenth and twentieth centuries, for example, attempted to mimic Aboriginal melodies and rhythms within "art" music for the concert hall; by clothing it in what some scholars referred to as "European garb," however, their "transcriptions" soon became quite removed from their original source.

12 John Hunter, *An Historical Journal of the Transactions at Port Jackson and Norfolk Island* (Glasgow: Good Press, 2019).

13 William Bradley, *A Voyage to New South Wales* (State Library of New South Wales, 1802), 60.

14 This attitude somewhat stubbornly persisted in the post-colonial Australian psyche. In 1924, for example, Melbourne musicologist Henry Tate suggested possible sources of raw material that may be used in the formation of a distinctly "Australian" music, particularly emphasizing the rhythmic, melodic, harmonic, and modal characteristics of native bird calls. He further encouraged the incorporation of Australia's unique environmental features, such as the topography, native flora and fauna, and soundscapes of the "bush"; daily life "reflecting the Australian experience"; and theoretical developments from the "Old World" (i.e., Europe). Tate generally rejected, however, utilizing Aboriginal culture, as he believed it is "estranged from the psychology of the modern Australian" and thus too remote to be an effective mechanism of nationalism. [News], *The Hobart Town Courier* (16 October 1830), 2. http://nla.gov.au/nla.news-article4206714.

TWO

Earliest Compositions and Institutions, 17844–1834

1 Kay Dreyfus, "In Search of New Waters: Australian music studies in the 1990s," in *Essays in Honour of David Tunley*, ed. Frank Callaway (University of Western Australia: Callaway International Resource Centre for Music Education, 1995), 162–163.

2 Graeme Skinner, "The Invention of Australian Music," *Musicology Australia* 37/2 (2015): 298–299.

3 [Advertisement], *The Sydney Gazette* (28 April 1825), 1. http://nla.gov.au/nla.news-article2183967. See also: Graeme Skinner, "Joseph Reichenberg and family," *Australharmony* (an online resource toward the history of music and musicians in colonial and early Federation Australia). https://sydney.edu.au/paradisec/australharmony/reichenberg-joseph.php

4 Graeme Skinner, "Toward a General History of Australian Musical Composition: First National Music, 1788–c. 1860," Ph.D. thesis (Sydney Conservatorium of Music, 2011): 90.

5 Charles Bertie was librarian and historian who gave initial impetus to the systematic study of Australian history through his association with a Sydney group of zealots. Among his many publications are *The Early*

History of the Sydney Municipal Council . . . (1911) and *Old Colonial By-Ways* (1928). Additionally, he had been appointed as the editor of a proposed historical and biographical survey of Australia; this endeavor was never completed, but the initial work became a starting point of the first edition of *The Australian Encyclopaedia* (1925–1926).

6 Charles Bertie, *Isaac Nathan: Australia's first composer: a lecture delivered at the Conservatorium of Music* (Sydney: Angus and Robertson, 1922), 14.

7 Bertie, 16.

8 [News], *The Sydney Gazette* (16 January 1827), 2. http://nla.gov.au/nla.news-article2187390

9 James Hall, "A History of Music in Australia (15)," *The Canon* 5/8 (March 1952): 364.

10 Bertie, 5.

11 Frank Fowler, "Preface," *Australian Album* (Sydney: J.R. Clarke, 1856), unnumbered page.

12 "Mr. Wallace's Concert," *The Sydney Herald* (9 June 1836), 2.

13 In 1814, a governor of New South Wales held a conference with local and distant natives with the purpose of convincing them to send their children to the new "Native Institution," or school. From 1816 onward, similar conferences were held annually and would later be referred to as the "Corrobory, or Annual Feast" or "annual corroboree," and though there are only a few documentary references to singing and dancing at the event itself, actual corroborees were almost certainly held by attending bands on the night preceding and following it. It was also at later meetings that Indigenous elders had the opportunity to hear their children singing hymns they had been taught; at a Christmas feast, after Indigenous elders "had witnessed the progress of certain of their children in reading, writing, and singing hymns to the God of the Christians, they began voluntarily to place their children in the school." It is uncertain whether Indigenous acceptance of these institutions was truly as forthcoming as it is presented here, as these missionary establishments dually eradicated the cultural heritage and musical traditions of Aboriginal clans. "To Sir George Murray," *The Sydney Monitor* (29 November 1828), 5.

14 *The Sydney Monitor* (18 June 1836), 3.

15 Skinner, 29.

16 Bushrangers were originally escaped convicts of the British settlement in Australia who used the Outback as a refuge from the authorities.

17 A swagman is a "nomadic" laborer who traveled from farm to farm by foot, carrying his belongings in a "swag" (bedroll) on his back. They were especially common in Australia during periods of economic uncertainty, such as the 1890s. The "swag" was also referred to as "Matilda"; hence, the famous bush poem "Waltzing Matilda" by Banjo Paterson describes a "jolly swagman." This stock figure became a folk hero in colonial-era Australia, and it is still perceived as a symbol of anti-authoritarian values

considered central to the nation's character. Indeed, "Waltzing Matilda" is perceived to be so quintessentially "Australian" that it is regarded as the nation's unofficial anthem.

18 A.B. (Banjo) Paterson, *Song of the Pen, A.B. (Banjo) Paterson: Complete Works 1901–1941* (Sydney: Lansdowne, 1983), 464–465.

19 Charles Thatcher, *Thatcher's Colonial Minstrel: New Collection of Songs* (Melbourne: Charlwood & Son), 7.

20 *The Bulletin*, a weekly journal founded in 1880, emerged as the foremost literary enterprise for popular national literature. Its agenda was avowedly nationalist and radical-democratic, and its publications achieved a large circulation throughout the Australian colonies.

THREE

Revolutionary Figures and the First Enunciations of a "National Identity": Late Nineteenth to Early Twentieth Century

1 Marshall Hall, "The Cruise of the Nona," *The Field Quarterly Magazine and Review* 2 (August 1871): 170–171.

2 Thérèse Radic, "Marshall-Hall, George W(illiam) L(ouis)," *Grove Music Online*, 2014.

3 The first award of a degree in music (i.e., a Bachelor of Music) at the University of Melbourne was recorded in 1879, and the first Chair of Music (endowed by Francis Ormond, thereafter known as the Ormond Professor of Music) was occupied from 1891, despite the lack of a music department or other employed faculty of music at the university. Francis Ormond held strong convictions that music was beneficial for the moral character of the individual, and thus his endowing of a musical chair was less to advance the nation's professional musical atmosphere than to promote the colony's civic well-being.

4 John Runciman, "Professor Marshall-Hall," *Magazine of Music* 9 (June 1892): 109.

5 Frederick Ouseley (Professor of Music, University of Oxford) to Graham Berry (Victorian agent-general), May 3, 1888, Melbourne University Central Registry Correspondence, File 1888/31.

6 Ernest Scott, *A History of the University of Melbourne* (Melbourne: Melbourne University Press, 1936), 145.

7 Thérèse Radic, *G.W.L. Marshall-Hall: A Biography & Catalogue* (Melbourne: Marshall-Hall Trust, 2002), 7

8 John Runciam, "The Case of Mr. Marshall Hall," *The Saturday Review* (November 1898): 602.

9 Runciam, 109.

10 Much of the University of Melbourne's decision to reinstate Marshall-Hall was founded in their increasing inability to manage the Conservatory, both financially and publicly, without the leadership of its creator.

11 Peter Tregear, Review of *G.W.L. Marshall-Hall: A Biography and Catalogue*, by Thérèse Radic, *Context* 23 (Autumn 2002): 80.

12 Marshall-Hall's compositions and impact are gradually accruing greater interest in the Australian musicological community, and he has since been the subject of a number of dissertations, articles, and scholarly publications. For a thorough compendium of his life and work, see: Thérèse Radic, *G.W.L. Marshall-Hall: A Biography & Catalogue* (Melbourne: Marshall-Hall Trust, 2002). Furthermore, "The Marshall-Hall Trust" was established in 1993 by Marshall-Hall's grandson, Marshall-Hall Inman, to publish and promote Australian composition before World War II.

13 Ian Burk, *"Goodbye 'til next time": A critical biography of A.E. Floyd (1877–1974)* (Melbourne: Lyrebird Press, 2012).

14 *Radio Times*, August 4, 1945: 5.

15 Undated article, likely written for the *Argus*. Floyd Collection, Grainger Museum, University of Melbourne.

16 Rhoderick McNeill, "Migrant Symphonies—the symphonic contribution of British composers to Australian musical life," in *Migrant Security 2010: Citizenship and Social Inclusion in a Transnational Era, Toowoomba, 2010*: 155.

17 Christopher Mark, Review of *Australian Music and Modernism, 1960-1975,* by Michael Hooper, *Music and Letters* 101/4 (2020): 810.

18 Louis Esson, "The Composer in Australia: A Talk with Fritz Hart," *The New Triad* 1/5 (December 1927): 24.

19 Esson: 24.

20 Malcolm Gilles, et. al., *Self-portrait of Percy Grainger* (Oxford: Oxford University Press, 2006), 17.

21 Percy Grainger, *The All-Round Man: Selected Letters of Percy Grainger, 1914-1961* (Oxford: Clarendon Press, 1994), 37.

22 One work that Grainger long advertised as having achieved this ambition was his *Marching Song of Democracy*, stating that it "is the most representative and effective of my larger choral works, (I value it as an expression of a typically Australian democratic athletic sentiment otherwise perhaps not voiced in music)." Then, as now, however, the work was not received as a strong representative of "Australian" sentiments. Grainger, *The All-Round Man*, 109.

23 Peter Tregear, "'Nostalgia is not what it used to be': Exploring the kitsch in Grainger's music," *Grainger Studies: An Interdisciplinary Journal* 1 (2011): 102.

24 Percy Grainger, *Grainger on Music*, eds. Malcolm Gillies and Bruce Clunies Rosss (Oxford: Oxford University Press, 1999), 375.

25 Allan Marett, "Australia," *Grove Music Online*, 2001.

26 *Radio Times*, 12 February 1944: 5.

27 Clive Douglas, *Autobiography of an Australian composer*, unpublished, State Library of Victoria, Dr. Clive Martin Douglas papers, MS 7656, Box 15. The following program notes are likewise adapted from his papers.

28 Felix Werder, "Composing in Australia," *Meanjin* 16/2 (June 1957): 140.

29 David Symons, *Before and After* Corroboree: *The Music of John Antill* (London: Ashgate, 2015).

30 In the early stages of composition, Antill spelled "coroboree" with two lower-case Bs, in accordance with writings by Spencer and others in the anthropological literature. Antill, "Corrobboree: A Ballet Suite for Orchestra," 1946, Papers, National Library of Australia, MS 437/8a/9 Box 14, 2.

31 Antill, Corroboree drafts, first booklet, 3.

32 "Sundry Shows," *The Bulletin*, 21 August 1946, 24.

33 John Antill, 'Why I Wrote '*Corroboree*,"' *Australian Musical News* 37 (1946): 20–21.

34 Rhoderick McNeill, "Symphonies of the Bush: Indigenous encounters in Australian symphonies," in *Encounters: Meetings in Australian Music: Essays, Images, Interviews.*, eds. Vincent Plush, Huib Schippers, and Jocelyn Wolfe (Brisbane: Queensland Conservatorium Research Centre, 2005), 1.

35 Other scholars have sought to rectify the general negligence of Antill's remaining compositional output, and their works are valuable resources for the curious reader. Beth Dean and Victor Carell's *Gentle Genius: A Life of John Antill* (Akron Press, 1987), and David Symon's *Before and After* Corroboree: *The Music of John Antill* (London: Ashgate, 2015) are two substantial studies.

FOUR

"The Nerves of Nationality": ***Australian Musical Possibilities*** **(1924) and its Impact on Australian Music**

1 European composers, too, appeared to recognize the unsettling atmosphere of their own work. In the same year as Henry Tate's treatise, for example, Gustav Mahler commented on a performance of his *First Symphony*: "What sort of world is it that brings forth such sounds and shapes as its representation?" Bernard O'Dowd, Introduction to *Australian Musical Possibilities* (Melbourne: E. A. Vidler, 1924), 7.

2 Henry Tate, *Australian Musical Possibilities* (Melbourne: E. A. Vidler, 1924), 18.

3 This statement is not to suggest that the Balkan nations have shamelessly plagiarized from one another while formulating their own national folklores and identities, nor that they are all identical in character. Despite their discrepancies, however, their political and geographical histories (i.e., frequently changing borders, ongoing intercultural contact, etc.) have yielded many intersections throughout the long habitation of the Balkan Peninsula. This condition, in turn, has facilitated their formation of individual cultural identities, in that each is contextualized within a greater social, political, economic, and geographic circumstance.

4 One could, of course, argue that the United States of America is a "sister country" to Australia, in that they were both colonized by Great Britain

in approximately the same time period and have displayed similar historical trajectories in their development. The United States, however, has markedly different geographical, political, social, and cultural features from Australia. While parallels may be observed between the two nations in several regards, they are nonetheless distinct enough from one another that Australian composers could not reasonably model any nationalistic musics on identically labeled "American" musics.

5 Ted Gioia, *Music: A Subversive History* (New York: Basic Books, 2019), 277.

6 Ross Edwards, "The Tensions of Making Sacred Art in a Secular World," Canberra International Music Festival, 2014. https://www.rossedwards.com/the-tensions-of-making-sacred-art-in-a-secular-world/

7 For example, the pivotal Australian composer Peter Sculthorpe (1929–2014) indicated that he encountered Tate's work while he was a student in Melbourne and "was impressed that he exhorted composers to look to Australia for inspiration"; "I myself had begun to follow this path and Tate's writings made the journey feel much less lonely." Carolyn Philpott, "Peter Sculthorpe's String Quartet no. 14: A Musical Response to Social Injustice," *Context* 27 & 28 (2004): 93.

8 Tate, 12–13.

9 Tate, 15.

10 The "deflected scale" to which Tate is referring corresponds to the diatonic major scale (Ionian mode), but with a flattened second and sixth scale degree.

11 Tate, 20.

12 Tate, 34.

13 At the time of Tate's writing this treatise, obtaining permissions from, or otherwise collaborating with, Aboriginal musicians was not a consideration. Many of the transcriptions that Tate cites in his book are "Westernized" at best, or completely deformed at worst.

14 Clive Douglas, "Folk-song and the brown man—A means to an Australian expression in symphonic music," *Canon* 10/3 (July 1956): 82.

15 Roger Covell, *Australia's Music: Themes of a New Society* (Melbourne: Sun Books, 1967), 65.

16 The pied butcherbird is a songbird native to Australia, whose capacity to produce melodies (and, at times, harmonies in "choirs") of remarkable complexity and variation has earned it the title of a "magic flute." See: Charles Hartshorne, "Musical Values in Australian Bird Songs," *Emu-Austral Ornithology* 53/2 (1953): 109–128.

FIVE

Interlude: Patriotism, Nationalism, and Somewhere in Between—The Turmoil of the Twentieth Century

1 Michael Gill, "The Skin of Our Teeth," *Civilisation: A Personal View by Kenneth Clark*, BBC, February 23, 1969.

2 John Whiteoak and Aline Scott-Maxwell (eds.), *Currency Companion to*

Music and Dance in Australia (Strawberry Hills: Currency House, 2003), 5.

3 Roger Covell, *Australia's Music: Themes for a New Society* (Melbourne: Sun Books, 1967), 3.

4 Covell, 11.

5 Some unsuccessful "models" include attempts to commercially farm the arid land of the Australian Outback, graze sheep where grass growth was sparse and slow, introduce rabbits and foxes for hunting, and design "urban" centers in the likeness of European centers.

6 Stefan Zewig, *The World of Yesterday* (New York, 1943), 3–4.

7 Deborah Crisp, "The Influence of Australian Aboriginal Music on the Music of Contemporary Australian Composers," in *Australian Aboriginal Music*, ed. Jennifer Isaacs (Sydney: Aboriginal Artists Agency, 1979), 50.

8 Covell, 146.

9 An ethno-national conflict is a struggle between two or more parties in which the primary objectives are defined foremost in ethnic terms; the conflict itself, however, typically does not arise solely as a result of ethnic differences among the competing groups, but rather over political, social, territorial, economic, or cultural matters. The various ethnic groups differentiate themselves with two interrelated elements: first, the accentuation of predetermined cultural traits, and second, the assertion that these traits substantially distinguish the group from those who do not share those characteristics. Thus, an ethnonationalist conflict emerges from aims of power, dominance, and cultural survival, and it is perpetuated by the aggravation of ethnic and cultural disparities. Such condition is readily observed in Australia's colonial and post-colonial history, and indeed continues to be evident in continuously altered manifestations to the present day.

10 Judith Howard, "Social Psychology of Identities," *Annual Review of Sociology* 26 (2000): 369.

11 Neville Meaney is an Associate Professor of History in the University of Sydney, with a focus on international relations, foreign policy, and Australia's associations with Asia. Much of his research examines Australia's relations with the global community, specifically as they concern defense, cultural transmission, and economic interactions. Neville Meaney, "Britishness and Australian Identity: The problem of nationalism in Australian history and historiography," *Australian Historical Studies* 32/116 (2001): 89.

12 Meaney's suggestion is not only problematic when considering the legacy between settler and Aboriginal populations, but also when observing Australia's immigration policies throughout much of its history. For example, the nation's "White Australia" policy sought to effectively forbid the immigration of non-Europeans and fostered a racially insulated white society; these broad restrictions were not officially renounced until the late twentieth century.

13 The Gallipoli Campaign was an attempt from the Entente powers (Britain, France, and Russia) to compromise the Ottoman Empire by assuming one of the central Turkish straits. The amphibious landing at Anzac Cove on April 25th, 1915, was undertaken primarily by troops from the Australian and New Zealand Army Corps (ANZAC). It was a disastrous endeavor, however, as a result of poor planning, disorganized guidance, and minimal support from their directing commanders. The Entente powers were ultimately unsuccessful, and an inordinately large number of Australian and New Zealander troops were killed or wounded in the battle.

14 Army Recruit Training Centre, "The Aim of Recruit Training," retrieved August 1, 2021. https://web.archive.org/web/20070831230108/http://www.army.gov.au/artc/aim.html

15 The "Classical" period generally refers to the period from the mid-eighteenth century to the early nineteenth century, during which time musical composition was largely predominated by Austro-German traditions. Musical nationalism arose as a reaction against the imposition of a monolithic uniformity and was inspired by social revolutions in France and the United States, as well as novel ideologies from philosophers such as Diderot, Voltaire, and Rousseau regarding the relationship of the individual to the society. In essence, musical nationalism was often a reflection of concurrent political nationalism.

16 Richard Taruskin, "Nationalism," *Grove Music Online*, 2001.

17 Australia is designated a Federal Commonwealth realm and thus is considered to retain complete autonomy regarding its internal affairs; nonetheless, it still upholds a common allegiance to the British Crown and perpetuates the ceremonial participation thereof (e.g., hosting an annual visit from the Queen).

18 Though Aboriginal peoples certainly have a distinct and complex culture, the implication of an artificial uniformity within the term "nationalism" is not at all applicable to mainland Indigenous Australians. They refer to themselves as various "land-owning groups" rather than as a single "nation," and are united by very few elements: neither the complexion of their skin, nor language, nor cultural traditions, nor even specificities of their collective Dreamtime stories are alike across their self-defined clans. Indeed, it is only in their categorization of "other," imposed upon them by European colonizers, that one may speak of Aboriginal peoples as a collective whole. What underlies their diversity, however, is a shared post-colonial experience and desire to reestablish their relevance within the Australian continent. Thus, the discussion of "nationalism" between the colonizers and Aboriginal peoples is not practical and is therefore given the label of "ethno-national conflict" previously presented.

19 Luke Trainor, *British Imperialism and Australian Nationalism: Manipulation, Conflict, and Compromise in the Late Nineteenth Century* (Cambridge University Press, 1994), 9–11.

20 Jindyworobak was an Australian literary movement whose white members, mostly poets led by Rex Ingamells, sought to contribute to a uniquely Australian culture through the integration of Indigenous Australian subjects, language, and mythology. It ultimately fostered a romantic notion of the spirit of place and the literary importance of what could still be discerned of Aboriginal culture. "Jindyworobak" comes from the Woiwurrung language, formerly spoken around modern-day Melbourne, meaning "to join" or "to annex." It was first used in James Devaney's *The Vanished Tribes* (1929), in which he claims to have sourced it from a nineteenth-century Aboriginal vocabulary.

21 Such fanaticism for the "exotic," ironically, is quite common in periods of nationalism. One of the primary sources of musical inspiration throughout the Romantic era, which is commonly associated with the post-1850 rise in nationalism, was a fascination for distant, peculiar, or generally unfamiliar territories (e.g., the Orient).

22 John Antill is occasionally deemed a musical counterpart to the Jindyworobak movement as a result of his 1946 *Corroboree*, however, much debate exists around this application of the term, given the scant evidence that Antill was aware of (or desired to be associated with) this trend.

23 Katrina Cashman, "Life & Work," in *Margaret Preston—Australian Artist*, official website, February 22, 2017. https://web.archive.org/web/20171009051808/http //www.margaretpreston.info/life-work/

24 Similar characteristics would likewise become evident in the music of Australian compositions, as manifested in programmatic depictions of Aboriginal legends, austerity, asymmetrical meters and forms, and repeated melodic and rhythmic cells.

25 Jens Korff, "Are dot paintings traditional Aboriginal art?" Creative Spirits, 2019. https://www.creativespirits.info/aboriginalculture/arts/are-dot-paintings-traditional-aboriginal-art

26 Dennis Scholl, personal communication, July 2020.

27 Erica Corsano, "A chat with alumnus and art collector Dennis Scholl," 2020.

28 Didgeridoos are considered to be linked with the spirit of its owner; it is therefore customary to destroy a didgeridoo after its owner has passed away.

29 Valerie Lawson, *Dancing Under the Southern Skies: A History of Ballet in Australia* (Australian Scholarly Publishing, 2019), 160.

30 An Aboriginal word meaning "ancestral home, paradise."

31 Margalit Fox, "Colleen McCullough, Author of 'The Thorn Birds,' Dies at 77," *New York Times*, January 29, 2015. https://www.nytimes.com/2015/01/30/books/colleen-mccullough-author-of-the-thorn-birds-dies-at-77.html

32 Dudley Glass, "Australia's Contribution to Music," *Journal of the Royal Society of Arts* 111/5080 (March 1963): 302–303.

33 Ross Edwards, "Ross Edwards for ACO: Indigenous influences on his music," YouTube video, posted by "Pru Borgert," August 15, 2016, https://www.youtube.com/watch?v=6TmVKg3lLu8&feature=emb_title
34 "SYDNEY AMATEUR CONCERT," *The Sydney Gazette* (24 July 1826), 3. http://nla.gov.au/nla.news-article2186232
35 Graeme Skinner and Jim Wafer, "A checklist of colonial era musical transcriptions of Australian Indigenous songs," *Australharmony* (an online resource toward the history of music and musicians in colonial and early Federation Australia). https://sydney.edu.au/paradisec/australharmony/checklist-indigenous-music-1.php
36 Graeme Skinner, "Toward a General History of Australian Musical Composition: First National Music, 1788–c. 1860," Ph.D. thesis, Sydney Conservatorium of Music, 2011: 83.
37 [Advertisement], *The Sydney Gazette* (11 November 1834), 3. http://nla.gov.au/nla.news-article2217523
38 Alan E. J. Andrews (ed.), *A Journey from Sydney to the Australian Alps undertaken in the months of January, February and March, 1834 by Dr. John Lhotsky* (Hobart: Blubber Head Press, 1979), 108–109.
39 Allan Marett, et. al., "Australia," *Grove Music Online*, 2001.
40 Elizabeth Wood, "MORITZ HEUZENROEDER—A MUSICAL PIONEER": 4.
41 Wood, 5–6.
42 Glass, 303.
43 *Cumberland Argus*, 15 February 1922: 2.

SIX

"The great composer who came to define Australia's sound for the rest of the world" Peter Sculthorpe, 1929–2014

1 Graeme Skinner, *Peter Sculthorpe: The Making of an Australian Composer* (Sydney: University of New South Wales Press, 2007), 1.
2 Skinner, *Peter Sculthorpe*, 3.
3 Skinner, *Peter Sculthorpe*, 4.
4 Emil Chudnovsky, interview with Andrew Haveron, Kirov Academy "The Classical Music Podcast Ep. 2," podcast audio, June 23, 2020. https://www.youtube.com/watch?v=eu4JVyeLU8s&t=5833s.
5 Skinner, *Peter Sculthorpe*, 3.
6 Edward Masey, Review of *The Foundations of Australian Culture*, by P.R. Stephensen, *The Australian Quarterly* 8/29 (March 1936): 106–107.
7 Peter Sculthorpe, "Peter Sculthorpe 'Brings in the Sun,'" National Portrait Gallery, https://www.portrait.gov.au/stories/peter-sculthorpe.
8 Skinner, *Peter Sculthorpe*, 5.
9 Peter Sculthorpe, "Peter Sculthorpe 'Brings in the Sun.'"
10 Rachel Campbell, "'The Whole Work is Full of Primitive Rhythms': The Folk-Primitivist Origins of Peter Sculthorpe's National Music," *Musicology Australia* 41/1 (2019): 50.

11 Wilfrid Mellers, "New Worlds, Old Wildernesses: Peter Sculthorpe and the Ecology of Music," *The Atlantic* 268/2 (August 1991): 94–95.
12 Skinner, *Peter Sculthorpe*, 4.
13 Ross Edwards, "Peter Sculthorpe 1929–2014: Ross Edwards speaking at the Peter Sculthorpe Celebration Concert," October 25, 2014. https://www.rossedwards.com/peter-sculthorpe-1929-2014-ross-edwards-speaking-at-the-peter-sculthorpe-celebration-concert-25-october-2014/.
14 Graeme Skinner, "Composer of the Month: Peter Sculthorpe" (*Limelight*: Australia, 2018).
15 Interestingly, D.H. Lawrence is not an Australian writer, but a British one. *Kangaroo* is an apparently semi-autobiographical novel that recounts a visit by an Englishman to New South Wales.
16 "Irkanda" is an Aboriginal word meaning "a remote and lonely place," or so Sculthorpe described.
17 Peter Sculthorpe, program notes for "Irkanda IV," *Faber Music*.
18 High Cs as a representation of "God," or, more generally, the divine, are a recurring motivic element in Australian compositions in the generations following Sculthorpe.
19 A German-born Australian composer of classical and electronic music, as well as a noted critic and educator. He was a columnist for the Australian newspaper *The Ages*, in which he made the quoted comment regarding Sculthorpe's work.
20 Roger Covell, "Sculthorpe, Peter" (2011).
21 This event coincided with the establishment of the Musicological Society of Australia (1963) and the rapid rise in academic music positions—thus, Sculthorpe was at the forefront of Australia's institutionalized musical developments.
22 Suzanne Robinson, "Peter Sculthorpe: The Making of an Australian Composer," *Musicology Australia* 30:1 (2008): 122.
23 David Cairns, "Faber Music: News: *Sun Music I* Reviews," August 31, 1967.
24 Robert Henderson, "Peter Sculthorpe," *The Musical Times* 107/1481 (July 1966): 595.
25 Anne Boyd, "Peter Sculthorpe's Sun Music I," *Miscellanea Musicologia* 3 (1968): 4.
26 In his program notes for the work, Sculthorpe indicated that the second movement of *Sun Music* derives from a Balinese circular dance associated with a trance-inducing ritual song.
27 Graeme Skinner, "Some Makings of an Australian Composer (1964–65)," *Fontes Artis Musicae* 55/1 (January–March 2008): 113.
28 Graeme Skinner, "Some Makings of an Australian Composer," 116.
29 Robinson, 122.
30 Peter Sculthorpe, "Peter Sculthorpe on Australian music (from the ABC Archives)," YouTube video, April 30, 2019, https://www.youtube.com/watch?v=tyuZH5FAv6c.

31 Here, Matthews directs the reader to "a full and exemplary" account found in Michael Hannan's study *Peter Sculthorpe*, consisting of an overwhelming seventy pages of analysis. David Matthews, "Peter Sculthorpe at 60," *Tempo*, New Series 170 (1989): 12.

32 The six composers were Vincent Plush, Colin Brumby, Peter Sculthorpe, Larry Sitskey, Ross Edwards, and Miriam Hyde.

33 A billabong is a branch of a river forming a backwater or stagnant pool, made by water flowing from the primary stream during a flood.

34 Ross Edwards, personal communication, December 2020.

35 The original melody was recorded by A.P. Elkin.

36 Port Essington was the site of a failed British naval settlement from 1838 to 1849 and was the third failed attempt by the British to settle northern Australia. It collapsed largely due to natural disasters and disease, however, the eleven years during which it existed yielded significant cultural exchanges between the British and the local Indigenous peoples.

37 Paget, 102.

38 Perhaps the two most vocal proponents of this opinion are musicologists Rachel Campbell and Liza Lim, the latter of whom advanced the notion that Aboriginal cultures were merely lifted as artifacts representing a generalized view of indigeneity, thus perpetuating colonizing attitudes and behaviors. Others, such as Carolyn Philpott, subvert these notions and argue that his referencing of Aboriginal heritage and culture has actually advanced pressing concerns of "social injustice" within Australia. See: Carolyn Philpott, "Peter Sculthorpe's String Quartet no. 14: A Musical Response to Social Injustice," *Context* 27 & 28 (2004): 83–96.

39 The perceived relationship between environmental preservation and Aboriginal heritage was so pronounced that, during the late 1990s, the "Eco Warriors" movement fashioned a flag with the colors of the Australian Aboriginal flag (red, yellow, and black) and green (to represent the environment).

40 For a contemporary report that addresses the transferring of environmental preservation to native peoples, see: Victoria Tauli-Corpuz, "Cornered by Protected Areas: Replacing 'Fortress' Conservation with Rights-based Approaches Helps Bring Justice for Indigenous Peoples and Local Communities, Reduces Conflict, and Enables Cost-effective Conservation and Climate Action" (Rights and Resources Initiative: 2018).

41 In this same year, Australia was celebrating its bicentenary of colonization. Though Peter Sculthorpe expressed an increasing disdain for the fervent nationalism becoming increasingly rampant and commercialized as this landmark drew closer, he nonetheless composed *Child of Australia: An Australian Anthem* to commemorate the event.

42 Here, Sculthorpe is referring to Beethoven's 1824 set of variations for piano trio on the theme "Ich bin der Schneider Kakadu" by Wenzel Müller, which was subsequently nicknamed the "Kakadu Variations."

43 Peter Sculthorpe, "Programme Notes" in "Faber Music: Kakadu (orchestra)," 1988.
44 *Advance Australia Fair* has faced significant controversy and criticism from the Aboriginal Australian community, as they claim the lyrics erase their extensive presence on the land and negate their experiences of enslavement and oppression. Thus, there is advocacy from the Indigenous community, presently led by hip-hop artist "Senator Briggs," to alter or change the national anthem entirely.
45 Peter Sculthorpe, "Peter Sculthorpe at 50—ABC Four Corners Profile (1979)," YouTube video, April 29, 2019, https://www.youtube.com/watch?app=desktop&v=LR7KLPs54vs.
46 This phrase likely refers to Australia's practice of sheep herding, an activity that is widely successful in pastoral Britain but practically unsustainable in the arid Australian outback. By perpetuating this impractical activity, Australia continued to psychologically "ride on Britain's back."
47 Another example of an export practice likened by author and anthropologist Jared Diamond to those of a "third world country" is the selling of the wood chips of the Tasmanian blue gum tree for exceptionally low bulk costs. Australia, afterwards, purchases already manufactured paper at high prices. There is significant criticism for this economic exchange, as the Tasmanian blue gum is native to southeastern Australia, yet economic leaders have not negotiated a particularly beneficial monetary compensation for this resource.
48 In political science, the term "banana republic" describes a politically unstable country with an economy dependent on the exportation of a limited-resource product, such as bananas. Greg Melleuish, "Australian Identity in the 21st century," Submission 10 in *Nationhood, national identity and democracy* (2019): 3.
49 Faber Music, "Earth Cry," program notes, 1986.
50 Graeme Skinner, "Composer of the Month: Peter Sculthorpe." *Limelight* (Australia, 2018).
51 Peter Sculthorpe, "Peter Sculthorpe at 50."

SEVEN

"Sometimes I realize that the music I'm speaking has a broad accent": Ross Edwards, b. 1943

1 AM indicates a Member of the Order of Australia, established by Queen Elizabeth II in 1975, to recognize Australian citizens for significant achievement or meritorious service. Prior to the establishment of the order, Australian citizens received British honors; thus, this award in itself reflects Australia's individuality and cultural independence.
2 Higher doctorates are often awarded *honoris causa* when a university wishes to formally recognize an individual's achievements and contributions to a particular field. These degrees are considered equivalent to professional doctorate in the relevant discipline and are typically gained

not through a defined program of study, but rather, by submission of a substantial body of research-based work.

3 Ross Edwards, personal interview, July 2020.

4 Paul Stanhope, "The music of Ross Edwards: aspects of ritual," M.A. (honours) thesis (University of Wollongong, 1994): 9.

5 Stanhope, 3.

6 Antony Jeffrey, *The Many Faces of Inspiration: Conversations on Australian Creativity* (Adelaide: Griffin Press, 2011), 57.

7 Ross Edwards, "A Natural Way," Interview by Gordon Kalton Williams, http://www.gordonkaltonwilliams.com/A_Natural_Way_interivew_with_Ross_E dwards_900_words.pdf.

8 Don Featherstone (director), "Dance of Nature: The Music of Ross Edwards," audiovisual material published by the National Film and Sound Archive of Australia, 1995. https://aso.gov.au/titles/documentaries/dance-nature-music-ross-edward/clip1/

9 Toru Takemitsu (1930–1996) is considered among the most important Japanese composers who have written music in the Western tradition. His music preserves a fundamental Japanese identity yet synthesizes its traditions within Western (and largely modernist) aesthetics. Two distinguishing features of his work are the incorporation of both Western and Japanese instruments and his subtle manipulation of orchestral timbres, a practice that likely influenced Edwards's use of both European and Aboriginal scoring.

10 Stanhope, 13.

11 Stanhope, 52.

12 Ross Edwards, "Reflections," *Transforming Art* 4/1 (1992): 28.

13 Ross Edwards, "Address to the Conference on Belonging," lecture, Australian National University, Canberra, November 1999.

14 Featherstone, "Dance of Nature: The Music of Ross Edwards."

15 Edwards, "Address to the Conference on Belonging."

16 Ross Edwards, "Ross Edwards on String Quartet No. 4 'Ridley Gold,'" YouTube video posted by the Australian String Quartet, July 27, 2021. https://www.youtube.com/watch?v=Se0U9dLdF5I&feature=emb_title

17 Jeffrey, 59.

18 Jeffrey, 60.

19 Christopher Dench and Ian Shanahan, "An emotional geography of Australian composition," *Sounds Australian* (Winter 1992): 25.

20 Edwards, "Reflections": 30.

21 This is a relatively rare instance in which Edwards chose to invent a word rather than borrow an existing Aboriginal term.

22 Phillip Cooney, "Beyond sacred and maninya: developments in the music of Ross Edwards between 1991–2001," Ph.D. thesis, (University of Newcastle, 2003): iv.

23 Ross Edwards, "Reflections": 30.

24 Stanhope, 86.

25 This practice bears a strong parallel to Sculthorpe's tendency to recycle material, most notably in his *Kakadu* series.

26 Fred Watson, program notes for Ross Edwards's "Piano Concerto," 2003.
https://www.rossedwards.com/piano-concerto-1982-revised-2003/

27 Ross Edwards, "Composer Conversation with Ross Edwards," YouTube video posted by "UNSW Music Performance," 37:12, May 11, 2020. https://www.youtube.com/watch?v=-ZuqMFcFb8o

28 In performance, the percussionist is not placed at the front-center of the stage, but rather, obscured upstage. Furthermore, the music is not particularly virtuosic and is often overshadowed by the writing for the other instruments.

29 Ross Edwards, "Yarrageh: Nocturne for Solo Percussion & Orchestra (1989)," http://www.rossedwards.com/yarrageh-1989/.

30 The acoustic effect is not unlike that of a Baroque prelude and fugue or an Italian recitative and aria, as a result of its extreme metrical and timbral contrast.

31 This technique recalls Anton Webern's use of *Klangfarbenmelodie*, resulting in a pointillistic effect in which the pitch classes of a melody are played by various instruments with different ranges and timbres.

32 "Mantra," in Hinduism, is a hymn or prayer that is memorized and chanted to the various gods. These were often transmitted orally for many centuries prior to their notation in sacred texts.

33 Though Edwards dislikes the term, Philip Cooney identifies his works as "postmodernist" due to "his own rejection of the restrictive and elitist tenets of European modernism," non-traditional approach to texture, reduction of melodic material, use of modality and tonality, openness to a variety of cultural influences, and his embracing of spirituality and intuition. Philip Cooney, "Ross Edwards: I still wake up excited about the score I'm working on," *Resonate Magazine* (2013).
https://www.australianmusiccentre.com.au/article/ross-edwards-i-still-wake-up-excited-about-the-score-i-m-working-on

34 Cooney, "Beyond sacred and maninya": 362.

35 Ross Edwards, personal communication, July 2020.

36 Ross Edwards, program notes for *Sea Star Fantasy* (Sydney: Hal Leonard Australia, 2015), 3.

37 Edwards utilized this somewhat laden term in reference to his orchestral work *White Ghost Dancing*. He states that "the concept of a white ghost"—that is, early recorded instances of Aboriginal peoples mistaking Europeans for the ghosts of their ancestors, whom they believed were light-skinned—"came to symbolize non-indigenous Australia's innate Aboriginality—its capacity to transform and heal itself through spiritual connectedness with the earth." As mentioned previously, such attempts to "claim," or at least share, the perceived power of Indigenous peoples over the natural land (particularly by means of sheer cultural accident) is a problematic element of twentieth-century Australian "national" music.

His notions of this philosophy likely derived from Peter Sculthorpe, who, during his research into Aboriginal cultures, recognized the intimate relationship Aboriginal peoples share with their land and opined that modern Australian composers should seek a similar affinity. Ross Edwards, *White Ghost Dancing (1999)*, https://www.rossedwards.com/white-ghost-dancing-1999/.

38 Ross Edwards, "The Tensions of Making Sacred Art in a Secular World," Canberra International Music Festival, 2014. https://www.ross-edwards.com/the-tensions-of-making-sacred-art-in-a-secular-world/.

39 Australian Music Centre, "The Sonata Project: Bernadette Harvey," event details, 2017.

40 ABC Music, "Incantations: Chamber Music by Ross Edwards," 2018.

41 For example, Edwards has written that *Frangipani*, the second piece in his collection *Mantras and Night Flowers*, is the result of an invitation from Sonya Hanke, President of the South Pacific Liszt Society, to "produce a variation on a theme from one of the 'Hungarian Rhapsodies.'" The theme is "disguised," however, with a Japanese scale, as the composer admits he found its original form "just a little bit corny."

42 Stanhope, 11.

43 Frog calls feature prominently, for example, in mm. 6–70 of Bartok's *The Night's Music*, in which its presence is wholly detached from the established meter and tonality. Similarly, Edwards incorporates the subtle contours of insects and other nocturnal creatures within the *Sea Star Fantasy* in a manner that largely aims to disrupt the established modal and metric framework of the piece.

44 Ross Edwards, "The Tensions of Making Sacred Art," 2014.

45 Edwards, "The Tensions of Making Sacred Art," 2014.

46 Ross Edwards, personal communication, June 2020.

47 Edwards, "Ross Edwards on String Quartet No. 4 'Ridley Gold.'"

48 This slogan is particularly prevalent in Aboriginal Australian political protests against colonial and post-colonial infringements on their traditional land and culture.

49 Ross Edwards, program notes for collection of piano bagatelles entitled *Mantras and Nightflowers*, 2001.

50 Philip Cooney, "Ross Edwards: I still wake up excited about the score I'm working on," *Resonate Magazine* (2013). https://www.australianmusiccentre.com.au/article/ross-edwards-i-still-wake-up-excited-about-the-score-i-m-working-on

EIGHT

"An optimistic, personal geography": Paul Stanhope, b. 1969

1 Graeme Skinner, "Stanhope, Paul" (2011).

2 Paul Stanhope, *Jandamarra: Sing for the Country. Resource Kit* (Sydney Conservatorium of Music, 2020), 3.

3 Peggy Glanville-Hicks (1912–1990) was a prominent Melbourne-born composer whose work, particularly in operatic genres, achieved interna-

tional recognition, coverage, and acclaim and greatly advanced the wider reception of contemporary Australian music. In addition to her research and performance engagements, Glanville-Hicks actively supported emerging composers in Australia, in honor of which was established both her fund and a residency at her former home in the Sydney suburb of Paddington.

4 "Manikay," ancestral songs of Arnhem Land (northeastern Australia), are transmitted generationally and preserve sacred knowledge and belief of traditional spirits, land, plants, animals, people, and significant events. Performances are often accompanied by clapsticks and a didjeridu.

5 The two series that resulted from his research are *Morning Star* (1992–1993) and *Mularra* (1998–1999). The Indigenous "Morning Star" cycle, in particular, has a prominent association with death, funerary rituals, and spiritual release, and it is often sung throughout the burial process of a deceased community member. These works have since been withdrawn; their fundamental themes, however, remain prominent throughout Stanhope's output. For example, his *Requiem* (2020), discussed later in this chapter, addresses Indigenous mortuary rituals and symbolic renewal. Skinner, "Paul Stanhope."

6 Skinner, "Paul Stanhope."

7 Paul Stanhope, "Meet the artist . . . Paul Stanhope, composer," retrieved from https://crosseyedpianist.com, February 20, 2014.

8 Founded in 1973, the Australia Council for the Arts is the central arts funding and advisory body for the Government of Australia.

9 Stanhope, "Meet the artist . . . Paul Stanhope, composer."

10 Steve Hawke (b. 1959), the son of Australia's former Prime Minister Bob Hawke, is a well-known novelist and playwright. Though he is of non-Indigenous heritage, he has lived and worked in the Bunuba community for over three decades as a Land Rights Activist and, later, a creative writer. The premiere of *Jandamarra* was directed by Phil Thompson, who also directed the 2011 performance of Hawke's identically named play. For a video of the complete 2019 performance of *Jandamarra*, see: "Jandamarra - Sing for the Country: Ngalanybarra Muwayi.u," YouTube video posted by "sydneycon," 1:11:08, December 16, 2019. https://www.youtube.com/watch?v=FMQPTdTY_eI.

11 The Kimberly is a sparsely settled region of northwestern Australia, known for its large swaths of wilderness punctuated by rugged ranges, dramatic gorges, semi-arid savanna, and a largely isolated coastline. The Bunuba peoples are its traditional landowners.

12 Derby is a remote town in the Kimberly region of Western Australia.

13 Historically, the Bunuba community's reassertion of autonomy occurred over a period of approximately 130 years wrought with genocide, slavery, and loss of land. Within *Jandamarra*, however, the retelling of events was necessarily simplified to accommodate their presentation in a compact time frame and from the perspective of the Bunuba peoples.

14 Much like the portrayal of the Bunuba's reclaiming of traditional land,

this event of reconciliation within the cantata was both simplified and rendered more optimistic than its historical reality.

15 Steve Hawke, *Jandamarra: Sing for the Country: Ngalanyabarra Muway* (Australian Music Centre, 2014). For a thorough discussion on Stanhope's procedures and methods in composing *Jandamarra*, see: Paul Stanhope, "About Music Lecture—Paul Stanhope," YouTube video posted by "sydneycon," 53:46. https://www.youtube.com/watch?v=atCZV9mw6pc

16 The mixed-race Gondwana Choir performed in the premiere of the work in 2014.

17 An octatonic scale is a symmetrical scale composed of alternating whole tones and semitones. Throughout *Jandamarra*, Stanhope frequently utilizes this sequence in varying melodic and harmonic capacities.

18 In the 2014 premiere of Jandamarra, this melody was sung by Patsy Bedford, who is one of the custodians of the song and played the role of Jini, Jandamarra's mother. In the revised 2019 version, the three custodians of the melody (Patsy Bedford, June Oscar, and Molly Jalakbiya) perform it together with Lindsay's mother, thus reiterating the cantata's overall aspect of reconciliation.

19 These two narrators were, for the purposes of dramatic and artistic effect, cast "out of time." Thus, they are almost ghost-like, retrospectively commenting on events from contrasting perspectives but otherwise detached from their immediacy.

20 Paul Stanhope, personal communication, August 2020.

21 This juxtaposition is quite significant, as it suggests an overlap between Western and Aboriginal storytelling and, more fundamentally, shared cultural themes. For both civilizations, narratives are a primary mechanism of intergenerational transmission and preservation, and thus are an especially effective compositional "bridge." Steve Hawke and Paul Stanhope, "Jandamarra" (2014).

22 The University of Sydney, "Jandamarra—Sing for the County: Ngalanybarra Muwayi.u—Educational Resource Kit Interviews," unlisted YouTube video, posted by "sydneycon," July 9, 2020.

23 Stanhope, *Jandamarra [...] Resource Kit*: 6.

24 Stanhope, *Jandamarra [...] Resource Kit*: 9.

25 The "Junba," traditionally from the Western Kimberly region, is a form of storytelling communicated through song and dance. They are believed to be communicated to individuals in dreams, when the spirit from their "Old People" visits. Within Jandamarra, the "Junba" has three custodians: its composer, "AA" Adam Andrews, and his two sons, Dylan Andrews and Kristin Andrews. Kristin serves as the lead singer of the "Junba" and the "Wangga" (introduced later in this chapter) songs.

26 Sally Quinn, "Jandamarra—Sing for the Country," *The University of Sydney*, August 1, 2019. https://www.sydney.edu.au/news-opinion/news/2019/08/01/jandamarra—-sing-for-the-country.html

27 The "Wangga" is an Aboriginal Australian genre of traditional music and

ceremony that originated in the northern and northwestern territories of the country. Typically, its public dance-songs express themes related to the ancestral dead, their living descendants, and rejuvenation, and they are "passed down" (or acquired) by individuals through spirit agents while in an altered or dream-like state of consciousness. (In traditional cultures, these atypical psychological states are considered to transport the individual closer to the divine.)

28 The University of Sydney, "Jandamarra."

29 Stanhope, *Jandamarra [...] Resource Kit*: 3.

30 Sculthorpe's decision to incorporate a didgeridoo was rather unusual, given his avoidance of the instrument in previous compositions. He was adamant in his desire to give "the work a specifically Australian sound," however, and felt that "the didjeridu, reflecting the landscape in both a physical and spiritual sense, is the quintessential Australian instrument." Though Stanhope did not employ any Indigenous Australian instruments in *Requiem*, he was likely influenced by Sculthorpe's aim to produce a body of music that reflected a national, rather than stereotypically Western, "celebration of life." Peter Sculthorpe, program notes for "Requiem," 2004.

31 Stephanie Eslake, "How Paul Stanhope's Requiem evolved into a celebration of life," *CutCommon*, February 16, 2021.

32 Oodgeroo Noonuccal (1920–1993) was an Indigenous Australian poet, artist, educator, and political activist. She was the first Aboriginal woman to publish a book of verse and was widely recognized for her advocacy for Aboriginal rights, epitomized in her efforts to realize the landmark 1967 referendum that granted citizenship to Australia's First Peoples. In 1987, she famously protested the Australian Government's intention to celebrate the nation's bicentenary, which she described as "200 years of sheer unadulterated humiliation" of Aboriginal people.

33 Philip Eames, "A Collage of Remembrance: An Interview with Paul Stanhope," *Context* 46 (2020): 77.

34 In Aboriginal ceremony, these are referred to as "memorial poles." In recent years, such burial devices have assumed an ornamental and symbolic significance alongside their purely functional capacity, and they therefore feature heavily in contemporary Indigenous art.

35 About his *Requiem*, Sculthorpe stated that it sought to encapsulate "the sacred in nature" in its depiction of the Australian Outback.

36 Paul Stanhope, program notes for "Requiem," *Paul Stanhope: A New Requiem* (Sydney: City Recital Hall, 2021), 20.

37 Stanhope, program notes for "Requiem," 22.

38 Stanhope, program notes for "Requiem," 23.

39 Paul Stanhope, program notes for "Songs from the Shadowland."

40 Eames, 77.

41 Peter McCallum, "Standing ovation for 'major contribution to Australian choral music,'" *The Sydney Morning Herald*, March 15, 2021.

42 Alex Siegers, "Concert Review: Paul Stanhope: A New Requiem/ Sydney Chamber Choir," *SoundsLikeSydney*, March 15, 2021.
43 Paul Stanhope, "Paul Stanhope: A New Requiem," *Limelight*, March 2, 2021.
44 Eames, 78–79.

NINE

Compendium of Characteristics that Denote or Identify the "Australiana" Idiom

1 Bernard Berenson, *The Arch of Constantine: The Decline of Form* (New York: The Macmillan Company, 1954), 23-24.
2 Peter Sculthorpe, "Rites of Passage," *Limelight*, May 2009.
3 Roger Covell, "Sculthorpe, Peter" (2011).
4 The "harmony of the spheres" (also known as *Musica universalis*) is a theory proposed by Pythagoras that the Sun, Moon, and planets all emit a distinct pitch based on their orbital revolution, and that the quality of life on Earth reflects these sounds otherwise physically imperceptible to the human ear.
5 Edwards, "The Tensions of Making Sacred Art in a Secular World," 2014.
6 As dictated by their mythological and spiritual traditions, Aboriginal peoples consider themselves to be the primary custodians of the natural land. Indeed, defilation or disruption of the environment is punished with severe retribution from the perpetrator's native community.
7 The mythology of Australian Aboriginal peoples utilizes the term "Dreamtime" to encompass a "golden age" when their first ancestors, major environmental landmarks, and other noteworthy features of the continent were created. In turn, it represents the Aboriginal concept of "Everywhen," during which the land was inhabited by ancestral figures of often heroic or supernatural proportions. (The inability of these figures to manipulate the natural world, however, rendered them non-deific.) Though there are regional variations in its narrative specificities, the "Dreamtime" is largely considered a shared heritage of the native peoples; in Australia, references to "dream," "dreaming," or the Dreamtime are intrinsically associated with this body of creation stories. The term "The Dreaming" was first recorded by early anthropologist Francis Gillen and was quickly adopted by his colleague Baldwin Spencer. Thereafter, it was popularized by A.P. Elkin, who was an Anglican clergyman, an influential Australian anthropologist, and a proponent of the assimilation of Indigenous Australians into "European" society.
8 Allan Marett, et. al., "Australia," *Grove Music Online*, 2001.
9 Richard Taruskin, "Nationalism," *Grove Music Online*, 2001.
10 This is in contrast to musicologist Michael Hannan's suggestion that Sculthorpe's "nationalism" (or *Australiana*) was largely modeled after Aaron Copland's *Americana*.

11 Campbell, 40.

12 This approach is particularly ironic when considering that Aboriginal peoples did not gain citizenship until 1976 (nor official voting obligations until 1983); that is, they were not considered "truly Australian" under legal definitions, thus forming a cognitive dissonance in the Australian psyche with their representation in music as such. Campbell, 41.

13 Jonathan Paget, "Has Sculthorpe Misappropriated Indigenous Melodies?" *Musicology Australia* 35/1 (2013): 108.

14 A set of melodies of Indigenous origin that were constantly reused by Sculthorpe throughout the 1980s and 1990s, some of which make explicit reference to the Kakadu National Park.
This "recycling" is treated as an artistic enchantment, in which Sculthorpe reworks the material from varying perspectives to demonstrate its nuances.

15 Much of Sculthorpe's early work demonstrates strong influences of Asian music, many characteristics of which permeate later compositions.

16 Paget particularly draws attention to Sculthorpe's evolution of eco-centered thematic material from "more typically European reactions" (i.e., loneliness and estrangement) to "reflective of Indigenous attitudes" (i.e., a sense of deep connection and belonging).

17 Peter Sculthorpe claimed to be distantly related to Fanny Cochrane Smite, a Tasmanian Aboriginal whose wax cylinder recordings of songs are the only audio recordings of any of Tasmania's Indigenous languages. Paget does not specify if Sculthorpe's "identification with Aboriginality" refers to this assertion of heritage, or simply to a passionate interest in Indigenous culture.

18 Paget, 97.

19 Paul Stanhope, *Jandamarra: Sing for the Country. Resource Kit* (Sydney Conservatorium of Music, 2020).

20 Ross Edwards, "Address to the Conference on Belonging," presentation (Australian National University, 1999).

21 Several music scholars have strongly criticized the representation of Asian musical cultures in Australian compositions. Gordan Kerry, for example, states that "much Asian-influenced music is 'Orientalist,' in the sense that it portrays an Asia far removed from present day, or even past, realities." That is, composers fabricate a "dream world" in which the stereotypical "virtues of stasis, gentleness, and repetition are cultivated, but essentially unmoored from their cultural, often formal, context." This recognition of stilted artificiality has likewise been expressed in relation to the use of Aboriginal culture by such scholars as Kerry, Liza Lim, and Rachel Campbell, among others. It is worth noting, however, that the cultures of more geographically immediate Pacific nations, such as Melanesia and Polynesia, have proven less influential than Japanese, Balinese, or Chinese cultures. Gordan Kerry, *New Classical Music: Composing Australia* (UNSW Press, 2009), 62.

22 Featherstone, "Dance of Nature: The Music of Ross Edwards." https://aso.gov.au/titles/documentaries/dance-nature-music-ross-edward/clip2/
23 Paul Stanhope, "The music of Ross Edwards: aspects of ritual," Master of Arts (Hons.) thesis, University of Wollongong, 1994, 11.
24 These are considered the "Beneficent Spirit" and the "Harmful Spirit," respectively, which unite in the "Ahura Mazda" (the Supreme Creator) and dually influence the natural and supernatural world.
25 Edwards, "The Tensions of Making Sacred Art," 2014.
26 Edwards, "The Tensions of Making Sacred Art," 2014.
27 Ross Edwards, personal communication, June 2020.
28 "Maninya" is a nonsense "word" associated with Edwards's compositional period of fast, lively, dance-like works.
29 Edwards, "The Tensions of Making Sacred Art," 2014.
30 Graham Williams, *Life in Balance*, Lifeflow Meditation Centre, Adelaide.
31 Paul Stanhope, "The music of Ross Edwards."
32 Paul Stanhope, program notes for "The Magic Island," 2012. https://www.australianmusiccentre.com.au/work/stanhope-paul-magic-island
33 Deborah Crisp, "The Influence of Australian Aboriginal Music on the Music of Contemporary Australian Composers," in *Australian Aboriginal Music*, ed. Jennifer Isaacs (Sydney: Aboriginal Artists Agency, 1979), 54.

TEN

Final Questions

1 A "second-generation immigrant" typically indicates the second generation of a family to be natively born in a country.
2 Yan Zhuang, "Why is Australia Still Part of the British Monarchy?," *The New York Times,* December 3, 2020.
3 In January of 2021, the Australian Commonwealth changed a single line of the national anthem from "young and free" to "one and free," in light of mounting criticisms from Indigenous activists who argued that the word "young" ignored the 60,000-year presence of Aboriginal culture. This change, however, is considered but a minor remediation in a much greater national concern—namely, that of a firmly asserted cultural identity. Natalie Williams, personal phone communication, January 2021.
4 Natalie Williams, personal phone communication, January 2021.
5 Despite his many years in London, Williamson considered his work completely Australian, once describing his work as having "the sort of brashness that makes Australians go through life pushing doors marked pull."
6 Though Barton is more widely known as a virtuoso Aboriginal didgeridoo player than as a composer, he has produced numerous

remarkable works that deserve attention and recognition as substantial contributions to Australian culture.

7 For example, the Australia Council for the Arts published a 196-page document entitled "Protocols for using First Nations Intellectual and Cultural Property in the Arts" (2019), which represented the first attempt to establish a thorough foundation for collaboration between Indigenous and non-Indigenous peoples.

8 The Cummeragunju walk-off (in which Cheetham's grandparents were involved) was a 1939 protest led by Aboriginal Australians (predominantly the Yorta Yorta community) against the harsh working conditions, poor living spaces, and excessive restrictions on movement in the Cummeragunja station, an Aboriginal reserve in southern New South Wales. At the time, the reserve was managed by the Maloga Mission from the Church of Christ community, which furthered the "Stolen Generations" policies instituted by the Australian Government. (The "Stolen Generations" were the children of Aboriginal and Torres Strait Islander descent who were forcibly removed from their families by both Australian government agencies and various church missions. The majority of these removals occurred between 1905 and 1967, although documented instances exist through the 1970s.) *Pecan Summer* is the first opera composed by an Indigenous Australian and involving an Indigenous cast.

9 *Kalkadungu's Journey* was composed in reference to the development of events between the Kalkadoon people and European settlers during the 1860s. Though their initial relationship was conciliatory and somewhat amicable, the discovery of copper and increasing European incursions on traditional land ignited guerilla warfare that lasted over a decade. It culminated in a gruesome stand-off on Battle Hill, with popular folklore describing the remnants of bleached bones for more than fifty years afterwards.

10 *Terra nullius* is a Latin term meaning "nobody's land," which James Cook used to justify the acquisition of Australia for the British Empire. In doing so, he negated the occupation of Indigenous peoples and rendered them an infringement upon, rather than an inherent element of, the newly discovered continent. Governmental acknowledgment and assuaging of these conflicts often occur many generations after the events themselves—for example, it was not until 2008 that Prime Minister Kevin Rudd issued a parliamentary apology for the "Stolen Generations."

11 The only individuals who may quote a particular community's music are members from that community itself—for example, in Paul Stanhope's *Jandamarra,* Bunuba musical material may only be performed by members of the Bunuba community, or another community that has received explicit permission from the Bunuba peoples. Additionally, considerable regulations exist within individual communities as to who may perform particular songs, and many members are restricted on the basis of age, gender, and initiated status in the community.

12 For example, Paul Stanhope conducted ethnographic fieldwork in north central Arnhem Land to transcribe the *Mularra* clan-songs (*manikay*) of Rembarrnga-speakers, as part of a project at the University of Sydney in the early 1990s.

13 Michael Hooper, "Connecting with the Past: Thoughts on Earlier Compositional Journeys: Interview with Natalie Williams," *Resonate Magazine* (February 2008).

14 Natalie Williams, personal phone communication, January 2021.

15 Indeed, the vast majority of Stanhope's education was conducted within Australia. Although he studied in the Guildhall School of Music and Drama (London), as well a brief interlude in the University of York, he was welcomed as an *Australian* composer from a nation with an already distinct body of music. (Graeme Skinner, "Paul Stanhope," *Grove Music Online*, October 26, 2011.) Nonetheless, Natalie Williams states that it is still common for Australian students to go abroad for advanced or terminal degrees, as there is not much professional opportunity in Australia beyond a Master's diploma; this, in turn, contributes to a lack of cultural self-sufficiency. Furthermore, Australian education still follows a British model in which students are offered no graduate teaching, thus making opportunities abroad more attractive in terms of professional development and financial support.

16 Paul Stanhope, "Paul Stanhope: Featured Composer 2010," YouTube video, https://www.youtube.com/watch?v=yKz6AjDdhGo&t=31s/

17 This phenomenon was, in part, the result of the emerging institutionalization of academic organizations and funding sources that stimulated the development of a distinctive "Australian Music."

18 Regarding the prevalence of modernism in Australia, Gordon Kerry notes that the arrival and widespread dissemination of "modernism" as a musical movement was several decades behind its climax in Europe. Thus, composers such as Richard Meale or Nigel Butterly found themselves responsible for "modernizing music broadcasting" simply because it had conclusively established itself as the dominant aesthetic of the time. Kerry, 78. Michael Hooper, *Australian Music and Modernism, 1960–1975* (Bloomsbury Publishing, 2019).

19 Natalie Williams, personal communication, January 2021.

20 Ross Edwards, personal communication, June 2020.

21 Kerry, 45.

22 This term was coined by historian and economist Geoffrey Blainey in his book *The Tyranny of Distance: How Distance Shaped Australia's History* (Sydney: Macmillan Press, 2001).

ELEVEN

Overview of the Aesthetic Pariods of Australia's Musical Nationalism

1 Graeme Skinner, "Australian Musical First Modernism," in *The Modernist World* (New York: Routledge, 2015), 274.

2 John Williams, *The Quarantined Culture: Australian Reactions to*

Modernism, 1913–1939 (Cambridge: Cambridge University Press, 1995), 5–6.

APPENDIX

Timeline of Major Events Throughout Australia's History

1 Official counts approximate that, owing to a combination of introduced European diseases and direct violence, 600 to 900 Aboriginal peoples on the island were killed, nearly eradicating the island's Indigenous population. Nicholas Clements, *The Black War* (Brisbane: University of Queensland Press, 2014), 1.

Select Bibliography

[Advertisement]. *The Sydney Gazette.* April 28, 1825. http://nla.gov.au/nla.news-article2183967

[Advertisement]. *The Sydney Gazette.* November 11, 1834. http://nla.gov.au/nla.news-article2217523

[News]. *The Hobart Town Courier.* October 16, 1830. http://nla.gov.au/nla.news-article4206714

[News]. *The Sydney Gazette* January 16, 1827. http://nla.gov.au/nla.news-article2187390

Andrews, Alan E.J., ed. *A Journey from Sydney to the Australian Alps undertaken in the months of January, February and March, 1834 by Dr. John Lhotsky.* Hobart: Blubber Head Press, 1979.

Antill, John. "Corrobboree: A Ballet Suite for Orchestra." 1946, Papers, National Library of Australia, MS 437/8a/9 Box 14, 2.

Antill, John. "Why I Wrote '*Corroboree.*'" *Australian Musical News* 37 (1946): 20–21.

Army Recruit Training Centre. "The Aim of Recruit Training." Retrieved August 1, 2021. https://web.archive.org/web/20070831230108/http://www.army.gov.au/artc/aim.html

Beattie, James. *Essays on Poetry and Music: As They Affect the Mind: On Laughter, and Ludicrous Composition: On the Usefulness of Classical Learning.* Edinburgh: W. Creech, 1779.

Berenson, Bernard. *The Arch of Constantine: The Decline of Form.* New York: The Macmillan Company, 1954.

Bertie, Charles. *Isaac Nathan: Australia's first composer, a lecture delivered at the Conservatorium of Music.* Sydney: Angus and Robertson, 1922.

Boyd, Anne. "Peter Sculthorpe's Sun Music I." *Miscellanea Musicologia* 3 (1968): 3–20.

Bradley, Williams. *A Voyage to New South Wales.* State Library of New South Wales, 1802.

Brooke-Hitching, Edward. *The Phantom Atlas: The Greatest Myths, Lies and Blunders on Maps.* San Francisco: Chronicle Books, 2018.

Burk, Ian. *"Goodbye 'til next time": A critical biography of A.E. Floyd (1877–1974).* Melbourne: Lyrebird Press, 2012.

Cairns, David. "Faber Music: News: *Sun Music I* Reviews." *Faber Music.* August 31, 1967. https://www.fabermusic.com/news/sun-music-i-reviews-936

Campbell, Rachel. "'The Whole Work is Full of Primitive Rhythms': The

Folk-Primitivist Origins of Peter Sculthorpe's National Music." *Musicology Australia* 41:1 (2019): 36–57.
Cashman, Katrina. "Life and Work." *Margaret Preston—Australian Artist*, official website. February 22, 2017. https://web.archive.org/web/20171009051808/http://www.margaret preston.info/life-work/
Chudnovsky, Emil. Interview with Andrew Haveron. Kirov Academy "The Classical Music Podcast Ep. 2." Podcast audio. June 23, 2020. https://www.youtube.com/watch?v=eu4JVyeLU8s&t=5833s
Cook, James. *Captain Cook's Journal during the First Voyage round the World*. Frankfurt: Outlook, 2018.
Cooney, Phillip. "Beyond sacred and maninya: developments in the music of Ross Edwards between 1991–2001." Ph.D. thesis, University of Newcastle, 2003.
Corsano, Erica. "A chat with alumnus and art collector Dennis Scholl." *FIU News*. July 2020. https://news.fiu.edu/2020/inside-the-nside-world?utm_source=newsletter
Covell, Roger. *Australia's Music: Themes of a New Society*. Melbourne: Sun Books, 1967.
——. "Sculthorpe, Peter (Joshua)." *Grove Music Online*. 2011; Accessed 20 Oct. 2020.
Crisp, Deborah. "The Influence of Australian Aboriginal Music on the Music of Contemporary Australian Composers." In *Australian Aboriginal Music*, edited by Jennifer Isaacs, 49–56. Sydney: Aboriginal Artists Agency, 1979.
Cumberland Argus. February 15, 1922.
Dench, Christopher and Ian Shanahan. "An emotional geography of Australian composition." *Sounds Australian* (Winter 1992): 8–32.
Douglas, Clive. *Autobiography of an Australian composer*. Unpublished, State Library of Victoria, Dr. Clive Martin Douglas papers, MS 7656, Box 15.
——. "Folk-song and the brown man—A means to an Australian expression in symphonic music." *Canon* 10/3 (July 1956): 81–85.
Dreyfus, Kay. "In Search of New Waters: Australian music studies in the 1990s," in *Essays in Honour of David Tunley*, edited by Frank Callaway, 155–164. University of Western Australia: Callaway International Resource Centre for Music Education, 1995.
Eames, Philip. "A Collage of Remembrance: An Interview with Paul Stanhope." *Context* 46 (2020): 75–80.
Edwards, Ross. "Address to the Conference on Belonging." Presentation, Australian National University, Canberra. November, 1999.
——. "Composer Conversation with Ross Edwards." YouTube video posted by "UNSW Music Performance," 37:12. May 11, 2020. https://www.youtube.com/watch?v=-ZuqMFcFb8o
——. "A Natural Way." Interview by Gordon Kalton.

http://www.gordonkaltonwilliams.com/A_Natural_Way_interview_with_Ross_E dwards_900_words.pdf

——. "Peter Sculthorpe 1929–2014: Ross Edwards speaking at the Peter Sculthorpe Celebration Concert." October 25, 2014. https://www.rossedwards.com/peter-sculthorpe-1929-2014-ross-edwards-speaking-at-the-peter-sculthorpe-celebration-concert-25-october-2014/

——. "Philip Cooney: An Interview with Ross Edwards, October 2010." *Ross Edwards—Official Wesbite.* October 2010. http://www.rossedwards.com/philip-cooney-an-interview-with-ross-edwards-october-2010/

——. "Reflections: the performing arts." *Transforming Art* 4/1 (1992): 28–30.

——. "Ross Edwards for ACO: Indigenous influences on his music." YouTube video, 29:49. Posted by "Pru Borgert," August 15, 2016. https://www.youtube.com/watch?v=6TmVKg3lLu8&feature=emb_title

——. "Ross Edwards on String Quartet No. 4 'Ridley Gold.'" YouTube video, 1:45. Posted by "Australian String Quartet," July 27, 2021. https://www.youtube.com/watch?v=Se0U9dLdF5I&feature=emb_title

——. *Sea Star Fantasy.* Sydney: Hal Leonard Australia, 2015.

——. "The Tensions of Making Sacred Art in a Secular World." Lecture, Canberra International Music Festival, May 18, 2014.

——. "White Ghost Dancing (1999)." https://www.rossedwards.com/white-ghost-dancing-1999/

——. "Yarrageh: Nocturne for Solo Percussion and Orchestra (1989)." http://www.rossedwards.com/yarrageh-1989/

Ellis, Catherine J. "Developments in Music Education Among Aboriginals in Central and South Australia." In *Aboriginal Australian Music*, edited by Jennifer Isaacs, 27–40. Sydney: Aboriginal Artists Agency, 1979.

Eslake, Stephanie. "How Paul Stanhope's Requiem evolved into a celebration of life." *CutCommon.* February 16, 2021.

Esson, Louis. "The Composer in Australia: A Talk with Fritz Hart." *The New Triad* 1/5 (December 1927): 24–25.

Featherstone, Don (director). "Australia's finest living composer." YouTube video, 6:48. Posted by "Don Featherstone," April 10, 2015. https://www.youtube.com/watch?v=zLyoa45bVgk

Featherstone, Don (director). "Dance of Nature: The Music of Ross Edwards." Audiovisual material published by the National Film and Sound Archive of Australia. 1995.

Floyd, A.E. "New Musical Education." *Argus* (?). Black proof in Floyd Collection, Grainger Museum, University of Melbourne.

Fowler, Frank. *Australian Album.* Sydney: J.R. Clarke, 1856.

Fox, Margalit. "Colleen McCullough, Author of 'The Thorn Birds,' Dies at 77." *New York Times.* January 29, 2015. https://www.nytimes.com/2015/01/30/books/colleen-mccullough-author-of-the-thorn-birds-dies-at-77.html

Ghim, Walter. "Vita . . . Gerardi Mercatoris Rupelmundani." *Gerardi*

Mercatoris Atlas sive Cosmographice Meditationes de Fabrica Mundi et Fabricate Figura. Amsterdam: 1606.

Gill, Michael, director. *Civilisation: A Personal View by Kenneth Clark*. "The Skin of Our Teeth." BBC, 23 February 1969.

Gilles, Malcolm, David Pear, and Mark Carroll, eds. *Self-portrait of Percy Grainger*. Oxford: Oxford University Press, 2006.

Gioia, Ted. *Music: A Subversive History*. New York: Basic Books, 2019.

Glass, Dudley. "Australia's Contribution to Music." *Journal of the Royal Society of Arts* 111/5080 (March 1963): 302–311.

Grainger, Percy. *The All-Round Man: Selected Letters of Percy Grainger, 1914-1961*. Edited by Malcolm Gillies and David Pear. Oxford: Clarendon Press, 1994.

——. *Grainger on Music*. Edited by Malcolm Gillies and Bruce Clunies Rosss. Oxford: Oxford University Press, 1999.

Hall, James. "A History of Music in Australia (15)." *The Canon* 5/8 (March 1952): 361–380.

Hartshorne, Charles. "Musical Values in Australian Bird Songs." *Emu-Austral Ornithology* 53/2 (1953): 109–128.

Hawke, Steve and Paul Stanhope. "Jandamarra: Sing for the Country: Ngalanyabarra Muway." *Australian Music Centre*. 2014. https://www.australianmusiccentre.com.au/work/stanhope-paul-jandamarra-sing-for-the-country

Henderson, Robert. "Peter Sculthorpe." *The Musical Times* 107/1481 (July 1966): 594–595.

Hooper, Michael. *Australian Music and Modernism, 1960-1975*. Bloomsbury Publishing USA, 2019.

——. "Connecting with the Past: Thoughts on Earlier Compositional Journeys: Interview with Natalie Williams." *Resonate Magazine* (February 2008).

Howard, Judith. "Social Psychology of Identities." *Annual Review of Sociology* 26 (2000): 367–393.

Hunter, John. *An Historical Journal of the Transactions at Port Jackson and Norfolk Island*. Glasgow: Good Press, 2019.

Jeffrey, Antony. *The Many Faces of Inspiration: Conversations on Australian Creativity*. Adelaide: Griffin Press, 2011.

Kerry, Gordon. *New Classical Music: Composing Australia*. UNSW Press, 2009.

Korff, Jens. "Are dot paintings traditional Aboriginal art?" Creative Spirits, 2019. https://www.creativespirits.info/aboriginalculture/arts/are-dot-paintings-traditional-aboriginal-art

Lawson, Valerie. *Dancing Under the Southern Skies: A History of Ballet in Australia*. Melbourne: Australian Scholarly Publishing, 2019.

Marett, Allan, Catherine J. Ellis, Margaret Gummow, Roger Covell, Gordon Kerry, and Graeme Smith. "Australia." *Grove Music Online*. 2001.

Mark, Christopher. Review of *Australian Music and Modernism, 1960–1975*, by Michael Hooper. *Music and Letters* 101/4 (2020): 810–812.

Marshall Hall. "The Cruise of the Nona." *The Field Quarterly Magazine and Review* 2 (August 1871): 170–179.

Masey, Edward. Review of *The Foundations of Australian Culture*, by P.R. Stephensen. *The Australian Quarterly* 8/29 (March 1936): 106–107, 109.

Matthews, David. "Peter Sculthorpe at 60." *Tempo*, New Series, 170 (1989): 12–17.

McCallum, Peter. "Standing ovation for 'major contribution to Australian choral music.'" *The Sydney Morning Herald*. March 15, 2021.

McNeill, Rhoderick. "Migrant Symphonies—the symphonic contribution of British composers to Australian musical life." In *Migrant Security 2010: Citizenship and Social Inclusion in a Transnational Era, Toowoomba, 2010*: 153–158.

——. "Symphonies of the Bush: Indigenous encounters in Australian symphonies." In *Encounters: Meetings in Australian Music: Essays, Images, Interviews*, edited by Vincent Plush, Huib Schippers, and Jocelyn Wolfe, 1–5. Queensland Conservatorium Research Centre: Brisbane, Australia, 2005.

Meaney, Neville. "Britishness and Australian Identity: The problem of nationalism in Australian history and historiography." *Australian Historical Studies* 32:116 (2001): 76–90.

Mellers, Wilfrid. "New Worlds, Old Wildernesses: Peter Sculthorpe and the Ecology of Music." *The Atlantic* 268/2 (August 1991): 94–98.

Melleuish, Greg. "Australian Identity in the 21st century." Submission 10 in *Nationhood, national identity and democracy* (2019): 1–8.

"Mr. Wallace's Concert." *The Sydney Herald*. June 9, 1836.

Paget, Jonathan. "Has Sculthorpe Misappropriated Indigenous Melodies?" *Musicology Australia* 35:1 (2013): 86–111.

Philpott, Carolyn. "Peter Sculthorpe's String Quartet no. 14: A Musical Response to Social Injustice." *Context* 27 & 28 (2004): 83–96.

Quinn, Sally. "Jandamarra—Sing for the Counry." *The University of Sydney*. August 1, 2019.
https://www.sydney.edu.au/news-opinion/news/2019/08/01/jandamarra—sing-for-the-country.html

Robinson, Suzanne. "Peter Sculthorpe: The Making of an Australian Composer." *Musicology Australia* 30:1 (2008): 120–125.

Radic, Thérèse. *G.W.L. Marshall-Hall: A Biography & Catalogue*. Melbourne: Marshall-Hall Trust, 2002.

Radio Times. August 4, 1945.

Radio Times. February 12, 1944.

Runciam, John. "The Case of Mr. Marshall Hall." *The Saturday Review* (November 1898): 602–603.

——. "Professor Marshall-Hall." *Magazine of Music* 9 (June 1892): 109–110.

Scott, Ernest. *A History of the University of Melbourne*. Melbourne: Melbourne University Press, 1936.

Sculthorpe, Peter. "Programme Notes" in "Faber Music: Kakadu (orchestra)." *Faber Music*. 1988. https://www.fabermusic.com/music/kakadu-931

——. "Programme Notes" in "Faber Music: Irkanda IV." *Faber Music*. 1961. https://www.fabermusic.com/music/irkanda-iv-930

——. "Peter Sculthorpe at 50—ABC Four Corners Profile (1979)." YouTube video, 15:32. Posted by "ABC Classic," April 29, 2019. https://www.youtube.com/watch?v=LR7KLPs54vs

——. "Peter Sculthorpe 'Brings in the sun.'" National Portrait Gallery. https://www.portrait.gov.au/stories/peter-sculthorpe

——. "Peter Sculthorpe on Australian music (from the ABC Archives)." YouTube video, 1:46. Posted by "ABC Classic," April 30, 2019. https://www.youtube.com/watch?v=tyuZH5FAv6c

——. "Rites of Passage." *Limelight*. May 2009.

Homan, Shane, et. al. "Australien." *MGG Online*. Stuttgart: 2016. https://www.mgg-online.com/mgg/stable/11745

Siegers, Alex. "Concert Review: Paul Stanhope: A New Requiem/ Sydney Chamber Choir." *SoundsLikeSydney*. March 15, 2021.

Skinner, Graeme. "Composer of the Month: Peter Sculthorpe." *Limelight*. 2018.

——. "The Invention of Australian Music." *Musicology Australia* 37/2 (2015): 289–306.

——. *Peter Sculthorpe: The Making of an Australian Composer*. Sydney: University of New South Wales Press, 2007.

——. "Some Makings of an Australian Composer (1964–65)." *Fontes Artis Musicae* 55/1 (January–March 2008): 111–127.

——. "Stanhope, Paul." *Grove Music Online*. October 26, 2011.

——. "Toward a General History of Australian Musical Composition: First National Music, 1788–c. 1860/" Ph.D. thesis. Sydney Conservatorium of Music, 2011.

Stanhope, Paul. "Jandamarra - Sing for the Country: Ngalanybarra Muwayi.u." YouTube video, 11:50. Posted by "sydneycon," July 9, 2020. https://youtu.be/fse85z-WrdM

——. *Jandamarra: Sing for the Country. Resource Kit*. Sydney: Sydney Conservatorium of Music, 2020.

——. "Meet the artist . . . Paul Stanhope, composer." *Cross-Eyed Pianist*. February 20, 2014. https://crosseyedpianist.com/2014/02/20/meet-the-artist-paul-stanhope-composer/.com

——. "The music of Ross Edwards: aspects of ritual." Master of Arts (Hons.) thesis, University of Wollongong, 1994. http://ro.uow.au/theses/2247

——. "Paul Stanhope: A New Requiem." *Limelight*. March 2, 2021.

——. Program notes for "A New Requiem." *Paul Stanhope: A New Requiem*. Sydney: City Recital Hall, 2021.

——. Program notes for "The Magic Island." 2012. https://www.australian-musiccentre.com.au/work/stanhope-paul-magic-island

——. Program notes for "Songs from the Shadowland." 1999. https://www.australianmusiccentre.com.au/work/stanhope-paul-songs-for-the-shadowland

"SYDNEY AMATEUR CONCERT." *The Sydney Gazette.* July 24, 1826. http://nla.gov.au/nla.news-article2186232

The Sydney Monitor. June 18, 1836.

"Sundry Shows." *The Bulletin.* August 21, 1946.

Symons, David. *Before and After* Corroboree: *The Music of John Antill.* London: Ashgate, 2015.

Taruskin, Richard. "Nationalism." *Grove Music Online.* 2001. https://www.oxfordmusiconline.com/grovemusic/view/10.1093/gmo/9781561592630.001.0001/omo-9781561592630-e-0000050846

Tate, Henry. *Australian Musical Possibilities.* Melbourne, Australia: E.A. Vidler, 1924.

"To Sir George Murray." *The Sydney Monitor.* November 29, 1828.

Trainor, Luke. *British Imperialism and Australian Nationalism: Manipulation, Conflict, and Compromise in the Late Nineteenth Century.* Cambridge: Cambridge University Press, 1994.

Tregear, Peter. "'Nostalgia is not what it used to be': Exploring the kitsch in Grainger's music." *Grainger Studies: An Interdisciplinary Journal* 1 (2011): 97–113.

The University of Sydney. "Jandamarra—Sing for the Country: Ngalanybarra Muwayi.u—Educational Resource Kit Interviews." Unlisted YouTube video, 1:11:08. Posted by "sydneycon," December 16, 2019.

Watson, Fred. Program notes for Ross Edwards's "Piano Concerto." 2003. https://www.rossedwards.com/piano-concerto-1982-revised-2003/

Werder, Felix. "Composing in Australia." *Meanjin* 16/2 (June 1957): 140–144.

Whiteoak, John and Aline Scott-Maxwell, eds. *Currency Companion to Music and Dance in Australia.* Strawberry Hills: Currency House, 2003.

Williams, Graham. *Life in Balance.* Lifeflow Meditation Centre, Adelaide.

Wood, Elizabeth. "MORITZ HUZENROEDER—A MUSICAL PIONEER."

Zewig, Stefan. *The World of Yesterday.* New York: 1943.

Index